HELLENIC TRAVEL

1. Agîa Laura. The Monastery of Kalavryta

HELLENIC TRAVEL

A Guide

by

W. A. WIGRAM
D.D.

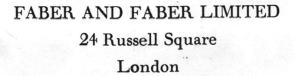

FABER AND FABER LIMITED

24 Russell Square

London

First published in mcmxlvii
by Faber and Faber Limited
24 Russell Square London W.C. 1
Second impression mcmli
Printed in Great Britain by
R. MacLehose and Company Limited
The University Press Glasgow
All rights reserved

To
the honoured memory of
SIR HENRY LUNN
Founder and Manager of
the 'Hellenic Travellers' Club'
Pioneer in the task of making Greece accessible
to tourists who can appreciate her marvels,
and who are unable to spare the time
for leisurely independent travel

CONTENTS

7

CONTENTS

ILLUSTRATIONS

9

MAPS AND PLANS

PREFACE

In these days, and for some time to come, most visitors to Greece are likely to rely on the 'Cruising ship' for their means of travel. This will take them to the more accessible ports—captains of comfortable and therefore costly ships fight shy of places where navigation is tricky and pilots hard to find—and from those ports it may be possible for some visitors to make expeditions of two or more days' length and rejoin their ship at a later point, thus visiting places otherwise inaccessible.

We therefore offer this book, the fruit of some years of experience in that sort of travel, in the hope that it will enable folk to understand what they have come some way to see.

It makes no pretensions to be a complete treatment even of the aspect of Greece with which it deals. We can touch but a few places, even on the mainland, and all the islands of the Aegean Sea have to go undescribed. Yet there is hardly one of them, from Rhodes, Delos, and Santorin down, that has not an enthralling tale to tell of its history or pre-history.

Present conditions of book-production now limit all schemes of bookmaking, and in consequence we have not told a tenth of what Greece has to reveal. Further, we have had to leave out the whole of that tale of melancholy heroism, the Story of Greece in the Second Great War of 1939–1945. When all the facts are available, that will be a volume to itself in the history of that great struggle, and not the least interesting in that library. Till then, it seemed best to leave untold what we have neither knowledge nor space to deal with as it deserves.

In the event of any reader wishing to go further in the study of what we have dealt with so briefly, we mention a few of the books from which we have benefited.

On the whole subject, Pausanias' Description of Greece remains the primary authority, and it should be studied in J. G. Frazer's great edition, if that be accessible.

Jane Harrison's books *Prolegomena to the Study of Greek Religion*, and *Themis*, with Farnell's *Cults of the Greek States*, are mines of

PREFACE

learning; and Lawson's *Modern Greek Folk-Lore and Ancient Greek Religion*, with Hamilton's *Greek Saints and their Festivals* show how continuous is the common Greek mind of today with that of their classic and pre-classic ancestry. Plenty of books deal with the special places that we touch on, and there is a library on Athens; we mention

Van Millingen	*Churches of Constantinople*
	Walls of Constantinople
Pears	*Fall of Constantinople*
	Siege of Constantinople
Poulsen	*Delphi*
Gardiner	*Olympia*
Miller	*Latins in the Levant*

as authorities on the points named in the titles.

Some of these works are, we fear, now only to be found in libraries, such as that of the Hellenic Society, 50 Bedford Square, W.C. 1. Independent travel in Greece may be difficult for a while, till roads have been repaired and hotels and motors are once more available. For those content to go in the old way, i.e. on mule or afoot, at least the mountains will not be altered, and the old tracks will not be any rougher, or the peasants less kindly than of old—so soon, that is, as there is any food to spare.

1946.

I

THE ACROPOLIS

*Approach—Piraeus—Modern Athens—Making of the Acropolis—
Beulé Gateway—Agrippa Monument—Propylaea—Artemis Brau-
ronia—Athena Nike—Promachus—Erectheum—The Priestesses—
Porch of Maidens—The Parthenon—The Altar—The Bouphonia
—The Venetian Siege*

'He that fareth to Athens', if we may adapt Sir John de
Mandeville, 'may come by many ways,' but seeing how
uninteresting the approach to any city by rail is apt to be,
he will be well advised to make his first approach by sea. There, he
cannot go wrong; let him come as he will, either round the Peloponnesus, or through the Corinth Canal, or round by Cape Sunium to get
his first glimpse of a Greek temple in the columns of the fanes of
Poseidon and Athena that crown it. By the first he will see the peaks
of the 'Violet Crown' of Athens, the hills of Parnes, Pentelicus and
Hymettus, that go purple-blue in the evening light and still justify
the ancient name. Presently Lycabettus shows up as a grey pyramid
with a stain of black pines at its foot, and gradually a white speck
shows against the black, which a field-glass may tell you is the
Parthenon on the Acropolis. Or you may come round from Sunium,
where once the flash from Athena's spear-head beckoned her children home; leaving the peak of Aegina on your left and the long
slope of Hymettus on your right, where you may pick out the black
dot of the cavern where Pan is worshipped yet, you see the long
arm of the 'Dog's Tail' promontory, where Salamis was fought,
lying out ahead of you. Either way you turn into the harbour of
Piraeus, past the headland where the dust of Themistocles lies still,
and bring up in that ancient-modern port.

13

Piraeus was never interesting, and always rowdy. In old days it was a model of classic town planning, with wide roads and right-angled turns, as dull as a modern American city. In that, it still keeps its old character, with nothing ancient save the lowest courses of the wall that once guarded its headland—there is no trace of the 'Long Walls'—and for those who know just where to look for them, the launching slips for the old triremes in the dock-yard harbour of Munichion. Rowdy the place is still, being a focus of that communism that is the bane of modern Greece; and which has this excuse, that the town has been more than doubled in size by the colonies built for the refugees from Asia Minor. Those who have lost their all may be pardoned for thinking that nobody else has the right to keep anything.

In a busy modern harbour, out of which it is hard to get without fouling other folks' anchors, it is hard to believe that only a hundred and twenty years ago Byron used to canter down to what was then 'Porto Leone' to get a swim in quiet. Yet so it was, though even then the Lion that gave the place its mediaeval name had been taken from it. He may still be seen—and those who make Venice their starting point for Greece should see him—in front of the Venetian arsenal where Morosini put him in 1685, and one would that the taking of this had been the worst thing he did to Athens. Yet English folk have a lawful interest in the Lion, poor beast though he is artistically, seeing that Greek artists did not usually have the chance of studying him, as they did their horses, in the flesh. He still bears the names of English and Norse members of the Varangian Guard—Harold Hardrada himself among them they say—who being on duty in Athens 'cut our names on this beast, the Greeks not liking it'.

Athens, as a modern town, gets scant justice from visitors. Yet take out everything classical—though that is a big concession—and what remains is a good modern capital. But, say one hundred years ago, this modern capital was a third-rate Turkish *Kaimakamlik*, containing perhaps four hundred houses, most of them roofless. On the Acropolis the Parthenon (its interior filled with a cheap mosque) stood among a crowd of wooden Turkish houses, picturesque and tumbledown, at the mercy of any chance conflagration there. Every capital and town in the countries that once were the Turkish empire shows what Turkish rule meant for them, by the progress they have made since that glacier was removed, and in none has the progress been more marked than in Greece.

Of course, one can see, after the event, that things might have

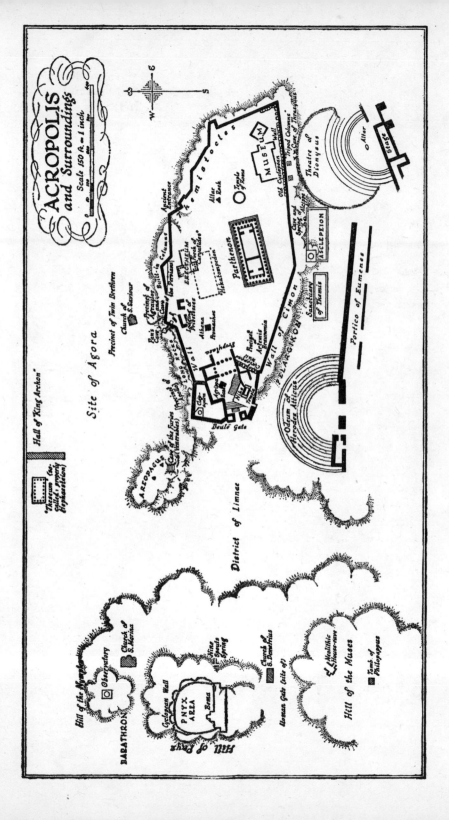

ACROPOLIS and Surroundings

Scale 150 ft. = 1 inch

ACROPOLIS

been better done. In 1829, the circuit of the old walls was still visible, and a German-Scot architect, of the name of Ross, had a grand scheme. 'Forbid all building within the old walls. Buy out the old shanties as chance offers. Lay out the modern city outside. Keep classical Athens as a park, with the Acropolis as its centre.' Had that been done, the capital would now have a park unrivalled in the world, and we should know more about ancient Athens than we are ever likely to know; but 'vested interests' forbade. Still, if things might have been much better, they might also have been much worse. The architects of the King's palace wanted to put it on the Acropolis 'where one end of the Parthenon will make a fine portico for it. The other end we can destroy'. One can see that Palace, portico and all, in Constitution Square today, and thank all the gods of ancient Athens for what they have saved us from.

The Acropolis has always been a natural citadel and sanctuary. The higher and stronger hill of Lycabettus—which was just far enough from the Acropolis to have then no military significance for it—was always neglected, most likely because it has no water supply. It plays no part in history, is the peg for just one legend, and now only carries an unimportant monastery. The Acropolis has always been the national home, from the days when the Athenians were a tiny tribe and Eleusis and Hymettus the abode of hostile foreigners. Then the rock top was the city, and the Cyclopean wall that we still trace its fortification, the work of the Cyclopes whom Athena brought to wall the city of her favourite Cecrops. Gradually the city crept down from the plateau, first to the hollow below and then to the plain to the north, while the King came down from his palace, and sat in the gate by the sacred rock of Areopagus, to do judgment and justice. When the Persian came, the Acropolis was still both citadel and sanctuary for the 'wheel-like' city at its foot, and served as such, as we see in the episode of the 'wooden wall'. It was only when the triumphant Athenians came back to their ruined homes, that they determined that the place should in future be a sanctuary only, and so it has ever since remained—with the exception of two dolorous episodes in modern times, 1685 and 1829.

The Acropolis, then, as we see it, dates from the triumph over the Persian, when all things fell together to give the Athenians a grand opportunity, most grandly used. There was a great feat to commemorate, a feat in which they had borne the most heroic part by far; there were abundant funds to devote to it—if we do not ask too closely about their right to devote them to that end! There was an outburst of genius among their artists of which the world has but once seen the like since; Mnesicles, Ictinus, Pheidias, are the tallest by but a few inches in a generation of artistic giants. There was a statesman at the head of affairs who would give those artists a free hand. They had the best material at call; whereas they had built in stone hitherto, they now realized that Pentelicus is one block of the finest marble in the world. Finally, they had a site that was sacred already, but which was practically a *tabula rasa* for their art. With one exception, they were not annoyed by the existence of shrines that were too sacred to disturb. Hence we get work done in one lifetime which was recognized as a masterpiece from the day of its completion to our own.

The very hill had to be remodelled before the work could be begun. The original gable-shaped ridge, with a precipice to the north and a steep slope to the south, was revetted by the erection of great walls on both sides, Themistocles undertaking the one and Cimon the other. The V-shaped space between the walls and the hill was filled with the rubble and broken statues from the older buildings that the Persians had destroyed, including the old 'Hundred-foot' Temple of Peisistratus, with its decorations. This made a level platform on which the new temple of Athena could stand, though its foundations were carefully carried down to the solid rock, a precaution that not many Greek architects would have been wise enough to insist on.

The process of revetting blocked one of the ancient entrances to the Acropolis—a ravine in the rock on the northern side—and Themistocles erected, at this point, one of the most enduring monuments of history. At the moment of the invasion, it would seem that the stone-built temple of Peisistratus was in the act of being surrounded with a new marble peristyle and the rude stone sculptures of its pediments being replaced by marble groups, appropriately representing the combat of Athena with the giants. The scaffolding gave the Persian a good opportunity of burning these, and the fire spoilt the marble for its purpose. Themistocles built the drums of the columns and the blocks meant for the cornices into his wall, 'to be a memorial for time to come for ever and ever', and they are there unto this day. How many of our war memorials, one wonders, will last as long?

The one regular entrance left to the Acropolis was the present one, at the western end, where the old fortifications of the Nine Gates were destroyed, to make room for a grand ceremonial portal. This as we see it now is partly blocked by later constructions, put up when the Acropolis had to serve as a citadel once more. These are the Beulé gate—so called from the man who rediscovered it in 1850—which is an extemporized protection made of scraps from older monuments, and dating from the Gothic invasion under the Emperor Decius, when the Pax Romana began to fail; and the 'bastion of Odysseus' enclosing the old Clepsydra spring which supplied the Acropolis with water, and recalling the War of Greek Independence in the nineteenth century. There has been some idea of removing these, under the impression that all that is not 'classic' and Hellenic ought to go, but it is to be hoped that nothing will be done. History is after all continuous, and these are part of the story of the place—and not its least interesting portion.

The dream of Mnesicles in erecting the Propylaea was 'a far-seen portal'. His white colonnades were to stand on the base of bare blue rock, with the blue sky behind. A zig-zag track—the remains of it are to be seen—was to be the one means of approach, and on great occasions the Pan-Athenaic Ship, the Chariots, and so on, had to remain below, though the sacrificial animals could be led up the road and of course the human element in the procession went up easily enough. Still, the girls who on these occasions wore long robes and carried big baskets on their heads, must have been well trained, if the procession was never to lose dignity. Of course, men will try to improve the work of a genius, and Mnesicles' design was not left alone. Marble steps of Roman date—the workmanship of which would have infuriated the original foreman—replaced the track, and statues adorned the whole. The big blue base of one of these, 'the Agrippa Monument', remains, and by it hangs a tale.

Athens, as subject to Rome, always took a hand in any civil war that was going, and always on the wrong side. Always the victor was apt to say, 'these rascals shall pay', but always there was somebody at his elbow to beg them off, and say 'Of course they deserve all you are likely to do, but, I have served you well, and I am an Athens university man!' (The city had practically become the Oxford of the Roman Empire.) In the civil war of the 'Second Triumvirate' she went in on the wrong side with her accustomed zeal. She put the statues of Brutus and Cassius, the 'liberators of the world', side by side with those of Harmodius and Aristogeiton, the 'liberators of Athens'—and the act took a deal of explaining when that side went down. The undergraduates of the 'university' joined the republican army, Horace among them. The fact that he was given rank as battalion commander (Tribune) at once, throws some light on the quality of the corps of officers in that force, for Horace's virtues, though they were many and great, were by his own confession not military!

Tecum Philippos et celerem fugam
Sensi, relicta non bene parmula.   (Odes II. vii. 9).

One fears that Trevelyan does not do injustice to the arguments by which the recruits were gathered to that force.

Whoever joins us shall get lots of booty,
And someone else shall do his turn of duty.[1]

It was Vipsanius Agrippa, general of Octavian, and friend of the jolly tribune in better days, who begged Athens off this time and the size and position of the memorial erected to him is presumably the measure of the Athenian fright on that occasion.

Mnesicles' great Propylaea (the word means no more than portals) were never finished, any more than the older set that preceded them and that are hidden under and behind them. Even the portions built still carry the *óta*, the 'ears' by which the blocks of marble were to be slung into position, which were meant to be chipped off afterwards. One can also see half-smoothed surfaces. There are, however, more important omissions than that. On the north wing, where the tiny Pinakotheke, or Athenian National Gallery, was situated, the whole colonnade that should finish the eastern face is missing, a fact for which we probably have to thank the Peloponnesian war.

The southern wing, which should run out like its fellow to the edge of the precipice, ends in a blank wall some twenty feet short of it. This was because the revised plan for the Propylaea, as made by Mnesicles, trespassed on one of the ancient shrines of the Acropolis. It would seem from the look of things that the authorities of the shrine have said: 'This new portal of yours may be a very fine thing, but please do not trespass on ground holy from of old. Remodel your plan.' The artists have said among themselves; 'No, do not cut up a good plan. Stop exactly where we are. Give Pericles five years, and he will put the parsons in their place, and we can go on.' Right or wrong, however, the parsons have won!

The precinct in question was that of Artemis Brauronia, a local deity (Brauron is in Northern Attica) who is not quite the same as the maiden huntress whom all know, but has much more in com-

[1] 'Horace at the University of Athens.'

mon with the grim Great Mother whom we meet again and again in Hellas, and is one with the Artemis Laphria of Patras and (perhaps) the Artemis Orthia of Sparta.

On her festal day, a great bonfire was lit in her precinct, and anyone who wished for luck in the coming year brought up some beast or bird and drove them through the fire—a ritual that we meet in many lands.

The Priestesses of the goddess, who were little girls aged from eight to twelve years, danced round the fire arrayed in bear-skins (or in saffron tunics in a later age) and ended the ceremony by jumping through or over the fire themselves. Obviously, the bear was somehow connected with this Artemis, as is natural enough for the 'lady of the wild wood'; and hence we get the one surviving relic of this shrine—a small bear that is now in the Acropolis museum.

The Propylaea was one of the things of which Athens was most justifiably proud. We read that in one evil day, when Athens found herself obliged to pay a heavy war indemnity to Thebes, and declared that she simply had not the wherewithal to raise the money, Epaminondas suggested that in that case, she might pay in kind and not in cash. Thebes would take over the Propylaea, and re-erect it on the Cadmaea. Athens paid, in cash!

As it was never a sanctuary, this great portal was never desecrated, but it could be used for mean ends notwithstanding. When the Frankish Dukes ruled in Athens in the XIIIth century—for Shakespeare wrote better history than he either knew or cared when he referred to 'Dukes of Athens'—it became their residence, as the Parthenon was their cathedral. Hence the erection of that great tower, now removed, which we see in pictures of the Acropolis, up to 1860, and hence too the holes hacked in the marble walls, to show where floors have been inserted.

The Propylaea, though disfigured by this barbarism, remained structurally uninjured till the fatal seventeenth century. During the Turkish occupation it served as a powder magazine, and in the year 1656 it so happened that there was a festival of some sort in the streets of Athens, and the Turkish governor, *more Turcico*, told the soldiers to assist the jollifications by throwing down a few bombs. As they went about the work with Turkish casualness, they blew up the magazine and thus reduced the Propylaea to the ruin that it is today.

The tiny temple of Athena Nike, 'Athena the giver of victory (as we are now bidden to call what we once styled Nike Apteros), stands out in front of the great Portal, on a bastion that was part of the original fortification of the Acropolis. In almost any ancient castle such a bastion will be found, so placed, that an assailant of the main gate must expose his right (his unshielded) side as he advances to the assault. This building is actually earlier than either Parthenon or Propylaea, being the first temple to be rebuilt by the Athenians when they returned to their homes after Plataea. Originally its altar stood in the tiny precinct in front of it, and the whole bastion was surrounded with a parapet—and a marvellous one for it embodied the 'Frieze of Victories' that is in the Museum now.

It adds something to the interest we feel in these ladies—who are just a little conscious of their own wonderful beauty—if we remember that they were the gift of Alcibiades, his trophy for the victories he won in the last act of the Peloponnesian war, by which, if he had been left to himself, that wayward genius might have given an honourable peace to the mother whom he had so wronged but whom he yet loved.

The temple stood uninjured till 1685, but in the fatal Venetian siege of that year it was thrown over the edge of the bastion by the Turks, who wanted (for nothing is sacred to a sapper) to put a battery in its place. The fragments lay in rubbish heaps below till Lord Elgin recognized parts of its frieze and rescued them for the British Museum, and thereby called attention to the rest. Be it remembered that Lord Elgin did not take these from their proper place, whatever may be said of the rest of his prizes. The temple was reconstructed in 1836, but a few pardonable blunders were made in the process; and small wonder, seeing that this was the first work of the kind attempted. Archaeologists were always anxious to take it down and do the work over again, the rather as they wished to secure an accurate plan of an older and pre-Persian temple that underlay the later one. In the thirties of the present century, their opportunity came. An earthquake so shook the structure of the bastion, which consists of a solid core of rock surrounded by masonry, that an examination had to be carried out, and the discovery was made that the Turks had so damaged the whole structure that the only marvel was that it had stood up for as long as it had. They had sunk water-cisterns in it. The whole therefore had to come down and a better reconstruction based on maturer knowledge could be commenced. This work was still in process when the war of 1940 began.

As one passes through the Propylaea and enters on the platform of the Acropolis, what one sees is, the two famous temples with the ribbed line of the Sacred Way running between them; and also, a wilderness of marble blocks, kept religiously in the hope that the proper place may yet be found for each one. Indeed, it has been found for some of them. In old days, the area must have been at least as full of statues as it is now of stones, for one sees the matrices that mark the sites everywhere in the rock, and one suspects that it must have been, like Delphi, overcrowded and confused.

Take the groups which, as Pausanias tell us, stood just by the Propylaea. Here were the statue and altar to 'Athena the Health-giver', commemorating the recovery of a valuable workman, who fell from the roof of the portico on to the rock; and the 'Wooden Horse of Troy' with heroes emerging from between its ribs. Could even a Greek make much of that? 'Lemnian Athena' (by common consent the most beautiful thing Pheidias ever made[1] stood just by it, and by Athena's side in strange companionship the 'Tongueless Lioness' of brass, in memory of the Hetaera Leaena, who cut out her own tongue lest she should betray her conspirator-lover, Harmodius, under torture. The statue of Conon, who pulled Athens to her feet after the disaster of 404 B.C., had a right here; but by its side stood that of Cleoetas, whose one title to fame was the invention of a new starting-gate for chariot races. Could even Westminster Abbey show a more amazing mixture?

Over them all towered Athena Promachos, the colossal figure of the goddess at guard over her city, Pheidias' own design.[2] She stood at her post long enough to save her city from Alaric in the Vth century, whose Goths saw her on her own citadel and fled. Soon after, she seems to have been taken to Constantinople, leaving only her stone base behind, and there she stood for nine centuries more, to meet a melancholy fate at last. When the buccaneering Crusaders attacked the city in 1204, the mob of Constantinople pulled her down and broke her up, because they got the idea into their collective mind that the outstretched arm of the statue had beckoned the invaders from the west. After the sack the plunderers, being short of money, melted her down—and, with her, other statues like the original Bronze Wolf of Rome—and coined her into ha'pence.

If however the statues of the greatest age have all gone, those of

[1] There is a contemporary reproduction of the head of this at Bologna Museum.
[2] The old tale, that the light on Athena's spear could be seen from Cape Sunion, is impossible. Hymettus is in a direct line between the two, and the figure was not taller than the hill. A ship coming up to Piraeus from Sunium would see it, if the sun was at the right angle.

an older day have come to light in our own time. In the days of Peisistratus and later a priestess of Athena seems to have been allowed to dedicate her own likeness in the temple when her time of service was done, and this resulted, in course of time, in a great collection of figures. All of them were knocked down and broken by the Persians, and when the Athenians returned, though the custom of dedicating the statues lapsed, the fragments were reverently put away in the 'revetment spaces' (see p. 18). Only a few years ago, it occurred to some fortunately obstinate archaeologist, that these spaces had never been examined; so though he was assured that there could be nothing there he dug and looked, and was rewarded by the discovery of the series of statues that now adorn the museum and prove that Athenian art did not spring to life fullgrown as men once thought, but evolved like every other human product.[1]

Of the two great temples, the Erechtheum really stands first in order of time and even of religious importance, though its present fabric is later than the Parthenon in date, and of course relatively insignificant. It was built by Nicias, the luckless general of the Peloponnesian war, and is recognized in every architectural treatise as the standard specimen of the Ionic style at its best. The fact that it was used as the residence of the Disdar, or Turkish governor, of the Acropolis, and that the wonderful northern porch was his *haremlik*, at least served to save it so far that repair was not impossible. Originally, when the city was all on the Acropolis, and the 'well-built house of Erechtheus' (relics of which still remain) the palace, the city temple was on this spot, for which reason it remained always the most sacred of the Athenian shrines.

As the original temple of the city, it was a place where many cults gathered, and it was probably for that reason that when Nicias built the temple that we see—and which again was never finished—his architect had to accept the exceptional, indeed abnormal, shape that we know. The sacred spots were there already and could not be moved, and the plan of the temple had to be made to accommodate them somehow. Of course all these shrines, and all the old divisions of the interior, perished when Justinian made it into a church, and

---

[1] The statues are known by the delightfully absurd name of 'the Aunts'. On their discovery the leading French archaeologist of the day naturally dashed up to see them, and was led into the shed where they were placed. He stood at gaze for an instant before one, and burst out 'Mais mon Dieu, c'est ma tante elle-meme!' And the 'Aunts' they accordingly became. Many are probably portraits.

hacked the old entrance portico at the east end to make room for an apsidal sanctuary. One feels that both here and in the Parthenon his men were sacrilegious 'temple-breakers' who were sinning against architectural light. Those who could build the church of Hagia Sophia could not plead ignorance. We have a general idea of what these various shrines were, though even classic Athens had forgotten, in many instances, all about both gods and worship due to them. Here, in this most sacred of shrines, was the original Xoanon, or wooden image, of Athena, and here dwelt her sacred snake, the original *genius loci*. Here was the scene of the great contest with Poseidon, as to who should be patron of Athens. Was not the sacred olive there to testify to it, which the Goddess produced at the time, the ancestor of all olives in the world? The marks of Poseidon's trident on the rock were there too, signs of the blow that produced the warhorse, and though the god of sea and earth-quake was defeated in that battle, yet courtesy extended him a corner in the temple too. It is true that there was another explanation of the marks that are there to testify to this day. Some said that it was there that the lightning-god entered into and impregnated Mother Earth, when he begat Erichthonius upon her. These could point to the undeniable fact that the spot was—and is—a 'bidental' which must never be protected from rain. The tombs of deified founders like Cecrops and Erechtheus were here too (we do not profess to explain how one minor figure came to give his name to the whole), to say nothing of the shrine of Zeus Orkios, guardian at once of the homestead and of the sanctity of oaths.

Hence it was natural that this most sacred spot, and not the Parthenon, should be the goal of the Pan-Athenaic pilgrimage, and that the Xoanon here should receive what is always a mark of great antiquity, the periodical gift of the sacred robe that her priestesses had woven. Yet, was it really Athena's after all? What does the armed virgin who wears the aegis want with any peaceful robe? The excavation that gave us the 'Aunts' has also brought evidence that there was an older goddess here before Athena was heard of, or maybe before the Athenians had come in. A goddess of peaceful arts to whom the olive was sacred ages before Athena invented it! Poor Pandrosos (if that was her name) found that Athena had taken her tree, her shrine, her people—and even her very frock![1]

---

[1] These ancient sculptures make it clear that there was also a shrine of Heracles somewhere on the Acropolis in pre-Persian days. It was not restored after the destruction, and its site is unknown.

Athena's priestesses lived, presumably, in the buildings the foundations of which run along the north side of the Acropolis, and they necessarily numbered a good many. A girl nominated to the office served, normally, for the four years from her twelfth to her sixteenth year, thus being sure of one innings at the great Pan-Athenaic festival. That done, she was free to leave the service and marry, as she or maybe her family determined.

Of course she might continue to serve, and the High Priestess of the Virgin Goddess had a high rank and privileges in the city, being entitled to a measure of corn, a measure of barley, and three obols, for every birth and every death in the city.[1] She was always free to marry if she would, though she had to vacate office of course if she did. Plutarch tells of one lady who was virgin priestess of Athena for three score years and ten, and who when she died at the age of 82 had attained 'through long practice, unrivalled skill in the art of turning down proposals of marriage'.

The girl priestesses had to weave the robe that was to be put on the goddess at the Pan-Athenaea, and one is glad to find that in the intervals of work they were allowed to play ball. They also officiated at the festival of the Arrhephoria. This 'procession of the un-nameables' was the pendant of the Thesmophoria on the Pnyx which we describe later, and the lasses had to carry the basket, that they might not open, down by the 'passage by which the Persian ascended'[2] and deposit it, unopened, in the Precinct of Agraulos below, near to the little temple of 'Aphrodite of the gardens'. As a wholesome warning, they were told how Athena served as nurse in the household of Cecrops, and went off to Pentelicus to bring back a stone to make the Acropolis higher, leaving her basket with her

[1] She did not always get these however. When Sulla was besieging the Acropolis, the Priestess, who was at her post, asked for an instalment of her dues from Aristion, the commander, urging that if there were few births then, deaths at least were plenty. He sent her three bushels of pepper. It would seem that luxuries were more abundant than necessities up on the Acropolis just then; Aristion had to yield for lack of water. Two hours after Sulla had got in, an unseasonable rain-storm filled all the empty cisterns once more. These cisterns, that supplemented the Clepsydra spring, are in the rock on the north side of the Parthenon.

[2] The cleft in the rock, by which the Persians stormed the Acropolis, can still be seen in its northern side, and British officers have found it not inaccessible to good cragsmen. No doubt the priestesses used a ladder of sorts. Quite close to it, and by the ancient houses of Mycenaean date preserved there, are the 'steps down to the cave of Pan'. It is by these steps that the faithless comrades of Lysistrata try to make their escape 'just to get home and card the wool' when she and the other women of Athens are defending the Acropolis against their husbands.

26

charges, with orders not to open it. Disobeying, they found Athena's snake therein, coiled round their brother Erichthonius. The crow told Athena, who at once dropped the block she was bringing from Pentelicus (it is there unto this day, as the hill Lycabettus!) and came back looking so furious that the girls jumped over the precipice and broke their necks. 'And that is what will happen to you, young ladies, if you dare to open the holy basket!'

On the southern side of the Erechtheum is the famous caryatid porch, or Porch of the Maidens, as it is now called. Structurally, it is not a porch, for there is no door behind it, but is a mere ornament, the beauty of which is its own justification. Once, this use of the human figures as pillars was thought unique, but actually the motif was not an uncommon one, and we know of other instances at Corinth, Agrigentum, Delphi, and so on, though this is *facile princeps* among them all for beauty. One of the maidens, as is known, was taken to London by Lord Elgin, and her place is now filled by a cast in hard cement. This is at least better than the brick pier that Lord Elgin left to carry the cornice, though, as the cement reproduction shows exactly what the 'Maidens' were like a hundred years ago, it also shows how painfully they have wasted in that interval. One must own that the air of Athens under modern conditions is not what it used to be.

The Maidens look straight across the foundations of the older temple of Athena to the Parthenon, which one can hardly dare to describe. When the two men who of all children of Adam were perhaps the most richly endowed with genius in their own way have put their absolute best into a building an ordinary man had best hold his peace. Yet no plan can be simpler than this, an oblong box with a row of uprights round it, and the temple was merely intended as a support for the ornaments, the carving without and the treasures within. It is true that those ornaments became 'classic' as soon as they were made, and have been models for sculpture for all time. It was said that Pheidias handled every theme in the conventional way, yet when he had done it there was something there that none had ever put in it before and that all felt to be indispensable after. Something like that is true of Ictinos also. His work can lose all its decoration and be smashed to pieces beside, and yet remain a marvel at which the world holds its breath.

We know that the work is all straight lines, and yet not a line in it is straight; there is the curve of the *crepidôma* on which the pillars stand, the *entasis* or swell and taper of the pillars themselves, and

27

the inward tilt of each one, so that if the centre line of each were produced, all would meet at a point two miles up; while the whole is made without cement, and with joins into which you cannot put a needle, and which will resist water-drip like a continuous surface. How was it done? Let us put the problem as an engineer put it to us, and maybe others will find the answer that we could not. 'How did these men make their straight edge? A straight edge they certainly had, to make those subtle departures from it, and if you have the plane surface that gives you the straight edge, from it you can make the cylinder and the screw; so, in all mechanical engineering, it is the true plane surface that is the key. We know where ours come from, in modern engineering. They are all descended from a set made in 1844, by Joseph Whitworth. Where did Ictinos get his?'

The problem of the recent reconstruction of the northern colonnade—on which the southern will probably follow—is one on which two opinions are allowable. Is it a gain or no? We think that it is. Archaeologists said it could not be done right. It was three thousand to one against getting each drum in its right place in the right column, and one blunder would be enough to mar the whole. The reply of Professor Balanos, who has done the work, was as follows: 'Take the detached vertebrae of a dozen human spinal columns. Mix them in a bag and throw them out on a table. Any decent anatomist will be ashamed of himself if he cannot put each bone in its right place in the right column—and a Doric column of Ictinos' is at least as living and articulate a thing as any human back-bone.' The result seems to justify him.

Of course all this wonder was meant to be no more than the setting for the masterpiece that it enshrined, Pheidias' Athena. Of it, not a fragment is left, nor could it be otherwise, for the chryselephantine technique (ivory and gold and plaster on a wooden core) is not very durable.[1] Only an uninspired but accurate copy in the Athens museum gives us some idea of what it may have been like. To us, knowing the size of the statue and the dimensions of the *cella* in which it stood, the idea of so colossal a figure in so confined a space seems jarring, and gives a sense of disproportion. Indeed, one can only solve the problem by an act of faith. If a man and a set of men with an infallible eye for proportion did the thing, it must have been right. At least we know that they repeated the expedient

[1] One fragment of a chryselephantine statue remains—half of an eye from the Aphaea of Aegina. However, see Chap. vi. Delphi, p. 126.

2. Parthenon from North East

3a. Acropolis: Olive tree
in the Erectheum

3b. Cave of Pan. (Acropolis: North Side)

again and again elsewhere—at Olympia, in the Heraeum of Argos at Aegina, at Epidaurus. They must have felt it right. Of course, the statue was meant to be seen only in a dim light, for it is thought that the only illumination of the Parthenon was through the door,[1] from which the worshipper saw Athena towering between the two white colonnades that divided the interior into a nave and two aisles.

Once built, the Parthenon was recognized at once as a part of the world's inheritance. Even those who aspired to destroy Athens, like Thebes and Corinth after Aegospotami, assumed that it must be preserved. Desecrators like Demetrius and Cleopatra, who aspired to divine rank, and were granted it by degenerate Athenians, could only claim to receive it in the Parthenon, as the highest—and also the most inappropriate—of honours. When Alexander conquers the Persian, he must put his trophies there, and the square holes in the architrave of the eastern face once carried the golden shields that were the spoil of Issus. When megalomaniac Nero wins his marvellous triumph and, first of all mankind, is awarded the crown at every one of all the great choric contests of Greece, an inscription in gold letters on the Parthenon has to commemorate it. We can see the traces to this day, again on the east front.

Yet one feels that, with all the glory of the Parthenon[2] it was the glory of Athens that was worshipped there rather than Athena. It was never a very holy shrine, and could accept, without any feeling of incongruity, a temple of 'Rome and Augustus' at its eastern end. So much was this the case, that even when the great statue of Athena was in its first glory, Pericles could count it as part of the state reserve of bullion, and tell the people that they had still plenty in the treasury, and that if they wanted more, there were still the robes of Athena to use.

To the last, the strangest prehistoric rites went on under the very shadow of the Parthenon, and perhaps made a more real appeal than any worship practised there. The original altar of the fane is still standing by the north-east corner of it, for it is no more than

[1] Some suggest a skylight immediately over the head of the figure, and anyone who has seen the marvellous effects that the Egyptian architects could produce by that expedient in a temple otherwise dark, will not be in too great a hurry to reject the idea. Translucent marble tiles sound very attractive, but those that survive are 1½ inches thick.

[2] Oddly, this familiar name was only given by accident to the temple. It was confined at first to the western chamber of the *cella*, perhaps because the priestesses lodged there then, as the word means 'the maidens' chamber'. It was only after a generation or two that men felt that they had hit on the ideal name for the whole building.

the original rough summit of the Acropolis crag, the old 'High Place', like another 'Rock', Es-Saqqarah at Jerusalem. Its dedication, not to Athena, but to Zeus and Athena, shows its antiquity.

Here was celebrated 'the Bull-killing' a thing that even Aristophanes laughs at as old-fashioned, but which nobody could dream of stopping, and quaint enough it was. Once in the year, all the official world went up to the Acropolis and strewed barley cakes and meal on this altar. Six bulls were then driven up, and the one that first went up on to the altar and ate the cakes was taken for sacrifice, and offered with the queerest of ritual. One man, (let us call him A) happened to come along with an axe, and left it on the altar. B, who was a girl, strayed along with a grindstone and left it by the axe. C, struck by this conjunction, took the axe and sharpened it, and then left it where it was. D chanced to find it there, and handed it on to E, who had a sudden brain-wave, and killed the ox with it. Then all present raised a howl of execration, and hurled stones at E, who ran for dear life, but the populace, finding that 'brother ox' is undoubtedly dead, proceed to make use of him, and prepare him for a banquet; while some take the skin, stuff it with straw and set it up on four sticks in a caricature of life. By this time E has been captured and brought back, and now begins the trial, 'who killed brother ox?' All the high dignitaries of Athens shouted out an old nursery rhyme:

> *It was E, it was E, that wicked one, he*
> *Took the axe that he hit brother ox with.*

E in defence passes on the guilt to D, 'for he took the axe and he gave it to me'; D in his turn accuses C, 'for he sharpened the axe and he gave it to me'; and C of course passes it on to 'the naughty girl B, for she brought the grindstone and put it by me', and finally it is decided that the really guilty party is the axe, which is duly tried for the murder and thrown into the sea. Guilt being thus done away with, a feast on 'brother ox' can follow with a clear conscience. The whole ceremony must go back to primitive days, when killing an ox was far worse than killing a man, for in murdering him you kill the food supply of the tribe—you cannot plough without him. Yet, man *will* have beef on high days and holidays, so brother ox must die; and the guilt of killing him, admittedly tremendous, must be divided up among as many as possible, till the share of any individual is negligible.

An odd custom, of course, but one that we can hardly laugh at, for such nursery rhymes as 'Who killed Cock Robin?' and 'How the old woman got home that night' reflect something very like it; while if the Athenians were childish in finding the inanimate axe guilty of murder, it was quite late in the XIXth century before the law of Deodand went off our own statute book; and by it the cart or tree that had killed a man was held guilty of homicide, and 'given to God' in the persons of His poor. It was only railway trains that put a stop to it.

Even with the triumph of Christianity, however, men felt that the Acropolis, the supreme instance of human genius, was a thing by itself. Practically all other pagan temples were dismantled and desecrated, and only after a stage of existence as a ruin did some of them become places of worship once more. The Parthenon and the Erectheum became churches at once. If the former did receive barbarous treatment as regards the interior, it became a cathedral, sacred to the Virgin of another faith. None dared to desecrate its sculptures, and they still adorned the church of the Panagia when the frescoes of Basil the Bulgar-slayer, that still survive, struck an entirely new note in its interior.

It became a Latin Cathedral when Latin replaced Greek as the ruler, a mosque when Ottoman replaced decadent Florentine, and the Greek bowed before another master. It was the lot of Mahommed the conqueror to take over to his faith the two most wonderful buildings in the world, the Parthenon and Hagia Sophia.

So it remained, unaltered externally, till the dolorous day in 1685, when the Venetian Morosini besieged the Turk in the Acropolis, and the German adventurer in his service, Königsmark,[1] turned his guns upon it and blew it up. Nor did the destruction end there. Morosini, the Venetian general, contemplated the great sculpture of the western pediment, representing the contest between Athena and Poseidon for the patronship of Athens. The chariots of the gods

---

[1] This adventurer is curiously connected with English history. Resident in London under Charles II, he made our country too hot for him by sharing in the murder of Lord Thynne, in the Haymarket, and thereby secured for himself an appearance—as one of the murderers—on the monument in Westminster Abbey. His nephew, Philip von Königsmark, made an almost successful attempt to elope with Sophia, wife of George, Elector of Hanover —afterwards George I—and lost his life in consequence. Hence the quarrel between George and his son, Frederick, whom George never believed to be really his son. Aurora, the beautiful sister of Philip, was out for revenge for her brother, and to obtain it became one of the numerous mistresses of Augustus the Strong, of Saxony. Augustus would not start a European war, even to oblige her, but the result of their *amour* was the Marshal Saxe who beat us at Fontenoy.

appeared in this group, and Morosini declared that he would give St. Mark a second, and even a finer team of horses than those that stand above that Cathedral door. Accordingly he gave orders for the removal of this central part of the great composition, but the ropes by which the statues were being lowered broke under the strain, and the whole was smashed on the rock below.

A second and smaller mosque was built in—and out of—the ruined fane, and it continued standing till the beginning of the nineteenth century, while anyone who cared to *bakhshish* the Mahommedan authorities was allowed to take away 'mementoes' of what had absolutely no interest to its owners. Then came the firman of the Sultan and the removal of the sculpture *en bloc* by Lord Elgin. We do not propose to enter into any discussion of his action, but it must be pointed out that he certainly saved all that he took from destruction, either by the curio-hunter or by war, when Turk and Greek got at one another's throats, and both alike were pointing their guns in turn at the Parthenon.[1]

[1] Apropos of the return of these sculptures, there is one point that ought not to be forgotten. The process of weathering, which we noted has so damaged the 'Maidens', has not spared that section of the Frieze of the Parthenon that remains *in situ*, viz., that at the western end. Anyone can get proof of this by a visit to the British Museum, where that section is represented by casts. The casts are in duplicate, one taken by Lord Elgin about 1810, the other about 1870. The difference made in the carvings by sixty years of weathering is painful, and now that process has been going on for seventy years more. If the sculptures were returned, we do not think that the Greek authorities would venture to put them back *in situ*, even where that is possible, but would do what they have done, quite rightly, at Delphi. That is to say they would keep the originals in the Acropolis museum, though they might replace the metopes and pediment sculptures by casts of hard cement. Only a very small portion of the Frieze could go back into position, for the wall of the *cella* is not there to receive it. There is then no question of putting back these works where they were. It is a case of Museum against Museum, and ought in fairness to be argued on that basis.

II

THE SKIRTS OF THE ACROPOLIS

*The Limnae—St. Marina—Anthesteria Feast—Pnyx—The Long
Walls—Thargelia—The Thesmophoria—Cave of Pan—Theseum—
Areopagus—Metroön—Odeum—Asclepeion—Theatre of Dionysus
—Choragic Monuments*

A really conscientious traveller, having seen how Athens took her origin on the Acropolis, will follow the stages of her growth, going next to see the area of her first extensions. There is little to be seen of the first of these, the Pelargikon or Pelasgikon on the south-west slope of the rock. Part of its old boundary-wall can be traced, and it was so sacred a place in later days that even the refugees of the Peloponnesian war were not allowed to squat therein. It seems to have contained one venerable shrine, that of Aphrodite Pandemos. To one's astonishment, one finds that this aspect of the 'triple Aphrodite' (i.e. the 'Popular' the 'Heavenly' and the 'Evil-Averting') was a most respectable divinity, and her high-priestess a matron of high position, even if she did ride a brazen he-goat on days of big festival.

When we get down a little further to the Limnae or Marsh, we find more to see—for those with archaeological eyes and imaginations. The name of the place seems odd, for it is an elevated saucer between the limestone hills of Acropolis and Pnyx, and is dry enough now. However, those who know Yorkshire moors know that such a place can hold water, and the cisterns and shallow wells that are there in abundance justify the name. There was only one spring in it, in a grotto under the Pnyx rocks, and this would seem to be where Peisistratus, in his efforts to increase the water supply of his city, put up his Nine-spouts fountain, Enneakrounos. If we use the term of the 'Old Town' of Athens for that which is given that name today, round about the agora, then here in Limnae, now deserted, we have the 'Older Town' and up on the platform of the Acropolis was the oldest of all. The main street of the Limnae district, traceable still, was the Sacred Way by which the procession of the Pan-Athenaea went up to the Acropolis; and when the Knights came galloping up it four abreast, as the Frieze of the Parthenon assures us that they did, one suspects that spectators kept to the flat house-roofs, for the road is seldom more than twelve feet wide, or fifteen at its largest. Side streets are narrower still.

Houses in classic Athens were simple enough, built of mud brick on the stone foundations that remain, and running up only to two stories, round a pillared court. There were no external windows, (burgling was house-breaking in the most literal sense) and the door that was the one opening in the wall swung outwards. Hence the need of a knock to warn passers-by that it was to be opened, as otherwise they would be precipitated into the unsavoury gutter in the middle of the narrow street. There was little domestic display even for the wealthy. It was that young scape-grace Alcibiades who started 'ostentation' in his own home, introducing paintings and marble there, and making it 'finer than a Temple'. Yet a woman of reputable character was seldom allowed outside these tiny hovels. Even Xenophon—and he was a model husband—thinks that if a woman wanted change and exercise, she could always go and wash the clothes, or re-fold the linen in the cupboard.

But it is here, in this old quarter, that we find evidence of the older strata of Athenian religion still living, when the later and grander have often perished. Here there was nothing of use as a quarry, and no statues to tempt the iconoclast, so here we get the old gods of popular worship, whose observances often go on to this day. Here, for instance, dwelt the god whose modern name is St. Marina, though what his or her old one may have been we know not. St. Marina appears in modern art as a most beautiful maiden, who is holding the Devil by the horn with one hand, and is banging the poor fiend on the head with a hammer. According to her legend, she was a fair virgin, who was so ascetic in habit that she put on boy's clothes and entered herself as a monk in a monastery. But it so befell that a wicked woman, who had tempted the beautiful monk in vain, accused 'him' falsely of being the father of her child, so that poor Marina had to choose between doing penance for a sin of which she was manifestly innocent, or disclosing her secret. Preferring the former, she was expelled the monastery with ignominy, but set up a hermit's cell near by and lived a life of such asceticism that even the strictest of monks held that 'Marinus' had atoned for a slip of youth, and invited 'him' to be their abbot. However, she refused, and it was only at her death that her secret became known.

So much for her story. Now for her observance. This most ascetic of Virgins specializes in providing large families for all that desire them, and ladies can secure such by sitting on a certain slope of rock close by the church, and sliding to the bottom of it. The rite is not so fashionable now as it was of old time, but the rock still retains the high polish the practice has given it. Now one may be sure that this was not started by the Holy Marina. That good lady is masquerading as somebody else again, and somebody much more ancient and less scrupulous. Only, one would like to know who it is!

Here, too, in Limnae is the really ancient shrine of Dionysus, one far older than the bigger one that all know of. However, that junior one superseded the older, and it was only opened for public worship once a year, though it did serve in between for the Dionysiac rites of a Thiasos or Masonic lodge of Orphic initiates, the Iobacchi.

Its one festival however was a great one, the three days of the Anthesteria—days of Jar-opening, Pitchers and Pots (*Pithoigia, Choes, Chutroi*). It was a three days' spring fair—it fell in February —in honour of Dionysus when the jars of the last year's vintage were opened, and anybody and everybody might blamelessly get drunk. 'A gentleman does not take too much wine, except of course at a feast of Dionysus' says Plato. It was then that the wife of the highest official, the King Archon, was ceremonially married to Dionysus and there were dramatic contests too. It was at this feast that the *Frogs* was first produced, as the chorus makes clear to us,

> *In Limnae we sing the divine*
> *Nisaean giver of wine,*
> *When the people in lots*
> *With their sanctified pots*
> *Come reeling around thy shrine.*

(Harrison: *Themis*)

But the feast was not a jollification only, but an 'All Souls' Day' as well. The connexion is not too clear to us, but to a Greek pots served, not only to hold wine, but to put on graves for offerings there, so that the Opening of the Pots is also the Opening of the Graves, and the dwellers therein can come out and share in the feast with their descendants.

Thus the final offering of the rite is the untasted dish that is holy to Hermes Chthonios, the Guide of Souls; and the last act, the dismissal of the spirits, the Keres, under his guidance, to their place. A solemn rite of exorcism followed, and one that survives to this day. Even now, at the beginning of Lent, folk will observe 'Clean Monday' by doing as their fathers did at Anthesteria. The house is clean-swept and herbs like buck-thorn hung up at the door—the prehistoric *Eiresione*—to keep evil spirits out. Meantime all humans adjourn to the open country, and make sure of expelling any devil that may have effected a lodgement internally, by solemn chewing of garlic.

But it is not only Aristophanes who is present in spirit with us in Limnae. Just by the shrine of Dionysus is a little *Ziaret* or place of sacrifice, dedicated originally to one Amynos, a local 'healer' whom Asclepius annexed in classic days. But, before Amynos had quite vanished, he secured a measure of permanence by taking in a colleague, a hero recently 'canonized', in the person of Dexion. But Dexion, as an inscription tells us, is really no other than Sophocles, 'deified' under that name. Dionysus does honour here to the man who did most honour to him in his greater shrine.

One goes up—or might go up, if modern walls and roads did not intervene—from the Limnae to the Pnyx, as a good citizen should to attend the daily meeting of the Ecclesia. Here the whole hill is fortunately clear, so that one can trace the old arrangements of the place of assembly, though the alterations are great. In classic days the whole top of the hill was artificially levelled—or more probably given a slope the reverse of the one it now has—and the platform thus made was retained in place by a wall of 'cyclopean' masonry. This wall has lost a good deal of its height, and in consequence the whole Assembly area slopes away from the *bema* that is still *in situ* at the top, instead of down towards it. If the area is gone, however, the speakers' platform is there (it is hewn from the living rock and so is immovable enough) and one can still stand where Pericles, Cleon and Demosthenes addressed the people, or sit on the steps where expectant speakers had to wait. Behind the speaker, in a position where.they probably heard little of his eloquence, were the seats for the Prytaneis or presidential board, but the area where the people gathered was apparently unseated.

The other two hills that one sees from this point, the 'Museum' Hill to the south, and that 'of the Nymphs' to the north, are less important. The very conspicuous monument to Philopappus, that nobody can avoid seeing on the summit of the former, is a grief of mind to every true lover of Greece. This nobody—he was a Roman Consul in days when the Consulate was the equivalent of a modern bought peerage—got his tomb put in this finest site in Athens; and a freak of fate has preserved it, when the memorials of Pericles and Plato have vanished utterly. The craggy hill 'of the Nymphs' opposite is more interesting. In the clefts of its rocks, there still dwell the three terrible Old Women, whose names are Cholera, Vlogia and Panoukla (Cholera, Plague and Small-pox) and who are quite undisturbed by the modern and scientific atmosphere induced by the Observatory on the top, or the more effectual presence of Hagia Marina on the slopes below. Just over the ridge one can trace the old site of the Barathron, the pit in the rock in which, outside the old wall, the bodies of criminals were thrown, and one must remember that it was from somewhere about this point that the Long Walls took off from the fortification of the city, and went away in parallel lines to the town of Piraeus, where they finally merged in the city walls of that place. The ground-plan of the classical Athens must have resembled a long-handled dumb-bell.

Of the walls themselves, not a trace remains above ground, though excavation would probably discover their foundations. Destroyed by the Spartans after Aegospotami, they were restored by Conon but destroyed again by Sulla and this time were never replaced. The very excellence of their construction made them a tempting quarry. Had they been of mud brick, we might see their traces still.

This area was the scene of some of the most ancient and the most reverenced of the religious rites of old Athens, which were by no means those of the great classic temples. Hereabouts, by the Barathron, was the grand consummation of the Thargelia, that very rugged outcrop of primitive strata in the Athenian religious system, a ceremony which, like the Bull-killing, was as incongruous with the rest as a granite boulder in the turf of a rose-garden—and as hard to remove.

It was neither more nor less than the Scape-goat ceremony of Hebrew custom, in an even grimmer form, for this culminated in a human sacrifice—as was very probably also the case in the Proto-Hebraic form of the Biblical ceremony, in the days before Moses reformed the primitive Semitic ritual. The Scape-man and the Scape-woman were selected somehow—from among criminals in historic days—and were labelled the Pharmakoi of the city. This word, familiar enough in its form of Pharmacy now, did not mean a drug then. It signified, what would carry off evils from the body politic, and only by analogy has it come to mean, what will remove them from the body physical. The luckless Pharmakoi, wreathed with figs black and white, were whipped round the city at the great May festival of the Thargelia, driven up to the Barathron, and there in the old days were burnt alive, thus effectually getting rid of the evils of the people that had been symbolically laid upon them. It is true that in later time, including all that we call historic now, the victims were not burned, but were allowed to jump through the fire and run; thus 'carrying the iniquities of the people' at least into a foreign land, if not 'into one not inhabited' (Levit. xvi. 22).

When we find human sacrifice in Greece, it is natural to ask how long that barbarity went on, and the answer is, very much longer than we have been inclined to think. It could be soberly proposed in the days of the Persian war, just before Salamis. In that time of strain, men felt that they must do something to compel the favour of the Gods. Still, it was not actually done, even then. Aristophanes, who always points his gibes with familiar fact, observes how in these degenerate days we Athenians make our high dignitaries out of

> *Any chance fellow we come across,*
> *Not good in old days for a Pharmakos,*
> *Mere dross and refuse, these we use—*

to make cabinet ministers and generals in short!

As a ritual ceremony, the thing went on long enough. That most respectable of 'Deans of a provincial Cathedral', Plutarch, tells us how he performed it at Chaeronaea about 90 A.D., whipping a slave round and out of the town with rods of *agnus castus*, chanting the while, 'Out with hunger, in with health and wealth,' and wondering in his own antiquarian mind what it could all mean. To this day, most honourable Jews in Palestine will practise a ritual burning of their children to Moloch, cutting off a lock of their hair, and throwing it into the furnace at the annual 'Meiron burnings'. In really old times, when the Pharmakos was burnt alive to carry away the evils of the people, that Pharmakos was usually a volunteer.[1] Men believed in their people and their religion then.

[1] People will say, no doubt, that that is flatly incredible. Yet in August 1555, at St. Alban's, George Tankerfield insisted on being burnt alive for his faith, when all Queen Mary's officials as good as begged him to get up and walk away.
> *They were our fathers, those men of yore:*
> *Little they recked of an easy death*
> *They would dip their hands in a heretic's gore;*
> *They stood and burnt for a rule of faith.*

A volunteer, too, was the last case of human sacrifice among Greeks, and that was in the nineteenth century. The rough islanders of Tenos and Santorin were leaders in the war of Greek independence, and the patriots found themselves with their backs fairly to the wall. Something had to be done to make St. Nicholas, their patron, understand the urgency of the position and the need of his help, and a man volunteered to go and tell him. He was sent to St. Nicholas, for his friends cut his head off. It seems horrible to us, but an earlier age accepted it as natural, even as we accept the doctrine that the officer must be the first over the top, or the captain the last to leave the sinking ship. There are times when, as in the case of Codrus, it is the obvious duty of the 'One Man', usually the King, to die for the people.

The area set apart for the Assembly does not occupy more than half the hill of the Pnyx, and the rest was the sanctuary of Demeter. Here there took place annually, in the month of October, the great women's mystery of the Thesmophoria, the Carrying of the Sacred Objects. For the four days of that ceremony, the Pnyx was given over to the women exclusively and any man who trespassed on it was likely to have an even worse time than Mnesilochus in Aristophanes' play. 'Thesmophoriazousae'. The rite was by no means peculiar to Athens; Thebes certainly, and other places probably, had an analogous solemnity. All will remember that Rome had one. The matrons were of course the principal actors, but an old notion that they only were allowed to be present is corrected by Lucan, who makes it clear in his *Dialogues of Courtesans* that maidens, and even ladies of the *demi-monde*, were present too. One of his girls, Myrtion, gives a tremendous dressing-down to her lover Pamphilus, because she thinks he is about to throw her over and 'settle down' respectably. Among the stones in her sling is the statement 'and the girl they are going to marry you off to has not got any good looks to boast of! I saw her at the Thesmophoria!'

The place still bears the name of the goddess—or rather what used to be her name. At the little col between the Pnyx and the Museum hills there once stood the Itonian Gate, a portal that had its share in the Mysteries of Eleusis, as we shall see; at this spot there still stands the Church of St. Demetrius, quite undistinguished deacon and most respectable martyr of the fourth century. Thanks to a similarity of name that has worked in the same way in many other cases, he has been served heir to Demeter here and elsewhere, and spears Turks as he sits on his brown charger in a way that he never did in life.

The Thesmophoria ceremony (magical rites that were to secure the fertility alike of land, animals, and human stock for the year) lasted three days. The crown of the ceremony consisted in the sacrifice of a pig, who always symbolizes fertility, and the solemn cutting of him up. His *disjecta membra*, together with certain phallic emblems—corresponding to the *Arreta* or nameless objects which the girls in their ceremony were not permitted to see—were carried down into one of the numerous pits on the hill and deposited there. Then the earth into which last year's pig had been resolved by this time was brought up again, and scattered on land and worshippers as a fertility charm. Demeter is of course no more than Mother Earth, giver both of life and food to her children. As such there was a statue of her on the Acropolis in a place of honour, in which she appeared accompanied by Persephone, her daughter, and the inscription that can still be read on the rock just by the matrix of the statue actually calls her Fruit-bearing Earth, *Ge Karpophoros*.[1] What her sanctuary contained is unknown. Pausanias knew, and was ready to tell us, but was warned in a dream that to do so would be a violation of his vow of secrecy as an initiate of Eleusis.

The north side of the Acropolis is one where visitors seldom go, as guides are so apt to lead them by easier paths to the Theatre of Dionysus. Yet all who have the time may be recommended to spend a morning wandering—and at times scrambling—here. Here one can trace the Altar of Apollo, where once the Archons took the oath to the State when they entered on their year of office. Here too the youth of Athens when they passed out of the boyhood stage, took their oath too at the moment of enrolment among the Ephebi, swearing to reverence the gods, to stand by their comrades, and to give their lives for their country if need should call.

The little Clepsydra, the Steal-water spring (so-called because it was and is variable in its flow), which was the main natural water-supply of the Acropolis, really belongs to this district, but owing to its enclosure in the later fortifications is now easier to visit from within the Acropolis Gate. It has become a shrine of St. George in these times. Here too, visible as a black door-way from below, but only to be reached by a scramble on the spot, is the cave of Pan, once the scene of the loves of Apollo and Creusa, daughter of Erectheus,

[1] The position is marked by a guard-rail, on the north side of the Parthenon.

whence came the boy Ion and through him all the Ionian race. This was the goal of the Torch race at the Thargelia, which theoretically started from Delphi and was the bringing of New Fire from the very shrine of Apollo. Actually, the competitors who had to end with this climb, started from the Altar of Prometheus in the town.

The position of 'Beloved Pan' here was a little peculiar. Of old he had no sanctuary in Athens (indeed, what should he do in a town at all?) and it was not until the days of Marathon that he had one assigned him. Then, when Pheidippides was on his return journey in his famous run to Sparta (and was possibly getting into a state when an exhausted man might see anything) Pan appeared and ran awhile alongside him, explaining that the Athenians had not treated him too well in the past, but that he would overlook that and help them now in their need, though he expected them to treat him better in the future. At Marathon, Pan did good service as all knew, and was given this very nice double cave to be his house as a reward. Here it was that in later days Lucan climbed up to have an interview with him, and found the Goat-god sitting on the little grass-plot in front of his abode.

Pan is no longer to be found in his Athenian house, but the natural man must rejoice to know that (Christian tradition to the contrary notwithstanding) he is not dead yet. He never got really admitted into the rather exclusive club that met on Mount Olympus, but while its members are all dead now (with the possible exception of Lady Aphrodite in her own land of Cyprus) Pan is still alive on the hills he has always haunted, and, as we shall see elsewhere, in the hearts of his own people.

A cavern in the Long Rocks marks the point of exit of the Cleft of the Persians running down from the Acropolis above, by which the girl-priestesses used to descend to the Precinct of Agraulos. That therefore is obviously to be found here, and we know that it was close to the Precinct of the Saviours, the local name for the Twin Brethren. Here we have another instance of the way in which the conservative Greek will keep the old names of his sanctuaries even when they have passed to another faith, for here stands one of the beautiful old churches of Athens, the tiny shrine of The Saviour. Somewhere below us, but on sites that have not been identified as yet, was the Prytaneion or Town Hall of Athens, and the real Theseum, which was a *temenos* or sacred enclosure with walls adorned with pictures, and not a regular temple at all. Here too was the Painted Colonnade or Stoa Poikile, which in early days was the place where Zeno taught, and so gave its name to Stoicism, and in the time of Pausanias was still adorned with the Spartan shields captured at Sphacteria,[1] and in the days of Synesius (say 420 A.D.) still kept its paintings. That worthy squire-bishop was much disappointed in Athens: 'The place is like the skin of a sacrifice—there is nothing sublime left but the name! Even a tourist can only admire the Academy and the Stoa. It was the dwelling of the wise once, but now has only the beekeepers to do it honour.' He had however a good word for the local tailors, even if he has none for the Parthenon. The Bishop bought his episcopal gaiters—or whatever may have been their fifth century equivalent—in the classic city.

Having referred to the real Theseum here, we may touch also upon the temple that usually goes by that name, which is at least in full sight of the area where we now are. Properly, it is probably the Temple of Hephaestus, as Pausanias refers to one of that name 'on the Hill, just above the Agora'. The identification is fairly certain, and it gives us some idea of the architectural wealth of Athens, that our ancient Baedeker should give only one line to so conspicuous a monument. As a temple, it would be counted wonderful anywhere else, but it is hard on the work of a good ordinary architect to put it where it must be compared with the Parthenon. The fact that its metopes (so far as they were sculptured at all) represented the labours of Theseus, gave the reason for the popular identification. Most of them, however, were only painted, and fifty years ago traces of colour were still visible there and in the two pediments, where the background was, as usual, a strong red or blue. The building owes its survival, where so much has perished past recall, to the fact that it was consecrated as a Church under the name of St. George, and in later days, when it was clearly indecent to leave so fine a building in the hands of Christians, became a mosque.

After the evacuation of Athens by the Turks, its stone vault (which is of course post-classic in date) was about the only roof left standing in the city. It did not become a church again, fortunately, and was used as the burial place of foreigners of note, including important phil-hellenes, or strangers who had fought for Greece in her war of independence. Hence the dust of more than one Englishman rests there, though that of General Church, the greatest of them, was given a monument in the Orthodox Cemetery.

[1] One of these, marked 'from the Spartans, at Pylos', has actually been discovered at the bottom of a well.

HALL OF THE 'KING ARCHON'. AREOPAGUS

The ground falls steeply at the east end of the temple, and in the hollow below there have been excavated the foundations of the Colonnade of the King Archon, which was, as Plato shows us, the real site of the trial of Socrates. His prison—though late tradition gave the name to the house of a neolithic cave-dweller under the Museum hill—was most certainly somewhere in the city and near the Agora, as is shown by e.g. the case of Theramenes, who was dragged, Xenophon tells us, to execution 'from the Senate-house to the Prison, through the Market'. This happens to be in exactly the opposite direction to the Museum hill.

Our meandering course now leads us from the Theseum up to the Areopagus. Not that this is the nearest object of interest, but (if pedantic archaeologists would only believe it) neither tourists nor writers always follow a straight course. It has been soberly argued that, because Pausanias described one unidentified site just after dealing with another that is known, therefore the unknown place must be quite close to the known one. It needed a student with a human sense of humour to suggest that the most conscientious sight-seer sometimes goes back to his hotel for lunch and starts out again.

The Areopagus is the rocky knoll, never defaced by building, that stands at the main gate of the Acropolis. It is the place where, when Athens town was beginning to creep down from the citadel limits and spread in the Limnae and other places, the King would come down from his palace citadel and sit in the gate to do judgement and justice. When kings passed away, the spot was already holy, and legend said that even the gods had condescended to submit their causes to the court that sat there. Here it was that Ares, when sued by Poseidon for the murder of the sea-god's son Halirrothius, pleaded gross provocation in the shape of the wrong done to his daughter Alcippe, and got his verdict of justifiable homicide. It was this episode that gave its name to the hill, even though others did say— and perhaps with more historic probability—that the real interpretation is, the Hill, not of Ares, but of Arai, solemn invocations of the Gods. Here too Orestes, when pursued by the Furies, put his case before the Athenian court with the goddess Athena as his counsel, and the Avengers are obliged to resign their victim. In consolation for their disappointment, the Eumenides[1] are given the right to a sanctuary, on the spot. The cave at the Acropolis end of

[1] These deities were never known by that name at Athens, and of course nobody would ever dream of calling them the Furies. They were known locally as the Semnae, the Venerables.

43

the Areopagus rock (it is no longer a cave, because the roof has fallen in, but the site is plain) was theirs, and into it anyone who wished to do reverence to these fearsome powers of the underworld could go, and worship in silence. Only, it was not prudent to do this if by any chance you had ever been reported dead. That fact, even if untrue, apparently gave the underworld a lien upon your person; and its powers, if you were rash enough to put yourself in their reach, were entitled to confiscate you!

Thc Areopagus was the court that tried homicides—a power that was left to it when other and more political functions were withdrawn from its purview; and the ceremonial that it employed in these cases was awe-inspiring in the extreme. To begin with, the court met always by night, the idea being that it was to give judgement on the evidence only, and absolutely without respect of persons. In theory, it was not even known who was addressing it. Then it must meet in the open air, on the bare rock of the hill. It would be trying cases of homicide, which implies blood-feud. Now you cannot possibly come under a roof with the man with whom you have a blood-feud; hence there never was, in ancient days, a roof over the court. In fact, there never was one on the hill at all, though it is true that in later and comfort-loving times, the court held its sessions in the hall of the Colonnade of the King Archon by the Theseum. Then the method in which the parties to a suit were put on their oath was equally impressive. Each had to go, separately, into the shrine of the Eumenides, and there worship in silence before them: that is to say, he had to put himself into the very presence and power of the awful beings who avenged guilt upon the guilty, and commit his cause and himself to them. Then he could go up, take his stand upon the 'Stone of Injury' or the 'Stone of Ruthlessness' as the case required, and set his case out before the half-seen human judges.

But when the ordinary reader thinks of appearances before the Areopagus, he is pretty sure to think only of one, and that a rather late instance that was not considered important at the time—the occasion when the Apostle Paul stood before the court on Mars Hill, or at least some members of it. It is true that this was not, it seems, any very formal hearing of a criminal case; the apostle was not being tried for his life or for any legal offence, such as would then have been heard in the Hall below. It seems however that at that time, when Athens had become the great university town of the day, the Areopagus had some jurisdiction over the teaching given, and 'certain Epicureans and Stoics' who were curious about the new

doctrine that was being proclaimed, asked the apostle to come 'up
on to' the famous hill informally, and there 'let them know what
this strange doctrine that thou teachest is'. That is the impression
given by our very accurate authority. When the explanation had
been given, most of the hearers seem to have been of the same
opinion as Browning's Cleon,

> *Thou canst not think a mere barbarian Jew*
> *As Paulus proves to be, one circumcised,*
> *Has access to a secret shut from us!*
> *Why, as I gathered from a bystander,*
> *His doctrines could be held by no sane man.*

Of course, there were some who listened, and among them one
whose name was destined to be great in later ages—though not for
any works of his real writing—Dionysius the Areopagite.[1] The foundations of a church that was dedicated to him can still be traced
below the hill, and here there was discovered in the seventeenth
century the last survivor of the many statues that once stood on this
spot. It was a figure of Peace nursing Plenty, and a work of one of
the giants, Cephisodotus, the later contemporary and pupil of
Pheidias. It was acclaimed at once as a figure of the Virgin and
Child and as such there seemed hope that it might be spared, yet it
met a dolorous fate. The Archbishop of Athens had it destroyed at
once; not that he denied its authenticity, or the identification, but
because he held that a good and orthodox saint like the Areopagite
ought never to have allowed himself a graven image. He would
certainly have had an eikon!

Another sanctuary was close by, the Metroön or precinct of the
Great Mother, which included in its circuit the site of the Senate-
house, and a Vesta-like temple with its daily sacrifice and ever-
burning fire, an observance that we find at Olympia also, and
probably in other cities of Greece. The observance goes back to
very primitive days, when fires were hard to light and when lit
must be kept going. Such an office was the obvious duty of the girls
of the tribe, though a later age might assign the duty to certain
selected maidens. If they should be careless about their duty and
let the fire go out, what could be more natural than that they
should receive—at least at Rome, for we admit ignorance of what
was done at Athens—a sound thrashing from the Pontifex Maxi-
mus, as representing the father of the family?

[1] The R. C. Cathedral of Athens is dedicated to this Saint.

THE SKIRTS OF THE ACROPOLIS

As we go down from the Areopagus to the southern side of the Acropolis, we pass first a monument which anywhere but in Athens would be of itself an attraction that men would come far to see. The Odeum of Herodes Atticus is worth more than the passing glance that is all it usually gets. Its donor was a millionaire of the reign of the emperor Marcus Aurelius, say 180 A.D., and it is for this reason that so important a structure is not mentioned by Pausanias. It was not there in his time. A man of rather oppressive generosity, Herodes scattered his enormous gifts broadcast, and you can hardly find one great classical site in Greece that has not been adorned by a rather ponderous building of his erection, which has his name on it in large letters. Here at Athens he gave not only this theatre, but also the great stadium that is so conspicuous today. Of course, that existed before his time, and the story goes that, sitting in the old stone seats at a Pan-Athenaic gathering, he observed casually, 'We'll have this in marble before next feast'. His gift was not allowed to survive the middle ages, though a Greek millionaire of our own day has repeated the gift and restored the present stadium. It was said that Herodes 'exhausted the quarries of Pentelicus' in this magnificent gift, but that has been said of a good many donors. As a matter of fact, Pentelicus is practically all marble —and there is quite a lot of it left to this day, fortunately for all concerned, even after providing the duplicate Stadium and the big dam for retaining the Reservoir that now supplies Athens with water.

The Odeum, however, is at least a very fine monument, and it was the donor's memorial to the wife whom he loved, which gives it a human interest. As a theatre, it is interesting to students of the history of that art, for its double storeyed stage is an anticipation of a modern experiment in theatrical art, and it shows how a later convention was taking the place of the familiar *ekkyklema* that all schoolboys used to know of, when a god or hero had to appear with suitable dignity.

In later times the building was of course degraded. The discovery of huge amounts of murex shell in the course of the excavation of it shows that it was once used as a dye-works, and the magnificently solid construction of it joined with its position to make it only too unfortunately attractive as an outwork for the Acropolis in various mediaeval sieges, of which the last, as a memorial tablet shows, was in the war of Greek independence.

We go on through the old enclosure of the Pelargikon, the wall of which has been practically buried in the big Colonnade of

Eumenes, which now forms the retaining wall of the slope that we are traversing. This was the gift of a king of Pergamus in Hellenistic days—about 140 B.C.—when Athens was relying on her old renown, and accepting gifts from outside, rather than producing new works of her own. Looking south as it does, it was warm all winter and cool all summer, and was therefore a favourite haunt of the 'philosophic students' of that period. It is this that gives the point to Lucan's jibe, when he puts his 'Mr. Free-speech' (Parrhesiades) up on the parapet of the Acropolis, and sets him to 'fish for philosophers in the Pelargikon' with a gold bait.

As we approach the great theatre of Dionysus we pass the small precinct of Asclepius, which is another of the most ancient shrines of Athens. A small spring, originally hot though it is so no longer, wells out of the rock at this point, and the place has been a healing centre from very early days. In fact before Asclepius was heard of here this was the sanctuary of Alcippe; Hellenic myth made her into the Daughter of Ares, whose violation by the son of Poseidon gave its name to the Areopagus, though actually this pre-Greek deity is far older than her supposed father.

It was only in the days of the terrific plague of the Peloponnesian war that Asclepius was brought from Epidauros to Athens as a last resource, and took over this shrine from its original owner. Now Asclepius has lost it in his turn, though the influence of the sacred snakes that he introduced still hangs about it thus far, that the modern shrine is sacred to St. Michael, who keeps, if not a snake, at least a dragon, though he has to share it with the Panagia, our Lady. The place has been continuously holy for nearly four thousand years, if the object of devotion there has varied. The spring too is still used locally for cures, though it is to be feared that foreigners who drink of it are more likely to need healing than to receive it! Greek peasantry seem to have a hereditary immunity to typhoid.

As for the Asclepion, the little precinct is a sad confusion now, but all who enter it with the classic guide to this particular site, the *Plutus* of Aristophanes, in their hands, will not find much difficulty in identifying every important point. Plutus, readers of the play will remember, has obviously gone blind, or why else does he always give his special gift of wealth to the undeserving? He is conducted to the shrine of the god by the slave Cario, where he performs his ablutions at the tank at the entrance (still *in situ* at the western end), makes his offering on the altar, which stood before the little temple the foundations of which are still to be seen, and finally is

47

bidden to lie down under the colonnade reserved for invalids, and to sleep if he likes, but in any case not to move whatever he hears, for that will mean that the God is going his rounds. Cario, however, has eyes if Plutus has none, and though he had to wrap his head up in a cloak, 'by the grace of heaven mine has plenty of holes in it', so that he sees all that goes on. Thus he sees the priest come round first and 'consecrate all the offerings into his big bag', (saving the plum-pudding that Cario has thoughtfully annexed first,) and then retires. Presently Asclepius himself comes out of his temple accompanied by his two daughters, Iaso the healer and Hygeia herself. They go the rounds of the sick under the colonnade, and thoughtfully put a mustard-plaster on the eyes of the notorious cheat who is lying next to Plutus, but a real healing ointment on those of the poor god. Then the gods vanish, and there is a hissing and a rustling, and the big snakes come out of their pit (the pit here, as at Epidauros, is a feature of the shrine) and they crawl under Plutus' cloak and seemingly begin to lick at his eyes. At any rate in the morning the god gets up seeing.

The suggestion is that the undoubted cures were brought about by the mixture of the best medicine of the day with an element of pure charlatanry and a good deal of faith-healing. It would not be difficult, probably, to train tame snakes to go and lick where the sweet stuff that they were accustomed to eat had been put. And one may assume that the man whose faith would make him lie quite still while even a harmless snake crawled over him and licked at his eyes, had also faith to be healed.

The Museum contains many votive offerings from this shrine, including Silon's model of his club foot, which the snake licked at and cured, and even representations of the lancets and cupping-glasses presented by grateful doctors.

To anyone of literary mind, the great Theatre of Dionysus, to which we come next in this wander round Athens, is perhaps the most interesting place of all, with the possible exception of the Parthenon itself, for it is the home and shrine of drama, the very birth-place of comedy and tragedy both. Yet, if this is the place that has given us Aeschylus, Sophocles, Euripides and Aristophanes, it is well to remember, that just as the artists of the Parthenon were only a little group of the greatest of a school of great men, so none of the great four whose works, or some of them, have come down to us, were by any means sure of always winning the prize at any of the great contests. Horace, for instance, puts two other names, Eupolis and

Cratinus, on a level with that of Aristophanes in Comedy. One of them at least could often defeat him and their works are lost; while if it had not been for the fortunate chance that St. John Chrysostom (as the tradition goes) had more robust tastes than we generally credit him with, and always slept with his Aristophanes under his pillow, those works might not have come down to us either.

Further, when we study the place itself, we must remember that the theatre which is the conspicuous monument now was itself no more than an appendix to an annexe to the shrine of Dionysus that was the real centre of things, and that if we are to understand the drama, we must make some effort first to grasp what the god meant to those who worshipped him.

Dionysus was the latest comer to the Hellenic Olympus, and was only admitted there after a good deal of hesitation, and after he had had to prove himself a god by his works. The whole plot of the great tragedy of the *Bacchae* turns on this fact, though it is true that he had secured his throne before the days of Homer. Of course he is the god of the vine, and so of wine, and also of fermented drink generally. He is certainly one with Bromios and Sabazios, who are Beer-gods up in Thrace.

In Greece he is quite frankly an importation, a foreigner as the *Bacchae* plainly declares him, who has come in from Asia Minor or more distant lands, by the road of Thrace, and brought the vine with him. In Crete his story is different, and there he has an independent development. Once in Hellas he is adopted into the circle of the gods, and made into the son of Zeus and Theban Semele—whose name would seem to mean really Earth—and the legend of his birth in the land and of his subsequent travels to India and return with the vine is fitted on to him. On this return to what is now regarded as his birth-place, he brings his 'rabble-rout' with him, the Satyrs and the Maenads or Bacchanals. The first of these are probably his original followers, who have come down with him from Thrace, and are like the Centaurs who are closely akin to them, originally wild men and half brute in nature, from the north. Neither in ancient art nor modern folk-lore are they always of the conventional type, half men and half goat or horse. Sometimes they are quite human, except that they are provided with a tail.

The Maenads, the girl devotees who go out and revel on the mountains, seem to be a strictly Hellenic development, and one that the Greek knew well. Actual Satyrs and Centaurs must have been a rarity in historic times, though it is a joy to find that neither beast is by any means extinct in modern folk-lore, as we hope to show later; but real girls did go out on the mountains to revel and rove. It is true that sober-minded scholars have asserted that Hellenic girls could not possibly have done anything so strenuous, or so improper, and declared that plainly the Maenads were not human, they could be no more than a personification of drifting clouds. However, Plutarch tells how the Bacchanals in his time got caught by an untimely snowstorm while on their wanderings, and how the men of Chaeronea, in spite of the risk of sharing the fate of Pentheus, went out with wraps and warm drinks to succour them. At Amphissa also, on the other side of Parnassus, the Maenads belonging to some other town that happened to be at war with the place in 200 B.C. wandered unknowing into the very agora of the city and there dropped and went to sleep, utterly worn out with their exertions. When they were recognized and the men proposed to hold them as hostages, the women of Amphissa rose in rage at the impious proposal. They brought wraps and stood sentry over the sleeping maidens till they woke, after which they escorted them safe to the boundary of the town territory. Apropos of this, it is well to call attention to the beautiful recumbent statue of the Exhausted Maenad in the Athens Museum—where the girl has clearly dropped and gone to sleep in just this fashion.

At Athens, Dionysus was an importation in a double sense, not only as a foreigner in Greece, but also because he was brought in from Eleutherae, a village on the slopes of Cithaeron, the place where, according to tradition, the vine was first cultivated in Attica. Hence the God was always Eleuthereus, in Athens, and the title is inscribed to this day on the throne of his priest in the theatre, though it was a title that lent itself to a double interpretation. The god who gave wine might be either 'of Eleutherae', or the 'Freedom-giver'. He always kept a memory of his old home, and the ancient wooden image, the Xoanon, that stood in the temple and attended the dramas in the theatre, made an attempt to escape and get back to Eleutherae every year. He was always caught before he had got far beyond the Dipylon Gate by which the road to Thebes and elsewhere goes out of Athens, and brought back in triumph to his temple.

To say that this god Dionysus, whom we associate with drinking and jollity only, and that not always of the most reputable kind, is also associated with the introduction of an entirely new idea into Greek religion, and an idea that implies a very long step forward in religious evolution, sounds startling but is the fact. The idea in question is that of mysticism, of personal communion with the Divine. There are two main thoughts in ordinary Greek religion.

The first of these is connected with the gods of Olympus, those normally respectable but distant deities, who lived first on the top of the high mountain under which the Hellenic invaders passed as they entered Greece, and then in a heaven above it. In historic times these gods no longer walked with men as they still did with the heroes of Troy, and even Athena is no more than the city of Athens idealized. Their worship was a business-like affair, conducted on the *Do ut des* principle, like Bismarck's diplomacy. I, the worshipper, will give to you, the god, the sacrifice that I am told you fancy, on the understanding that you will give me in return the benefit that I want and that you specialize in. There is also however a second idea, far older than this Olympic worship, the respect paid to the ghosts of the dead and the Keres (the Lemures of the Roman) who are closely connected with them. Here, as Miss Jane Harrison has pointed out, the idea is not *Do ut des*, but rather *Do ut abeas*—'I give that you may keep away'. I, the worshipper, will come to your grave and give you there the food that you require, because if I do not you will most likely come back to your old house to get it' ('Prolegomena to Greek Religion'). Then, later than these, though still in days that are pre-Homeric, Dionysus appears and brings with him the vine, and also the sense of personal communion with the Divine, and the idea that this communion may be ensured by the use of some outward and visible means— which is the sacramental system, with all that it has meant for religious growth. The means that he employs have an unfortunate side, it must be owned, for the mystic seeks for that most desirable sense of communion with the vine-god by getting very drunk, when he is clearly out of touch with earth, and so, it is to be hoped, in some sort of touch with heaven. The drinking is no more intended for enjoyment than was the chewing of the laurel at Delphi—though in actual fact it most likely was more enjoyable; both were done deliberately to induce ecstasy and the sense of union with the god. It will be seen that this is a crude form of sacramental teaching, and in the parallel growth of Dionysus worship in Crete the same thought is embodied in a fashion that is grim indeed, and one not far removed from cannibalism. Still, however strange to our thinking may be the forms in which the highest of human aspirations have been incarnated, we see that they can be taken up and used, in the holiest rite of the highest form of religion that we know.

This being the concept of Dionysus in men's minds, we can turn to see how his festival developed a feature that has survived the god in whose honour it was held, namely drama, in the form of either tragedy or comedy.

That folk should sing at vintage and harvest may be taken as a natural human instinct. It was not a Greek poet who said that 'they joy before Thee according to the joy of harvest' or who found the utmost expression of grief in the fact that 'even in the vineyards there shall be no singing'. That this singing at vintage time should produce a chorus of singers and dancers is a natural development enough, and the dance might take place almost anywhere. Of course a vineyard does not lend itself to the exercise, but there is one place in any primitive village that does, and that is the threshing-floor. There you are bound to have, from the conditions of life, a circular area of hard-trodden earth, some five and twenty yards or so across, and with an upright post in the middle. That is what you want for treading out the grain with oxen, and the space is always empty save just at threshing time. You have only got to put a carved head on the post, and there is your deity, your 'Herm', ready made. What better can you want for your orchestra, remembering that the word does not imply a lot of musical instrumentalists, or a pit in front of a stage in which to hide them, but a place where young folk can dance and sing, in chorus, with pipe and tabor to guide them? Often, in fact usually, the performers would 'dance out' some episode in the life of their god or hero, as tribes like the Masai in Africa will do to this day. 'There never was a mystery yet without dancing,' says Lucan, the fact being that the language of a primitive man is scanty, and he is apt to eke out his words by gestures, which become almost a language by themselves.

Of course this dancing is something very different from a valse or a minuet. Any ordered movement to music would come under the definition, and it was as definitely religious a ceremony as it is to this day, where it has survived in the great cathedral of Seville. The Greek would have described the ceremony of Trooping the Colour, or the ordered movements of the Celebrant and Deacons at a High Mass, as a dance, and would probably have added, 'and a very fine and religious dance too'. Still gesture and dancing do need some interpretation, and it is usually well to have somebody there who can explain to the ignorant what it is all about. Thus far, we find the ceremonial dance in practically every type of man, but it was the Hellenic spirit that took the next step, as it also beautified and dignified the whole. Some unknown genius was inspired to make a change, and instead of putting up one man to give the explanation in monologue, he put up two and made it a dialogue, and behold he had invented drama! That soon developed, relatively to the Chorus that it originally explained, and we get the play complete in its various acts or episodes, with the Chorus to sing their odes—that were originally the whole performance—in the intervals between them.

When we enter the theatre now, what we see is, the remains— very small remains, alas!—of two temples of the god; the ruins of various theatrical stages; the Orchestra with a very incongruous hedge of marble all around it; and finally what is most conspicuous of all, so that most people call it 'the theatre', the seating area or *cavea*. What there was originally and essentially was no more than this, a tiny shrine of Dionysus Eleuthereus, and by its side, a threshing-floor: a threshing-floor that is still traceable, we are glad to say, under all the additions of later ages, and which lay between the temple and the rising slope of the Acropolis rock, on which the spectators could sit.

The dramatic contests at the feast of Dionysus, with judges to decide which play was the best, date from the days of Peisistratus, who seems to have built the older of the two temples, in which the ancient wooden Xoanon had its home. In his time the theatre was still the old threshing-floor, and there was no stage; the two actors (there were no more as yet) were among the chorus, and it seems that the theatrical *cothurnus* with its thick sole was introduced simply to give them additional height and make them conspicuous. Things grew naturally. A wall with pillars provided a back-ground and by the time of Aeschylus (about 480 B.C. as he was 'one of the men of Marathon') there was temporary seating, and probably also a low stage that may have encroached on the orchestral space and pushed its circle back towards the slope of the hill. Sixty years later the second and more elaborate temple was built, and received the chryselephantine statue of Alcamenes; a permanent theatre was begun, and finished by about the time of Alexander the Great, or 330 B.C. Though this sanctuary was originally not the only place for dramatic contests, it gradually became so, and the old theatre in the Limnae was abandoned.

The present stage-front that we see is of Roman date, though the sculptures that adorn it are of earlier and better workmanship, and the Orchestra has been remodelled too. The stage has trespassed on its circle, a circle that we can still see in its old proportion at Epidauros and Corinth, and the barbarous marble hedge that stands between the dancers of the chorus and the spectators—the last thing that was needed there of old—is a monument of equally barbarous habits. The Romans used the theatre sacred to Dionysus for gladiatorial combats, and introduced the barrier because a gladiator had the extreme bad taste to go and die in the lap of a watching dignitary. The marble seats in which those dignitaries sat—which declare by their pattern that they are translations of a wooden original into stone—are still the most comfortable chairs in all Athens, where cabinet-makers have only just learned to avoid the upright back and horizontal seat, even with these models before them. Naturally, a restful seat is needed for the members of the jury, who were expected to sit all day in the hot sun, watching tragedy after tragedy, and at the end had to give a reasoned verdict, which of the series was the best, and why. Even the benches for the mere *profanum vulgus* above, however, are most beautifully designed. Where else will you find seats of just the right height to sit at ease, elbows on knees, while your feet rest in a groove that gives them comfortable space without incommoding your neighbour in the row below you? Only lateral space is denied you, for the little grooves that mark the space allowed for a sitter are a bare thirteen inches apart, as against the sixteen allowed in a London theatre. Athenians were either slim or squeezable, if they were to sit all day long in that space, as they most certainly did. Naturally the presidential throne in the middle of the front row is the perquisite of the High Priest of Dionysus, who entertained his fellow dignitaries at a banquet after the performance. 'My Priest, protect me! Take me home to supper!' cries the distressed Dionysus in the *Frogs*.

The seating capacity of the theatre is enormous, larger even than that of Epidauros. If all places right up to the Cave of Thrasyllus at the summit were occupied (and the row of seats is still to be seen there in the rock, to show that the theatre went up to that level), we believe that the full number is 20,000. The acoustics, as usual, are perfect.

Naturally, the use of such a place was not confined to the one great feast of Dionysus, or even to other occasions during the year when plays were produced. The area could be used for popular meetings, and even occasionally for the Assemblies that ought to be held on the Pnyx hill. One instance of this must be recorded, for it was here that Demosthenes delivered his famous justification for his whole career, the speech *On the Crown*. It could even be used for more vulgar displays, such as cock-fights, and one must own that it is magnificently adapted for so shocking a purpose! It is greatly to be feared too that the general public of Athens, even if they tolerated the tragedies on the opening days of the feast of Dionysus, and no doubt really enjoyed the comedies without the embarrassing presence of ladies, yet considered the real attraction of the festival to be—the cock-fighting that came on the last day. In the classic Calendar that now adorns the front of the 'old Cathedral' of St. Eleutherius, each of the great feasts of the Athenian year is represented in its proper month by its proper symbol, and that which is the natural emblem of the feast of Dionysus is neither sacrifice nor drama, but—a banquet and a cock-fight. There is further evidence of this in the theatre itself. Go to the splendid throne in which the High Priest sat in the centre of all things and look at its marble arm-rests. On each of them appears the figure of Eros in relief—and an exquisite figure it is—and Eros is putting down a cock to fight.

The prize received for success in the great dramatic contest, and for that matter in any one of the numerous choric contests of the year, in which almost anyone who liked might produce a chorus and compete, at his own expense or at that of some patron, was a tripod of bronze. However, the winner was not allowed to retain it, but had only the privilege of dedicating it, on a more or less elaborate marble base, as one of the city monuments. Of course, it was the kudos that was his real reward. A fashionable place for these memorials was the Street of Tripods that runs under the eastern end of the Acropolis, but of the numerous monuments that once adorned this only one remains. This, the Choragic Monument of Lysicrates, is certainly a most beautiful specimen; it was not this that secured its survival, but the accident that it was enclosed in a house belonging to the Capuchin Fathers, whose library it is said to have contained in its base. Byron stayed in this house during his first sojourn in Greece, and it shows the condition of the monuments then that the poet, with his head full of classics, walked right over the theatre of Dionysus without recognizing it for what it was, so deeply was it buried in debris. He thought that the Odeon of Herodes Atticus was the theatre of which he had read at Harrow. Another monument like that of Lysicrates, and as fine a one, the Lantern of Diogenes, had only recently been destroyed in Byron's day.

Round about the Theatre, however, there remain various other traces of these Choragic Monuments. The little natural cave of Thrasyllus mentioned above was utilized for the purpose. Two men of that name, father and son, each had a choric victory to commemorate, and they seem to have put their tripods in the cave, to which they made an ornamental marble frontage. There was a statue of Dionysus over it, which is now in the British Museum, and a Medusa's Head, to keep off the evil eye, on the gable. This figure won fame in the degenerate mediaeval days, when the Archbishop of Athens could say that the great misfortune of the city was—that it was so near the sea! Then, this 'Idol of the iron-bound niche' acquired the useful power of 'drowning hostile ships as soon as they appeared over the horizon'. Though still perfect in the eighteenth century, this monument was destroyed in 1826, and the cavern became a Christian church, which it still is, the shrine of the Panagia Speliotissa, Our Lady of the Cave.

The two odd detached pillars that stand above the cave, and are quite unconnected with any temple, are also Choragic Monuments, of a cheaper kind. They also carried votive tripods, and it will be seen on examination that their capitals are in consequence triangular, not square. Anyone looking down on those capitals from above (i.e. from the parapet of the Acropolis) will see the prints of the three feet of the tripods at once.

III

ATHENS CITY

Olympeion—Kallirhoe—Market and Library of Hadrian—The Tower of the Winds—Dipylon and Ceramicus—The old Churches— The modern Cathedral

T he most conspicuous of the monuments of the city is, of course, the gigantic temple of Olympian Zeus. Actually, this site was outside the ancient town and in the beginning was a sanctuary not of the great sky-god, but rather of the powers of the underworld. A cleft in the rock, some eighteen inches long, which was supposed to go down to Hades itself, was the original focus of the sanctuary, and offerings to the mysterious powers that ruled there were cast into this pit. It was also revered as a sort of Hellenic Ararat (though Deucalion's ark grounded on Parnassus), in that it was held that the waters of the deluge escaped down this rather inadequate sink, and if any doubted the fact, the tomb of the Greek Noah, Deucalion, could be pointed out in the precinct in proof of the statement. This monument has unfortunately not survived.

The foundation of the first temple here dates from Peisistratus in the VIth century B.C., from the very capable *tyrannus*, that is, who made himself despot of the city in an age which was calling out for one-man rule, and who governed, for the period of his life, a country that could neither rule itself nor select its own rulers. Of course there were revolts against him. 'Never was there a man yet, who gave himself to the service of the people, against whom the people did not turn in course of time' said Aristotle in a later age, but Peisistratus is the only case that we can remember of a *tyrannus* who has been able to return to rule after two 'abdications' and who died in power, and in his bed, at the last. He certainly had very big ideas and did big things, either to conciliate or perhaps, like

57

Napoleon when he gilded the dome of the Invalides, to dazzle his subjects.

The great temple on the Acropolis, as well as this in the city, was his idea, as was the provision of a decent water supply for the city, that last being a very favourite scheme of 'tyrants'. Besides collecting and editing Homer he organized the great Pan-Athenaic festival, the first dramatic contests at the theatre of Dionysus, and designed the stadium for the great athletic games of the Athenian year, the 'Olympian Games' of Athens, in honour of the Zeus of his temple. The Athenians might curse his memory, but there is no denying that most of their great monuments, mental and material, were of his designing.

It was perhaps as well that the two great temples that Peisistratus planned could not be carried out in his day, for a despot cannot produce genius to order, and the artists of Athens were not capable of executing in 550 B.C. what they could do a hundred years later. Peisistratus' Olympeion was of magnificent size—its columns were 7 ft. 10 in. in diameter, which is more than that of any existing temple in Greece proper—but was of stone not marble and its decorations were probably not superior to those of his Parthenon which survive. After the fall of his house, the Athenians did not care enough about the work of the tyrant to finish it, and it was left to be plundered by the Persians and remain as an unfinished sketch for centuries. The next ruler to do anything to it was, of all unlikely persons, Antiochus Epiphanes, some four hundred years later. This man, in whom there was a touch of genius and rather more than a touch of madness, was a thorough Pan-Hellenic enthusiast. Everything in his multiform and ill-compacted empire had got to be Greek, for the Greek was the highest expression of the true (i.e. western) civilization—a craze that has possessed other men besides. It was for this reason that he started out on his ill-omened effort to make the Hebrews into Hellenists, a scheme that failed completely with that stiff-necked people, and only produced the Maccabees at the time, and indirectly the case-hardened Jew of a later age. As a part of his general policy, he set about the re-building of this temple, using Pentelic marble as his material now, and commencing with the double row of colossal columns in the peristyle. Men said that he did this for effect, but actually it seems that this was the usual order of construction. However, he did not get far, and Sulla at his capture of Athens, plundered most of what he had done, carrying off many of the columns for the decoration of the temple of Jupiter

Capitolinus. Thus the place was left in such a state as to provoke one of Lucan's jests, for in a dialogue of his Zeus calls from heaven after Hermes—whom he has just despatched on some errand to earth— 'and Hi, lad! While you are at it you might just ask the Athenians whether they ever mean to finish my house.' In fact, Zeus had not to wait too long after sending his messenger, for the emperor Hadrian got to work and actually completed it, that colossal gift to Athens being only one of the many benefactions that the cultured ruler showered on the city that he loved. While about it, Hadrian enclosed all the suburb containing the temple—which had hitherto been outside the city—within a new wall. The entry to this was by a rather flimsy triumphal arch (we speak of its appearance, for it has at least stood for eighteen centuries) that took the place of one of the old city gates. There was a suspicion of 'swagger' about the inscriptions that we may still read on the two sides of the portal; on the inner side, 'This is the city of Theseus' and on the outer, 'This is the city of Hadrian'. The multitude of the statues of himself that the emperor scattered about the city suggested the same idea, but if they were numerous, his benefactions had deserved them, and at least it might be said that others had been worse. Soon after the days of Alexander (318 B.C.) Athens had the doubtful happiness of being ruled by a real philosopher-statesman, Demetrius of Phaleron, who was as ready to enforce all the last rules of correct living, and as sure of his wisdom in so doing, as any good socialist of today. At the end of 300 days this ideal ruler had put up 360 statues of himself—and then there came a revolt, and all but one of the statues were down within the month. One-man rule has at least this advantage, that there is just one obvious man to hang when things go wrong. It is so difficult to do that when the responsible ruler is a government department—or more probably several of them.

Hadrian was naturally given divine honours, with a regular priesthood, by the grateful Athenians, and it is interesting to note that the first man to be appointed High Priest of the emperor was Herodes Atticus.

Hadrian's was far from being the only statue that adorned the precinct of Zeus, but the only other one that deserves note is the portrait of the philosopher Isocrates. The inscription on the base of it said that this great teacher taught his pupils in the divine science till he attained the age of 98, after which he felt that he could no longer survive the loss of Greek independence under the Macedonians, and committed suicide. He may have done so, but unkind people quoted a letter written by him to Philip some years before, in which he congratulated that potentate warmly on winning the battle of Chaeroneia, because now, under a decent despotism, respectable philosophers would have a chance of living in peace.

In later days, the great temple became a quarry like many another and was reduced to its present condition, but it is to be noted that the material from it and other temples was not usually employed locally, for there were not buildings enough for the purpose there, no matter how unscrupulous the men of Athens might be. It was sent to Italy by ship. All the great churches of that land abound in marble that was put into them before the quarries of Carrara were worked. As early as the year 1340, the priest Ludolphus observes that 'there is not a marble column in Genoa that did not come out of Athens, or a carving of which the material did not come thence. The whole city has been built out of Athens'.

So, the great building—the superficial area of which was actually bigger than that of any English cathedral, though of course the arrangement was not the same—was gradually reduced to its present state. The architraves that still remain in their place formed the abode, until quite recent times, of the last of the long dynasty of 'Stylites', hermits who lived on the summit of lofty pillars. The writer was assured by Greek friends that this man was still there in the nineteenth century, which he could scarcely believe. On application to the then Minister of Education, however, he received prompt confirmation. 'Oh that is true enough; my old grandfather has often told me how when he was a boy, he used to be sent by his mother to fill the old fellow's basket'. It is true that this hermit was, as was natural in so degenerate a century, less ascetic than his predecessors. He had a little hut for shelter on the architraves, and they were large enough to provide him with a small promenade, which St. Simeon of the Pillar would never have allowed. The hut appears in sketches dating from the 'forties', by Lear of 'Nonsense' fame.[1]

The famous Kallirhoe, the Fair fount, is generally identified with a small spring in the bed of the river Ilissus, just where the stream (when there is any) pours over a bar of rock close to the Olympeion. The river is scanty enough normally, being often quite dry, though

---

[1] If hermits are a diminishing quantity in Greece, they are not extinct today. The tenure of an English-owned property in Euboea requires the maintenance of one, to pray for the owner. The Government has now 'taken over' the estate—but has not kept up the hermit! They also continue in plenty on Mt. Athos.

floods that can even be dangerous to life are not quite unknown. Whatever it may have been like in classic days, Ilissus is quite undrinkable now, and classic Athens depended far more on wells than on its few and scanty springs and streams. Wells are plentiful enough, for the local formation of limestone, porous above, rests on an impervious layer at a short distance down. A shaft sunk to this point usually finds a certain amount of water, though if you pierce the layer referred to in deepening the pit to increase the supply, all the water you ever had goes down the hole of your making. All admit that Kallirhoe was sacred from of old, for the maidens used to go to it from the ancient city to draw water for the marriage bath— a ceremonial that of itself proves ancient sanctity. Where it was, however, is a point on which archaeologists fight with their accustomed eagerness. That this spring in the Ilissus bed was so called at one age of antiquity is certain, for it is here that Plato sets the famous opening of the *Phaedrus*—though alas for him who now seeks there plane-trees and deep grass to bring Socrates for once out of the streets of the city and invoke 'beloved Pan, and all other gods who haunt this place'. Others insist that the true Kallirhoe is the fountain under the Pnyx, which we have referred to elsewhere as the Nine-spouts, Ennea-krounos.

One school of archaeologists says that the Ilissus spring is much too far for girls to go twice a day, carrying a heavy *stamnus* on their shoulders, while others triumphantly point out that the spring was far from the city, so far that girls who went to it ran some risk from the wild foreigners who came down from Hymettus—then outside Athenian territory—to carry them off. Whatever the true solution of an unimportant question, all can at least agree to see in this place the setting of one of the world's immortal compositions, and let us hope that some day Athenians may be able to make its appearance once more worthy both of Socrates and Plato.

The great Temple of Zeus was as we said by no means the only gift of Hadrian to Athens. A really good water supply brought by an aqueduct from Pentelicus, was another, and what Hadrian calculated as enough for the needs of a city of say thirty thousand inhabitants was made to do, right up to our own time, for one of twenty times that number, a fact that we fear argues some change in the ablutionary habits of the modern Athenians. It is only today that a big reservoir beyond the field of Marathon has brought abundant drinking water to the city, on which the visitor can rely. A very few years ago one drank water that was said to have been

61

brought in jars from a trusty spring at Amorousia or Morosi, ten miles away—and tried to believe that the classically shaped *stamnus* that supplied one's needs had not really been refilled at some much nearer and less cleanly source.

The aqueduct supplied baths in the city, which have perished altogether, but stood somewhere near the later Agora or market, and therefore close to the great library that was another of the gifts of Hadrian. Some part of this (though none of its contents, alas!) has been preserved by the fact that it was embodied in the mediaeval wall that defended the very small Athens of that date.

As for the Agora, we all know how the business quarter of an ancient city is apt to shift with the passage of centuries, and Athens was no exception to the rule. The classic Agora, where Socrates used to walk and button-hole any passer-by was down under the temple of Hephaestus, or the Theseum. It was really the 'Club', in which most citizens passed most of the day; for indoor life—for men— there was none. In Roman times it had shifted to where the library of Hadrian now stands, and the whole space was surrounded by fine marble colonnades, the gift of the same lavish emperor. Other buildings, such as the Stoa of Attalus (which is merely a big covered market, and suggests that kings who felt that they must give something to Athens were then being put to it to find something to give) were on its borders, as were such university buildings as the lost Gymnasia of Ptolemy and of Diogenes, and a Temple of Ares. These are among the buildings that the American excavators hope to find in the work that they are conducting in that area, works that are now being carried on at a terrible cost, and are only made possible by a generous millionaire. With all respect to his liberality and their skill, one must lament that so much has to be spent now, to do work that, had good advice been taken, might have been carried out quite easily long ago (see p. 17).[1]

Adjoining the market is the well-known Tower of the Winds, called more properly the Horologion of Andronicus, and dating from about 140 B.C. Actually, it is a combination of a water-clock,

---

[1] The first stages of this great work, now in progress, have been somewhat disappointing. Still they have given us the Altar of the Twelve Gods— the centre from which Athens counted her stadia—and several of the *ostraka* on which men voted for the ostracism of either Themistocles or Aristides. These last come out of the well into which they were thrown after counting. The shield of one of the Spartan officers at Sphacteria, found near the site of the old Poikile or Painted Colonnade, should be included in this.

a sundial, and a weather-vane and was a practical business man's gift for a business quarter. Visitors to the interior (where the structure of the roof may appeal to architects) can study the mechanism of the water-clock which was the real *raison d'être* of the whole, and may perhaps be able to hazard a guess at the principle of its working. At least, nobody will be able to prove them wrong!

The Winds, which have given the name not only to the building but also the Aeolus Street that conducts to it (and here let us say that those who laid out modern Athens were at least careful to provide fine vistas to their roads) are carved on the eight sides of the building, and it must be owned that they are evidence of the sad decline that art had undergone in the city in that Roman period.

The building, however, had an interesting history in the days of Mahommedan rule, a history which probably accounts for its excellent preservation. A *tekke*—which is much the same as a monastery, in the faith of Islam—was established in the old Agora, and this passed into the hands of Dervishes of the Bektashi order. This order have never had the reputation of being too orthodox in their faith, though their founder Haji Bektash was selected by the Ottoman Sultan Orkhan (about 1330 A.D.) to give his benediction to the newly raised regiment of Janissaries, and every member of that *corps d'élite* of the Ottoman army was always, in theory, an affiliated member of the order. However that may be, here in Athens they had one of their numerous *tekkes*, and they fell more or less under the influence of the place, for when this little classical monument came into their hands, they preserved it, 'graven images' and all, and declared that it was a chapel in honour of two local sages who were, beyond all doubt, among those who were Prophets of Allah before Mahommed, namely 'Aflatun' and 'Sakhratis' (Plato and Socrates). Few will be disposed to quarrel with their decision, or to think it anything but creditable to them.[1]

Close by the Tower is a fine Orthodox church which is XIIth century, and also has its own contribution to the long story of Athens, as follows. From the days of Justinian (say 550 A.D.) to the period of the Frankish conquest in 1206, the Orthodox Cathedral in Athens was the Parthenon. Then, when the Latins were supreme, the Orthodox were expelled thence, and it became a cathedral of the

---

[1] The Order maintains its tolerant character. A Bektashi Moslem of the writer's acquaintance in Crete was the ordinary local umpire in Christian quarrels. Legend has it that Saladin offered Coeur de Lion membership in it, in return for Christian Knighthood.

63

Roman obedience till Greece fell to the Turk, when as already
stated, it became a Mosque. The displaced Orthodox put their
Cathedral here, at all events for the time, but seem to have lost it
at some date during the Turkish occupation, as at the time of the
War of Independence the Archbishop had his throne in the tiny
church of St. Eleutherius, to which we shall refer later. At a guess,
the church was taken from the Greeks by the Turks, and turned by
them into the military bake-house as which it serves today. So far
as inserted floors and furnaces will allow a visitor to judge, it is an
unusually fine specimen of the architecture of its date—a period
of which there is only one other specimen in Athens—and it is a
pity that it cannot be restored to its proper use.

A road that presumably follows an old line leads from the Agora
to the Diplyon, or rather to a point just short of it, where it turns
off just by an ancient church known as that 'of the Bodiless Ones'
(i.e. of the Holy Angels), and leaves the traveller to find his way
thither from a point outside the old wall, and through the cemetery
of the Ceramicus.

The Ceramicus is one of those places which, if you visit them
without a guide who knows them, are about as interesting as any
other disused graveyard. If however you can be shown it by one
who knows its story, its every stone can throb with life in a way
rare even among the sites of Athens. We can only advise the visitor
on entry to go direct to the innermost portion of the enclosure, and
to commence his explorations at that point. He is standing just
within the inner one of the two double gates of the big Diplyon,
the main exit from Athens in this direction, by which the roads
both to Eleusis (the Sacred Way) and to Thebes left the city. The
gate was provided with a big barbican or external fortified court, but
this was, as was the custom in Greece, sunk within the line of wall
instead of projecting without it as was usual in mediaeval fortresses.
Just inside the gate, a large fountain or water tank was placed, and
the bare feet of the girls who came to draw water have so worn the
marble pavement, that one can see exactly where they stood, and
where were the pillars that supported the roof over the tank.

The Church of the Holy Angels, which is now just behind the
visitor, though out of sight, has this interest, that it about represents
the site of the original house of Alcibiades. Further, just by the wall
of the court or barbican of the gate is another building, standing
rather on the skew from it. This was the store-place, Pompeion,
where were kept all the properties and furniture required for the

64

great procession to Eleusis on the celebration of the Mysteries, which started from this court, as did also the procession of the Pan-Athenaea, though the former went outwards from the city and the latter inwards, up to the Acropolis. Now it will be remembered that Alcibiades, on one of the occasions that that scamp of genius had a fit of real reverence for religion on him—a thing that did happen sometimes, according to the confession that Plato puts into his mouth—went and got himself initiated at Eleusis. Then came the reaction natural after that week or more of strict retreat—and how natural it was we shall see when we come to deal with the story of Eleusis—and he and his friends, in a drunken orgy, parodied the holy mysteries in his own house. It was the unforgivable sin, far worse than serving Sparta against his own country. Here, we can see how easy the sacrilegious sport would be. The place where all that was needful to make it lifelike was next door to the house where he and his guests were drinking. Part of the penalty was, that the house where the deed was done was confiscated and dedicated to the gods. As we have seen how dedications of that sort last in this land, even when the shrine in question has been occupied by another faith, we do not find it impossible to think that the dedication of this church site may go back right to that scandalous episode.

To go back a few centuries in Athenian history, it was in the gateway of the Dipylon, while the Pan-Athenaic procession was forming up, that the rather over-rated heroes Harmodius and Aristogeiton stabbed their private enemy Hipparchus—for it was no more than a private quarrel and that not of the cleanest—having brought their daggers 'wreathed in myrtle' for the purpose on that sacred occasion.

The Dipylon and the wall about it seem to have been a weak stretch in the fortifications of Athens, for twice we find attacks in a siege being made at this point. One of them was when Philip IV of Macedon was besieging the place. His stormers got actually into the court of the gateway, but were driven out again, Philip carrying with him an arrow that had destroyed the sight of one eye. When it was extracted, it was found to carry the inscription, 'Aster to Philip: this death dealing shaft.' Philip, in natural anger, had scores of arrows shot into the city, each inscribed thus, 'Philip to Aster: gallows waits for you'—a threat executed a little later.

Just outside the outer portal of the gate, and indeed built against it, is the base of an equestrian statue. That also sets one thinking. There was a time when Cicero came to Athens, and, like the scholar and gentleman that he was, was profoundly interested in a place where, in his own words, 'each step you take, you tread on history'. But further, having an only too good opinion of himself, he felt that Athens really deserved to be honoured by a monument to the man who was the second founder of Rome. We remember his famous line—the one that has survived of all the hopelessly commonplace verses he wrote, for this finest writer of Latin prose that ever lived had the human ambition to be the poet that he could not be— *O fortunatam natam me Consule Romam*, which we may English,

Oh blest birth-date for the Roman state
Was the date of my great Consulate.

A triumphal arch in the Ceramicus seemed indicated, and he got tenders for one, but was staggered at the cost. His monumental mason, being an accommodating man, suggested that he should knock off the head from some statue, indicating one 'just by the Dipylon Gate', and then a new head and a new inscription would do all that was needed. Cicero, being a gentleman, if conceited, drew the line at that. But, dare we think it was this statue?

The roads, now barely traceable, go away towards their destinations, with the drains under them, drains that show how inventions may be made and forgotten. We remember showing this spot to a gentleman who was by profession a sanitary engineer, and finding him make a dead set at a sewer there. 'That drain I see, when was it put in?' 'Everything here is about 320 B.C.' 'But the thing is *oval!*' 'Well, why not?' 'But you say it is classic! Confound these Greeks, they steal all one's best ideas. The oval form of sewer is my firm's patent.' [1]

We pass along the line of the wall, to where the little stream of Eridanus, which flows through the city, comes out of it and goes down to join the Cephissus. It is little more than a drain at this point, and indeed a few yards lower down it goes underground and becomes one; the inspection chambers with their means of access roused the professional admiration of our sanitary friend. The stream issues from the wall at the bottom of a deep recess or 're-entrant angle', where a small sally-port gives the means of those counter-attacks likely to be necessary at this point. Here once more we plunge into history; it will be remembered that when the Athenians came back to their home after the Persian war and started to rebuild their city wall, the Spartans objected, and seemed likely to

[1] There is a parallel to this in the Roman Baths at Bath.

interfere. Athens could neither resist nor acquiesce, wherefore the wily Themistocles went off as ambassador to Sparta, to waste time as much as possible, leaving orders that in his absence every man, woman and child was to work day and night at the wall, to get it up to defensible height before the slow-moving Spartans could make up their minds to act. Any squared stone—monument, statue-base, anything—went into those walls in the need. Here we see evidence of how that work was done, in the 'tumultuary' character of the work at this important point, and at least one statue base can be found in the wall still. The marble statue was inserted into the stone base, and fixed with molten lead. Now when the base was to serve in the wall, the statue was broken off—if the Persians had not done that already—the marble roughly chipped off to a level, and the stone went into the wall, where it is to this day. In the Museum are two other instances of the same, though these are too precious to leave in the open. These also are statue-bases, but it is the subjects of the carvings that give them their charm. The date of the work must be, obviously, not later than from 500 to 480 B.C. as the blocks were put into the wall just after the latter year; and one of them represents boys playing hockey—they are 'bullying off', and the umpire is just giving the signal—another a pair of wrestlers ('Sikh wrestling, the first grip', was the comment of an officer of Indian experience who saw it) while if the third does not give a primitive example of Rugby football, it is something very like it. Where else do you get two sides lining up, marking their men, and where else is the ball thrown into play with that peculiar overhand swing?[1]

Here outside the wall we are in the Ceramicus—a boundary stone declares the fact legibly if there is any doubt—and this, the 'Potters' Field' as the name means, was a suburb of singular beauty that served as the Westminster Abbey of Athens, the place of burial for those whom the city delighted to honour. Hereabouts—and would that we could discover their graves—sleep Solon, Pericles, Miltiades and Phormio, that 'Cochrane of Athens' (see p. 200). Here too were laid—it is a recent discovery—the Spartans who were killed by Thrasybulus and his men, in the scuffles that cast out the 'Thirty Tyrants'. Athens could not afford a quarrel with Sparta so soon after Aegospotami, and went out of her way to do honour to these dead. So here they lie, 'Chairon and Thibrachus the Polemarchs, and Lacrates the Olympian victor, buried before the gates in Ceramicus'.

[1] The fourth side is—a cat and dog fight!

If it were possible, those who fell in battle abroad were brought home to lie here, as was the case with the heroes of the first year of the Peloponnesian war. They have two memorials, one the immortal speech of Pericles preserved in Thucydides, which was delivered here, and one, the exquisite funerary sculpture in the Acropolis Museum.

A few yards along the Via Sacra you come to family graves. A family could buy a 'cemetery lot' and wall it in as their fancy dictated, adorning it often with the family cognizance, bull or hound. Then generation after generation could be buried there, the name of each one being put on one common monument. Sometimes there is a personal note, as in the case of the monument to Dexileos, who was 'one of the five horsemen'—i.e. A.D.C. to the general in chief—in the Corinthian war. Normally, what the memorials emphasize is the 'farewell motive', and we have husband bidding farewell to wife or *vice versa*; at least once there seems to be a note of satire, and the object that the lady is bidding an affectionate good-bye to is her jewel-case. One very common object on a grave is a large pitcher or pot; or rather, a representation of one in solid stone. It may signify that the grave is that of a maiden, and that the pitcher stands for the marriage bath that was never needed; it may be merely the pot that, as we have seen, was regularly placed upon a grave for the reception of offerings. Naturally, tombs and funerals tended to be too costly, and the cemetery contains many instances of an attempt that was made to stop this. That Demetrius of Phaleron, whose really scientific government proved so intolerable to decent Athenians, ruled that no funeral was to cost more than just so much—and the sum was found only sufficient to provide a monument that much resembles a chimney-pot in stone, very ugly and unfortunately nearly indestructible.

The place however was not used only for funerals and the attendant ceremonial. When a Decree of Ostracism had been passed, the urns for the voting *ostraka*, which were to decide which citizen was to be exiled for the good of the State, were put up in this area, as also in the Agora, and several of the inscribed potsherds used have come to light. One bears the name of Thucydides, but one must own that it is not the historian but 'the son of Melesias', a luckless opponent of Pericles, that was the victim then. A more recent discovery made by the Americans in the Agora, bears the name of Aristides, and there was but one man of that name. One would like of course to believe that it is the very sherd that he inscribed himself, as the familiar story tells us, and that it therefore is his own autograph; but it must be owned that the odds are several thousand to one against that. A queer little precinct or *temenos* is included in the cemetery, the boundary stones of which make it clear that it was the property of one of the old and not too proper gods who never got into Olympus, in this case Tritopatores. He is not an exclusively Athenian deity, for he had a similar precinct at Delos, and it is not known who or what this 'Triple Father' really was, though he seems to have been an embodiment of all one's ancestors, to everybody. It is tempting to identify him with the triple-bodied deity who appeared on the pediment of the Pre-Persian' Parthenon, and who still beams with three benevolent smiles on the visitor to the Acropolis Museum. At least the 'Triple Father' provides yet another instance of the ever interesting 'persistence of dedications' in Athens, for his precinct is partly occupied by an ancient church,[1] and that was the only ancient dedication in Athens to the Holy Trinity.

Hereabout too one can feel that one is on the site of another historic episode, and even imagine that we can see, not a Roman camp, but something much more rare, a Roman *agger* raised to storm a city wall. Here Sulla made his attack on the city, and it was here that the civic fathers came out to surrender the city—not the Acropolis—and beg for mercy. They had put things off till almost too late, for the Roman had promised his men the loot of the town, and some of them were inside the wall and the massacre had begun, so that it was by no means certain that he either would or could call off his hounds. The Athenian embassy prayed for mercy, but the Roman was silent and the grim 'purple and white' face showed no sign of compunction. At last they were inspired to hold their peace, and merely point to where the Parthenon gleamed white against the sky on its rock. For a minute more, Sulla was silent still; then at last he growled out, 'I spare the living for the sake of the dead'. Cicero spoke the truth when he said that in Athens your every step is on history.

Further, that history does not really come to an end with the end of the classic period, and only revive with the beginning of the Greek War of Independence, though we fear that it must be owned that the heresy that it does is rather encouraged by modern Greeks. No doubt there is much in the story of the period of subjection to

[1] Was occupied, one ought to say, for the building which had no historic interest, has been moved to another site hard by.

Latins and Turks (it is six centuries in all, 1200–1800) that Greeks
would like to forget, and it is true also that in the period from
500 A.D. to 1200 A.D. there is little history to be found in Hellas.
For those centuries the story of the Greek race is to be found in
Constantinople, and a very great history it is. Still, mediaeval
Greece has its real national life too.

A proof of the fact that Athenian life was not over is to be found
in the very interesting series of beautiful, if tiny, churches that are
one of the artistic treasures of this period of Athenian and indeed
Hellenic history. Two of these, the church of the Saviour and the
former cathedral, we have mentioned on a previous page. A sister
church to the XIIth century cathedral is to be found in what is
known as the 'Russian' church (properly that of St. Nicodemus) in
Phil-hellene Street. English people may know it because it is close
by the English church, a building of which we may say that, seeing
that it was built in the 1840's, it might easily have been very much
worse than it is.

The church of St. Nicodemus, however, is a really fine specimen
of the architecture of its date (it was built 1040), and as it is used for
its proper purpose and not as a bake-house, can be studied with ease.
The fact that it came somehow into the hands of the Russian colony
in Athens in better days, and so provided one of the few churches
where in one critical period that persecuted church could be sure of
keeping its worship going, will not lessen its interest to English
people. St. John of the Column, just under the eastern end of the
Acropolis, certainly stands on the site of some classic shrine, some of
the pillars of which stand out in front of it to this day. The column
which gives the church its name stands within it, and is still a place
of cures. You write out your prayer to the saint on paper—which
St. John of the many you address we own we do not know—wet it
and stick it to the pillar. If it remains in place you can go away happy
in the assurance that your prayer is granted. The interest of the
church, however, is more anthropological than architectural. Far
otherwise is it with the remaining churches of the group, that of the
Ss. Theodore, of St. Eleutherius, and of the Presentation of the
Virgin, a group to which we ought to add that of the Saviour by the
Acropolis. Men will tell you that these are all of fourth century
building and attribute them, or most of them, to the piety of the
empress Pulcheria. There are no historic records available, so one
can only judge by the style of the building, and one must own that
the design, which is a very beautiful one, suggests a later date. A

church the plan of which is the Greek cross with a dome at the inter-section surely shows the influence of St. Sophia, which we all know as the work of a great original genius. If so, then these Athenian churches must be later than 550, a fact borne out by the numerous fragments of material from pagan temples that are built into their fabric. On the other hand, the lines of their architecture are in-variably broken up, internally, by a relatively large Eikonostasis that they were clearly never designed to carry. That plainly suggests that they were built before that ritual feature had become the dominant thing that it is in Greek Orthodox ceremonial today, and that they belong to periods when the altar screen which always existed was very much smaller, and was more of the older type of which specimens are shown in the Byzantine Museum in Athens, or which can be seen *in situ* in the interesting church among the ruins of Olympia. That would put their date of building at some-where about the eighth or ninth centuries, a conclusion supported by the fact that the central dome in each case is raised on a 'drum'—a fashion that began at that time. Sometimes, however, we find older features existing. The Church of the Presentation of our Lady, for instance, is a double one, two complete fabrics side by side. The smaller and older portion, the northern one, is a tiny basilica in plan whereas the other is a Greek Cross. That basilican portion may well be as old as legend asserts, and go back to the days of the Empress Pulcheria, and the end of the IVth century.

This little church is known popularly by the name of Panagia Kapnikarea, which we may interpret as 'the smoky Madonna', a name which is said to have been given from the fact that the sacred Eikon that it contains—which is not noticeably blacker than ancient pictures are apt to become—was damaged by smoke from a neigh-bouring fire. The building is said by legend to occupy the site of an ancient shrine of Athena, where the maidens of Athens were accustomed of old to offer their bridal wreaths to the Virgin Goddess. Whether that be so or no, certain it is that the very pretty custom still prevails here, though of course the offerings of the wreaths are now made to our Lady.

There was very little Orthodox Church building done in the days of Latin domination here, and of course none at all in the time of Turkish rule. Hence, of all later churches, the nineteenth century cathedral is the oldest, and it is admittedly not a success externally, though its interior has dignity. The principles of Gothic architecture were not understood in the 1830's, and those of Byzantine art had not been studied at all, being considered as barbarous as was once the style that was called Gothic for that reason.[1]

It contains as a relic the stone on which the water-pots of Cana were said to have been put—or at least what was certainly shown to pilgrims in the fourth century as such. It is also the burial place of one who was justly counted a martyr to Greek independence, though hardly the Christian religion. This was Gregory, eighth Patriarch of Constantinople of that name. When the Greek War of Independence broke out, he was seized by the Turks as he left the church on the morning of Easter day, and hanged in his robes in the gateway of Phanar, the Patriarchal residence in Constantinople. (Such a hanging, as usual with Turkish executions, means very slow strangulation.) The act was simply an expression of anger at the revolt itself, for the prelate had done what he could to damp it down. His body, thrown into the Golden Horn, was picked up by some Greeks and buried, and smuggled to Athens when the independence of Greece was secured. The gate of the Phanar has never been opened since, and it is said never will be opened—till an Orthodox Patriarch shall return from the reconsecration of St. Sophia.

The whole modern cathedral rather overshadows the tiny St. Eleutherius by its side—a building in which the Archbishop had his throne for several centuries, and which is interesting, not only on account of its architecture, but also because of the numerous fragments of classic work that it contains. One of these, that over the western door, is the complete festal calendar of ancient Athens to which we have referred on a previous page. As usual, the ancient church stands on a site holy before it was built, and is said to represent the temple of Eleithyia, the goddess who assisted women in childbirth, and whose other name of Eleutho is very near that of the saint.

The cathedral had its part to play in the Athenian troubles connected with the Great War. King Constantine was a most devout son of the Orthodox Church for whom indeed something like a miracle was once wrought. He was most dangerously ill with some form of internal abscess; the doctors dared not give an anaesthetic (his heart was feeble), and could not operate without. As a last resource, the most holy of all Eikons near Athens, that of the Panagia of Tenos, was brought from its island shrine to the king's

[1] This has been remedied now, and the Byzantine Museum in Athens is a collection that deserves much more attention than it usually obtains.

72

bed, being accompanied on its road from Piraeus by a long procession of bare-footed royalist devotees. (Let us add that five bare-foot miles on a Greek road in a Greek August is something in the way of a penance.) As it was brought into the bedroom the King, defying the orders of his doctors, raised himself in his bed and reverently kissed the holy picture. The exertion burst the abscess, and the King recovered.

Thus it can easily be understood that when the King decided, rightly or wrongly, to keep his country out of the Great War, there was at least a strong party among the authorities in the church that were ready to support him, and who joined in his strong opposition to the Premier Venizelos, who wished to put all on the hazard and join in the war. Feeling ran very high, so high that the King, when he dismissed the Premier, could order the then Archbishop to excommunicate him. Of course the step was a scandalous one, for the only charges against the Premier—other than merely frivolous ones—were political, and the Archbishop naturally demurred. He was, however, not a very strong man, and was terrified by the threat of the troops that if he did not, they would burn the cathedral over his head. 'It was a very great opportunity missed,' said architectural purists, but the prelate proceeded to do as he was told. A savant who was in Athens at the time—and whose archaeological interest in the ceremony almost balanced his political and religious dislike of it—described the ceremony, which was as follows. A trench was dug in the Champ de Mars in the city, and a severed bull's head put at the bottom of it. Then the Archbishop hurled a black stone at the head, ejaculating 'Anathema to Eleutherius Venizelos, who—performs various iniquities of which the details do not matter'. Everybody present followed suit, a supply of carefully blackened stones being on hand, till a cairn was raised above the burial place of the head. That evening, the Venizelist party wreathed the cairn with flowers, and the Royalists replied with more stones next day, and so on till both parties tired of the amusement. How far back that ceremony could trace its history we do not like to guess, but we should say till neolithic times as a conservative estimate. At least it will be seen that neither the historical nor the picturesque came to stop in Athens at so early a date as 600 A.D.

IV

DAPHNE AND ELEUSIS

Sacred Way—Monastery of Daphne and history—Rheiton—The Mysteries and their development—Eleusis—Duration of its rites—The Hierarchy—Demeter legend—Initiation ceremonies

It is naturally the Sacred Way that leads from Athens to Eleusis, the route of the great pilgrimage to that sanctuary, and it starts in theory from the Dipylon Gate, and through the Ceramicus, that we have just been examining. Actually the traveller must go by another street in Athens, but thereafter his road follows the general line of the Via Sacra, which is often traceable at its side. At the beginning, he goes out through the groves of the Academy of Plato, the site of whose college is roughly marked by the present botanical gardens, and whose actual tomb is known to be somewhere in the neighbourhood. Daphne is apt to be his first halt, at a distance of about seven miles from Athens. No doubt it was originally what its name suggests, a temple to Apollo, and one of the many shrines along this Sacred Way at which pilgrims could halt. Indeed there is just one Ionic column, and one of rare grace, built into the fabric of the present church to testify to this. In the time of Justinian the temple vanished, and one of the many fortified monasteries which that great builder used as guard-posts along his roads took its place. The Emperor's work still forms the lower courses of the enclosing wall. In the eleventh century, the basilica that Justinian built was replaced by the present church, which was erected in the period 1080–1100, and is therefore exactly contemporary with St. John's Chapel in the Tower of London. The contrast between the buildings is eloquent of the different levels of civilization at the two ends of Europe at that day. The wonderful mosaics that form one of the glories of the present church were inserted during the twelfth

74

century, and form an important link in the whole chain of the development of that art.

Soon after the year 1200, there came a change in the land, with the invasion of the Latins. 'Frankish' dukes (they were really Burgundian, of the house of De la Roche) ruled in Athens, and the Orthodox monks were expelled from the monastery. The repair of the mosaic in the present century brought to light a grim comment on what was done then by the invaders; all had wondered before at the curiously grim expression in the eyes of the great mosaic of Christus Pantocrator in the dome of the church, but when scaffolding was put up to repair it the mystery was explained; there were western crossbow-bolts in the eyes, for the Latin invaders had amused themselves by shooting at 'the Christ of the heretics'. It is a parallel to what was done in St. Sophia by these same 'crusaders'.

At least the Frankish Dukes kept the monastery for religious purposes, for they established Cistercians within its walls, and these fathers, who seemingly did not like the ordinary arrangement of an Eastern monastery, built one for themselves according to western ideas. Fortunately they did not alter the fabric of the church, and the result is a combination which we believe to be unique—a Western cloister attached to an Eastern sanctuary. The Dukes of Athens made this church their family burial place, and the stone coffins that are found in the enclosure, so familiar at home, and so unusual here, once contained their remains. One of those who were thus buried here was that Walter of Brienne who perished in the great disaster of Scripu on the Copais plain—an episode with which we deal later.

Gradually, the exotic growth of Frankish rule in Greece withered, though it succeeded in destroying with itself the more natural and valuable plant—the Byzantine Empire; and so allowed the Turk, more harmful than either, to take the place of both. The Burgundians had given place to an Italian house as the ruling family before the end—the Acciajuoli of Florence; and the episode with which those last ended shows how utterly rotten the whole state of the body politic had become. The last Italian duke had died, in 1454, and his widow, one Donna Chiara, presented herself as heir to her husband by expelling her nephew and marrying an old lover, whose wife she and he contrived to dispose of between them. The nephew escaped to Constantinople, where he told his tale of woe to Mahommed the Conqueror, then newly established in his new capital. 'El Fatih' heard his suppliant to the end, and observed, 'You have been turned out of your dukedom *by a woman* and ask help from me! We who are true believers do keep that sort of thing in the family at any rate.' This spurred this hopeful nephew to action, and he returned to Athens, where he was able to raise an *émeute* and drive his enemy to take sanctuary at Daphne. Then he followed her there, and (having apparently taken lessons in this art at Constantinople) he came behind her with a bow-string—and put an end to his aunt's life. In these circumstances it is not to be wondered at that a few months from that date, 'El Fatih' was lord paramount in Hellas.

Outside the walls of the monastery is a chapel-like building that is generally taken to be one by visitors, but is actually something so unfamiliar, and so characteristically Greek, as to merit a description. It is an ossuary, or place of deposit for the bones of the departed. The fact is that in Greece, good cultivable land is too precious to be employed on cemeteries; and uncultivable, too rocky for that purpose. So, though the dead must be buried in holy ground, they cannot stay permanently in it, but must give place to others. The bodies are placed in graves excavated in the hard rock. After three years, by which time the body ought to have been reduced to dust and dry bones, the bones are exhumed and either given to relatives or, in the case of a monastery like this, kept in an ossuary. If the body is entirely preserved, it is probably that of a saint and must be treated accordingly; but if certain signs are present, the chances are that the dead man has become a Vampire, a *Vrykolakas*, and the corpse should be burned for the safety of the neighbours, and indeed to save the soul of the departed.

Daphne is now a national monument, and is not used for service; thus it has lost, to our grief, an Eikon for which we always felt a special devotion. It was a picture of Elijah, going up to heaven in the fiery chariot, but it was the offering of the piety of that nearly extinct tribe, the cab-drivers of Athens, to the only saint they knew of who was ever recorded to have taken a carriage. Hence the chariot was the type of carriage they knew best, a small two-horsed 'Victoria.'

The road goes on down a gentle slope from Daphne on the way to Eleusis, passing first a fine shrine of our Lady Aphrodite—at which they say offerings are still made occasionally—and so going along the shore of Eleusis bay, and past the tarn of Rheiton, once the boundary of the Eleusinian territory, to the sacred town itself.

Here there centred a ceremony that was revered by all Greeks, and by all who were influenced by Greek culture, but which had its focus in this little country town, independent as late as the days of

Solon, but afterwards subject to Athens. 'There are just two things in all Greece' says Pausanias, 'which are in a class by themselves. They are the Games of Olympia and the Mysteries of Eleusis.' What was done there? Much that was quite public and that was known, but there was a great deal that, as the very name implies, was open only to the Initiates, or *Mystae*, and they kept their vow of secrecy in a way that we must admire even while we are annoyed by it. Yet, all literature has been ransacked for references, the site has been excavated, and we can eke out the scanty direct information that we have by comparison with what is now known of parallel rites elsewhere, and so attain knowledge of a good deal here also.

Every primitive people had, and some still have, a Mystery, a rite of Initiation, and Eleusis was no more originally than one of these, taken up and enriched by the most artistic minds of the race of man. All these primitive mysteries are much alike, whether they be found in Mexico among the Aztecs, among aborigines in Australia, or Negroes in Nyasaland. There is a deal of common human nature in man, and it comes out in these resemblances. All savage dances are much alike, and stone weapons have such a likeness that a modern stone axe from Fiji has before this found itself in the same case in a museum with some neolithic weapons, for the expert had confused the two, and it was only the fact that the Fijian weapon was of jade that put him right. Now, in the tribal mysteries, the object is always the same, namely that of initiating youth into the duty of life, which is the giving of strength to the tribe, and of averting dangers from it. What any tribe needs for its strength is a good supply of food and a good supply of men, and youth is told on initiation what to do, and also what to avoid, if he or she is to do his or her part in providing both. Thus the mysteries are usually corn ceremonies[1] and birth ceremonies, and as primitive agriculture is much the same all the world over, and the way in which babies come into the world always exactly the same, it is not unnatural that the instruction that deals with these two matters should be much the same also. This gave them a value, that is neglected and missed now, when the primitive race meets civilization, for it will be seen that they included instruction given from age to youth, as a matter of course, on subjects that it is vitally important that youth should know, and which instructors in our days find it very difficult

---

[1] Where the staple food is not corn, then whatever occupies its place is taken for the rite. On Melville Island, youth is shown how to sow and pre-pare the yam, and as the climax of the rite is given a yam to eat.

to teach. Hence we can see how, in later days, it was quite natural that good missionaries should call them obscene, in that they were certainly outspoken—out-acted would perhaps be a better word—and that they dealt with elemental facts in a way that might well seem shocking to an age that was prudish as well as moral.

Originally, there were many ceremonies of the kind in Greece, in that each tribe had its own Mystery, and Pausanias, writing as late as 160 A.D., mentions at least five as 'Eleusinian' in character, that is to say as like enough to those of Eleusis to be obviously of the same school, though as a matter of fact they were probably parallel and independent growths. Then there were others that were obviously of a different type, such as the Orphic rites, which had a most interesting development in Hellenic lands, though they were partly Thracian in origin. These were not quite extinct in Thrace in the year 1906, and we believe go on still in such remote islands as Scyros and Sciathos. There were also the Kabeiric rites whose name for the 'Great Ones' that they revered, (*kabir*) is almost enough to prove a Semitic or Oriental origin; and no doubt others besides.

Of all these, however, Eleusis became *the* Mystery *par excellence*, and we may take it as the standard initiation rite of a Pelasgian tribe at that place, assuming Pelasgian to mean no more than pre-Hellenic. Of course, other influences bore upon it; some of these were Egyptian, for according to the legend, Danaus brought the Thesmophoria from Egypt to Argolis and Attica, and his fifty daughters taught the rites of Demeter. As is usual, archaeology confirms the general lines of legend, for the oldest burial stratum at Eleusis has produced Egyptian objects, and objects connected with the worship of Isis the Egyptian corn-goddess, dating from the XVIIIth Egyptian dynasty, which is about 1500 B.C. Naturally, there was corn in Greece before that date, but it agrees well with the fact that Eleusis was a corn-mystery.

Then, there are also Orphic influences, which is as much as to say, Dionysiac. Dionysus certainly comes in somehow, and at so early a date that he can be identified with Iacchos, who is one of the original Eleusinian spirits, but in himself he is always an outsider, who brings with him the vine. Orpheus the singer comes with him, quite possibly as the prophet of those new and valuable influences in religion which we have seen appear with the vine-god, even though they are mixed with much that is lower. We have learnt to look on Orpheus as not merely the musician who goes down to Hades to seek a lost love, but as a definite historic figure, a religious reformer and

78

possibly martyr, who comes with the new faith from Thrace. The corn-mystery culminated here, as in many another land, in an initiation drama, in which Kore the corn-maiden, the divine being who dies and goes beneath the earth, to come back again bearing life for man, becomes a symbol of man's resurrection; and each candidate for entry to her mystery is taught, 'this is what you have to do to serve the tribe, and at last you will die—and remember this, that death is not the end.'

Such a rite as this, when the most mytho-poetic minds of history are left to work upon it, does not always remain the same in content, though it was only natural that each of the myriads who came to it should see in it, as it developed, something in proportion to what they had brought. Philosophers saw the story of the soul's entanglement in matter, and the winning of its release; Christian fathers—most unfriendly witnesses these—own that at Eleusis was taught the unity of God and the Resurrection of man. The very crude and primitive ritual was refined, till it became what was to the Greek a combination of a High Mass and a Passion Play, and this Pelasgian tribal mystery became something which could be revered, and that deservedly, wherever Rome ruled, and Greece influenced the minds of men.

To describe it would be hard, even if our information was more complete. Describe a High Celebration of the Mass, whether Roman, Anglican, or Greek Orthodox (and it is the last that is most like to what Eleusis was), as accurately as you will to somebody who has never seen its like, and would not the answer be, 'what is there so impressive in that?'—and yet we know that it is the central point of their religious life to millions. It is the atmosphere that counts, and atmosphere must be felt, not described. This is certain, that Eleusis meant very much to very gifted and religious men, and that what was taught there was a new concept of a future life. Homer can only give a shadow world, gloomy and unattractive as any Hebrew Sheol. Eleusis held out the hope of a paradise, open at least to the Initiate.

The rite developed gradually, and the precinct where it was celebrated, originally small, developed *pari passu* with the rite. At first, it was just the property of the tiny City-State, worked by the King-priest of the spot, and when the State was annexed by Athens the mystery was left as the heritage of the ancient houses. The royal house of the Eumolpidae became the Hierophants; a noble family, the Heralds; but it was understood that, though it was still Eleusinian, any Athenian who was otherwise qualified must be accepted there for initiation. This soon became 'any Greek', and the rite was Pan-Hellenic already when the incidents of the invasion of Xerxes increased its prestige a thousandfold. The Persian had stormed Athens and sacked it, and was now in full march on Eleusis, when as his force debouched on the Rarian plain in which the place stands, they saw before them gigantic columns of dust, whirling as they often whirl in summer heats,[1] and heard a sound which the Greeks present could at least declare to be the cry of the Eleusinian initiate, 'Iacchos, Iacchos.' The deserters and prisoners rushed up to Xerxes exclaiming 'You have prevented us from celebrating the Mysteries, and the Gods themselves have come down to perform them; go on if you dare.' Xerxes turned back (*Herod.*, viii. 65).

After the Persian had gone, Eleusis was taken up by Pericles. The great statesman had his Pan-Hellenic dream of a vast commonwealth of which Athens was to be the centre, and such a thing as that must have its religious consecration. Here under his hand was what would give it: something that was holy and Pan-Hellenic from of old, not Athenian but yet under the influence of Athens, and which had just received a tremendous access of prestige. So in his day the architect of the Parthenon is employed to make a new and worthy Hall of Initiation in the place of the little old one of varying date, and the Great Telesterion of the area of a small cathedral (220 feet by 180 feet), with seats for 4000 spectators at its sides, is the result. Hollowed out as it is in the living rock, its lower storey at least is indestructible. Later yet, in the Roman day, when 'Greece had taken her captor captive', it was ruled that not only any Greek, but any Greek-speaker (which meant any educated Roman) could be initiated there, and most great men took advantage of this, in the era of the shrine's greatest brilliance. In republican days Cicero was admitted, and so was Clodius his dearest foe, from which we gather that the *Mystae* were not always on those terms of happy concord on which it beseems brethren to dwell. At least eight emperors came, including Severus and Augustus, and one *Hierophantis* boasts that she herself initiated three, Hadrian, Aurelius and Commodus. Julian was the latest on the list. Yet the place earns most credit, not from the emperors whom it accepted, but from one whom it refused; for Nero applied for admission, and he was rejected. It is

[1] They are known as Nereids now—the term has come to mean any sort of spirit—and it is best to say on seeing them: 'Honey and milk in your path.'

4. Daphne: monastery

5. Castle of Eleutherae: East side; wall and towers

true that the authorities could plead *non possumus* and point out that there was a law, not theirs to break, which forbade the initiation of homicides. Blood-stained hands could not take Demeter's chalice. Yet even so to turn down the master of thirty legions is evidence of the existence of principles, and of a backbone, in the authorities of Eleusis.

The place was always known to be respectable. Even when the Emperor Valentinian forbids nocturnal rites, for good reasons, he makes an exception in favour of Eleusis, and such a Church Father as Gregory the Wonder-worker can only say that he knows nothing against it, but 'if there is nothing to conceal, why the secrecy?' A little knowledge of Church history might have made his judgement more charitable, for that was just what pagans had said of earlier Christians. It was not until the end of the fourth century that the Telesterion was officially closed by order of the Emperor Theodosius, yet nevertheless the rites went on under the rose all through the Middle Ages, and it was not until the nineteenth century that the last shadow faded away. Alas that we must confess that it was Englishmen who were responsible for doing away with the last relics. In 1820, folk of Eleusis were still dancing round what was believed to be a statue of Demeter (it really was one of two Caryatids and its fellow, then buried, is there to this day) and wreathing it with garlands, but these two men gave a *bakhshish* to the Turkish governor of Athens and got leave to take it away. Eleusis protested in vain, declaring that they had 'always' performed these rites—which really was very nearly the fact—and that the crops would not ripen unless Demeter was there. *Bakhshish* prevailed, and the bereaved folk could only say that the ship that carried off Demeter would surely be wrecked; and one cannot be sorry that the prophecy came true. However, the statue was rescued, and stands now in the Fitz-William Museum at Cambridge, with the heartless inscription 'Demeter. Much damaged'. Might not even a sincere Christian have left the Mother in her ancient shrine?

There was a big official hierarchy at the place, of which the head was the Hierophant or Exhibitor of the Sacred Objects. He was always of the old Eumolpid house, and had necessarily to be possessed of a fine presence and fine voice (the family name means 'the house of sweet singers') that he might pronounce the formulae with a rightfully impressive intonation. He was chosen by lot from among those eligible, and always wore royal robes—the purple cloak and golden fillet. He might be a married man, but must live in chastity

during the great festival—a fact which was secured by a mild dose
of hemlock. On taking office, he assumed a new name, writing his
old one on a lead tablet and hurling it into Eleusis bay (which must
contain many specimens of the kind) after which it was a grave
solecism to address him by the name discarded. Lucan finds a friend
in the stocks once, complaining that he has received more than his
share of the dead cats and rotten eggs—or whatever may be their
classical equivalents—natural in the position. All the sympathy the
luckless man gets from his acquaintance is: 'Well, old fellow, you
know you asked for it. Calling the Hierophant *by his old name!*'

The *Hierophantis* was his female counterpart, her part being to
initiate the women, and to crown the men. Other officers were, the
Dadouchos, or Torch-bearer, who took the part of Dionysus-Iacchos
in the drama, the Herald, and of course as many minor officials as a
well-staffed cathedral. All were bound to ritual purity, and in
particular must never approach a corpse, though we find the Herald
violating this taboo very nobly on one occasion. It was when Athens
had fallen on evil days, and was in the grip of the Thirty Tyrants
after the Peloponnesian war. The exiled patriots under Thrasybulus
had put everything on one cast of the dice, had come down from
their fortress at Phyle—which still remains much as they left it—
had seized the fort of Munychion, and repulsed an attack upon it.
The usual burial truce had been asked and granted, and both parties
were mixed together picking up the dead and wounded, when the
Herald of Eleusis who was with the Thrasybulus party, saw his
chance. He sprang upon a block of stone, and the wonderful voice
that had thrilled many there on their initiation night rang out over
that field of civil war. 'Oh fellow-citizens, why do you drive us out?
Are we not sons of Athens even as you, and those who have fallen
today, do we not mourn them as much as you do?' The word went
round: '*Amnestia*', 'Forgive and forget'.

As for the legend told, some story of the giving of the great corn-
gift is universal among men, and all know the tale of Persephone
and the field of Enna. At Eleusis, that was accepted, but told with a
local variant, thus detailed in the Homeric Hymn to Demeter (Loeb
Library: *Homerica*). When the world was young, and Eleusis had
not yet become Eleusis, but was Saisaria, it befell that the king's
daughters went down one evening from the palace to draw water as
usual. There on the well, they found an old woman in deep sorrow,
and the charitable girls took her into the house, where they offered
her food, which she refused. However, she was won to a smile by

the old nurse Iambe—won we regret to say by a jest quite un-
repeatably broad—and consented to take the *kykeon*, the wheat or
barley broth that they brought her.[1] Then as she seemed a know-
ledgeable old dame, she was asked to look after the baby prince,
Demophon, who was weak and pining. Under her care, the child
throve so amazingly that his mother Metanira hid herself in the
nursery to see what the old woman did. She saw her give the child
his usual bath, and then rake a deep hole in the embers of the fire,
put the boy in, and turn away. Naturally the mother sprang from
her hiding place with a scream, and snatched up the child, whom
she found quite unharmed and very loath to leave so comfortable
a bed. The old woman turned on the queen in wrath: 'Unhappy
woman, you have broken the spell.' She revealed herself as Demeter,
wearied of the search for the lost Persephone and ready to adopt this
child as her son, but now—! However, she abated her wrath at the
prayer of the girls who had shown her kindness, and though she
could not go on with the process that would have made the child
immortal, she did adopt him as her son, and promised that he should
become a hero, with the new name Triptolemus, and go round the
world distributing Demeter's gift of corn to man. The story ends
with the return of Persephone as usual to earth, and puts the scene
of that return at a certain pit in the holy precinct, in honour of
which return it is decreed that for all time to come Saisaria shall
bear the new name of Eleusis, Advent.

The initiation ceremony consisted of a grand ritual drama, containing, we read, 'things done, things said, and things shown.' It
was not all of equal antiquity, and while the public part was
necessarily known to anyone who cared to watch it, the private
portion was revealed to the sworn Initiate only. Of the latter we
know only scraps, yet these put together and compared with what
the site and parallel ceremonies can yield us, give a fairly complete
outline of the whole. Among the objects found on the site, we may
give a high place to what is known as the Ninnion plaque, a terra-
cotta slab which was the initiation gift of a maiden of that name,
and which gives a picture of the most essential episodes in the whole
rite. But when we try to describe it, it is, on the whole, rather as if
one was given an outline of a shattered mosaic, and a few handfuls
of *tesserae* that undoubtedly came from the original, and then was
bidden to restore the composition. The *tesserae* belong to the picture,

[1] This is a note of great antiquity, for broth of this kind is far older than
bread.

but one cannot always be certain that one has put them into the right place in it.

There were three main 'degrees' that might be bestowed on the candidate, of which two were compulsory, and one, that of *Epoptes* or eye-witness, was an extra. Further, there were no doubt various higher degrees beyond, of which one was that of Hierophant. We know that in later days this was sometimes bestowed, *honoris causâ*, on distinguished philosophers.

Of the first of these, that of *Agra*, we know little. It was given at Athens and was probably the old Athenian initiation ceremony dating back to times before the annexation of Eleusis. It was a dedication of the candidate to Persephone—or Perephatta as they called her there[1]—and the ceremony took place where the church of St. Photina, near to Kallirhoe, still preserves one of the goddess' titles—though she does appear now in the guise of a virgin martyr of Samaria. This degree was often bestowed on mere boys or girls.

It was the degree of *Mystes*, given at Eleusis, that was the really important one, and it is to this that we turn now. It fell in the month of Boedromion, August-September, when all the harvest was in, and the fields were in their summer sleep. Some weeks before, the *Spondophori*, the truce-bearers, had gone round Greece proclaiming truce of God and safe-conduct to anyone who wished to attend these sacred rites, no matter what war might be in progress. (This venerable custom was disregarded by Sparta during the Peloponnesian war.) On the fourteenth of the month, the full moon, Demeter left Eleusis to pay a ceremonial visit to Athens and Athena, and on her return, all who were qualified were welcome to accompany her, for reception into her company. That is to say, the *Sacra* (the symbols and probably the holiest image) of the Goddess were taken from the Megaron in her shrine, and marched upon a donkey to the capital. On a donkey, because we are back now in primitive days, when the horse if used at all, was used for war only. (For the fact, we have the evidence of the *Frogs* in which Dionysus appears on the stage proclaiming that, as there are no decent poets left on earth now, he will go down to Hades—going to Eleusis with the initiates *en route*, for that was the way thither—and will bring up Aeschylus, or one of the great three of the past. Then Xanthias the slave produces the lunch-basket and proclaims, 'and I am the donkey that carries the Sacred Objects.') The Goddess lodges in her Athens

[1] It is the name on the 'stall' assigned to her priest in the theatre of Dionysus.

84

house, the Eleusinion, and the *Sacra* are placed in their shrine there.

Next day, the great gathering of Candidates for Initiation took place at that centre. Anyone who could pronounce Greek properly (at least in later days) was eligible, legend saying that Heracles and the Dioscuri were the first non-Athenians to be accepted. Each candidate must have a sponsor, however, and neither barbarian nor murderer could approach. Otherwise, the slave was as eligible as his master; 'My master taught me letters and had me initiated' is the epitaph on one at Eleusis. Women could approach, and though that has been doubted, Lucian again makes the fact clear. 'So you are going to throw me over for that cat Glauce,' says one of his damsels to her faithless lover; 'I have just as good a figure as she has, and that beautiful complexion of hers comes off. I walked by her all the way to Eleusis when we were initiated, and so I know.'

Those who appeared on this day at the Eleusinion had already been through several days of 'retreat' and instruction, coupled with some measure of fasting, including abstinence from crab, gurnet, and beans. 'Every Initiate will know why' says Pausanias, 'and so I need not explain.' The names were now formally enrolled, and orders given for a second appearance next day. On that day (the 16th) all must appear at a certain hour at the Itonian Gate (which as we have seen was close to the Eleusinion and the Pnyx) furnished each with a young pig. Then the order was given 'Mystics, to the Sea', and everyone there had to drive his or her pig to the sea—a four mile walk—and wash it, with him- or her-self, in the sea on arrival. Then all the pigs were sacrificed, and the candidates sprinkled with the blood for purification. 'It was not an orderly procession' says one authority solemnly, and of that fact we have no doubt at all—say five hundred young folk, driving five hundred pigs. Nor need we doubt that those who appreciated Aristophanes appreciated the rollicking fun of it as much as we do. Yet a sound knowledge of human nature lay behind it. These boys and girls had been through several days of strict 'retreat', and had several more before them. Anyone with experience of that sort of exercise will know the wisdom of thus giving a lawful opportunity to them to 'blow off steam'.

Two days more of preparation followed, which included the giving of the final instructions, and the entrusting with the password which was most necessary at the great moment. Then, on the 19th of the month, came the gathering at the Dipylon for the Pilgrimage. All candidates for the degree of *Mystes*, or Initiate, were there, each with a sponsor: all who had received that degree on some previous occasion, and now hoped to go on to that of Eye-witness: all who, initiated once, wished to renew the impression now. The procession numbered thousands, each person provided with the long stalk of fennel, the *narthex*, as their badge—of which Plato said once that 'many may bear the *narthex*, but few are the real Initiates'. All formed up on the road, with the *Sacra* on their humble donkey in the van, while Dionysus-Iacchos came out from his temple near by in his car to join the procession. The march was about fifteen miles all told, in the August heat, and in theory was all done on foot though in practice concessions were made in later days, provided that you left your chariot at a certain point. Halts too at the many shrines on the road—some of which we can trace as we have seen— gave opportunity for rest. One of these was at the Rheiton tarn where the family of Krokonidae ('Saffronson') had the right of binding the bared arm and ankle of each initiate with saffron-coloured bands. Chants were sung on the way, with the burden of 'Iacchos' and 'Evoe', the Bacchanals' cry. ('Is it not fitting', says the angry Clement in reference to this last, 'that in their idolatry they should call upon the name of the woman by whom sin first entered the world!') Eleusis was reached after dark, and that night was the 'night of torches', which the candidates must spend wandering with their torches on the shore 'like a swarm of fire-flies', enacting Demeter's search for the lost Persephone. In the course of this they had to go and sit where Demeter sat, on the Stone of Sorrow by the well, where the king's daughters found her. It is for this reason that the sacred well was (as we can see to this day) kept outside the precinct, though the line of wall had to be altered to secure it. Those who had not yet the right to put foot on the Holy Ground must yet be able to go there. Meantime the priestesses (who acted the Princesses in the drama) kept vigil in the temple, re-enacting their old intercession with the angry Demeter, and praying for her favour for those who were to be, like Triptolemus, her adopted sons.

The next day was probably a day of rest and preparation for the Great Night that was to follow, and when the darkness fell, all gathered in the court before the gate. Those who had the right entered the precinct, but the candidates and their sponsors remained without in the great court, lit only by the glow from the altar fire of the temple of 'Artemis before the Gate'. There could have been no moon, for full moon was six days past, and we can picture the crowd there in their 'Initiates' garb; boys in a long cloak, some say a fawn-skin, that could be dropped in an instant, leaving them naked; girls in a tunic girded with a cord, their hair in a sort of turban; all barefoot, with no jewels, no metals, and it is specially said, no cosmetics. Before them was the high wall of the precinct, all of black stone, pierced only by the splendid portal that was an emperor's imperial initiation gift, its Pentelic marble wan-white in the gloom. Then the Herald appeared in the gateway to give his summons:

Come, all that are clean of body and pure of heart.
Come, those whose lives show righteousness and justice.
Come, those whose speech is reasonable and intelligible.
Stand back, stand back, all who are profane and unholy.

The pass-word was demanded and given (even as late as 200 B.C. two men who tried to get in without it paid the penalty of death) and the Herald issued his last summons: 'Children of men, about to pass through death, draw near.' And your sponsor slipped the hoodwink over your eyes and led you up the steps into the precinct.

So far, we have been on firm ground, but after this there is an element of conjecture. There is no doubt that the main motif of this *Mystes* degree was, that Dionysus-Iacchos, as *Dadouchos*, took charge of the candidate, and after putting him through a series of trials, presented him to Persephone at the last. As his conductor led him on, the candidate met the Torch-bearer (he must have been allowed a glimpse of him) and was told to follow him without fear. This we know, because in the Dialogues of the Dead, the soul emerging from Charon's wherry has an experience like this, and says, 'it is like being initiated over again.' He was led, as the track in the sanctuary shows, past the shrine of Pluto, up to the great Petroma, where two huge stones fitted together formed a safe in which the sacred rolls of the ritual were kept when not in use,[1] and where a second search for metals was conducted. Then, blindfolded and barefoot, he was led into the Telesterion, the great pillared hall with rows of seats round the sides, to undergo there a series of tests that must have been an awesome experience. Led blindfolded round and round that hall, with the feel of an invisible crowd about him, he would soon get the impression of an absolutely endless journey. Then he was made to pass through a series of obstacles that in his

---

[1] At least, Pausanias says that this was the custom in the like mystery at Pheneus in Arcadia, and stones of the kind are in their place at Eleusis. *Pausanias*, VIII, xv. 1.

blinded state could be made to seem terrible. There were sudden graspings by unseen hands, there was the roaring of thunder peals in the ears, there were visions (when again the hoodwink must have been raised for an instant) of Tartarus and the Furies, with lost souls wallowing in slime. 'The nearer the goal the greater the terror' we are told, and it is not surprising that girl candidates at least often fainted from fear, for everything was done to give the impression that you were actually passing through the underworld—of which you had always been taught that Eleusis was one of the mouths—and at least one educated man, Apuleius, when going through a like experience, fully believed that it was nothing less than that.

Finally, a 'great light' blazed up as the bandage was snatched from your eyes, and you found yourself before Persephone, who was seated on a low stool, with an empty throne behind her. A throne that was empty, because Persephone only represented a power beyond herself, her Mother. (It is worth noting here that the names Persephone and Demeter were never used at Eleusis, though for convenience' sake we employ them. They were always 'the Mother' and 'the Maiden'—womanhood that is in its two great stages.) 'The Maiden' now explained the mystery: 'You have seen what I passed through, and yet, I rose again, and so will you. Here is the Initiate's secret, that death is a passage and no more; now you know the charms lacking knowledge of which the non-initiate lies as you have seen, for ever in slime.'

It was by now near dawn, and the final act began. The Sacred Symbol of Eleusis was shown to those who had now the right to look upon it; it was an ear of corn. At the same time, he was made to perform the mystic ceremony. He was given a jar of water and ordered to pour it out on the ground, ejaculating as he did so the words '$\breve{v}\epsilon$ $\kappa\acute{v}\epsilon$'. The first word is addressed to the heavens, 'Give rain;' the second to the great Earth Mother, 'Conceive'. It is no more in origin than the old sympathetic magic, to make the corn grow. He was then given 'Demeter's sacrament', the *kykeon* (barley-broth) that 'the Mother' partook of in her sorrow and was ordered to perform certain ritual acts, taking the *Sacra* (that he might handle now) out of their basket and putting them into their chest;[1] and he was given the pass-word or form, which he might use, if anyone who had the right to ask should ever demand if he was in truth an Initiate of Eleusis:

[1] This may have been, as we conjecture, the ritual reaping and storing of the corn that is Demeter herself. The sowing may have come earlier.

88

I fasted, I drank 'kykeon'.
I took IT from the basket.
I put IT into the chest.

Finally he was dismissed with a benediction so ancient that even Greece had forgotten the meaning of the words, though folk today have tried, with the help of ancient Egyptian, to render them as 'Go in peace, be pure from Evil'. The actual formula was, 'Conx Om Pax.'

For the *Mystes,* all was now done, and he might return to Athens and indulge his natural reaction to the full in the licensed jestings at the bridge over the Cephissus on the way home, though it is to be hoped that he would not push them as far as did Alcibiades. For those however who had already received the *Mystes* degree and now sought for something higher, the ceremony was but begun. They could proceed—we presume after another day of rest—to the degree of *Epoptes* or eye-witness, a rite of which less is known, for the good reason that those who took it were fewer and were doubly bound to secrecy. This much however we do know. In this degree, as the Ninnion plaque assures us, it is 'the Maiden', to whom you were presented before, who becomes the Conductress now, and she (no doubt after another set of trials) presents you to 'the Mother', who is seated on the throne that was vacant in the earlier ceremony. As 'the Maiden' revealed her secret and pointed beyond herself to a power greater than she, so does 'the Mother' likewise. The secret that she has to reveal is that the reward of loyal *Epoptes* is not merely immortality, but some sort of Union with the Deity. This is shown in 'drama' by the symbolism of a marriage—we are specially told that the proceedings were free of the least hint of lewdness—and the birth and epiphany of a god. In this act the Hierophant and the *Hierophantis* entered the most holy part of the shrine together, to come out surrounded by flames and holding aloft a sheaf of corn, declaring 'Holy Brimo has borne the holy Child, Brimos. The Strong has brought forth Strength'. There was another Sacramental meal and a fresh pass-word, which is said to have been:

I ate from the Drum, I drank from the Cymbal.
I bore the basket. I passed beneath the Bridal Chamber.

There was another obligation to secrecy and (if Justin Martyr was well informed) this may have been of late introduction and have shown signs of influences that were Orphic rather than strictly Eleusinian, but was even so of a character to set one thinking indeed. You pledged yourself to loyalty to your obligation, 'so help me the Word of the Father, which He spake when He established the universe in wisdom.'

That 'the Mother' pointed, as 'the Maiden' had done, to a power beyond herself, is a fair inference from a sculpture that has been preserved; it was discovered in that shrine of Pluto which naturally has its place here, and which we have referred to above. It represents all the gods of Eleusis together. There are the figures of Pluto, Dionysus, Triptolemus, and the rest, and with them 'the Mother' and 'the Maiden'. Yet in this their own sanctuary all of them, even 'the Mother' are subordinate, and the central figures are—a deity without a name. Male and female, two persons but one divinity, those in the place of honour are simply called 'The God, the Goddess'. One cannot help asking the question whether this unnamed God of Eleusis may not count kindred with the unknown God of Athens, of whom one said 'whom ye ignorantly worship, him declare I'.

As for the meaning of it all, one must remember that to most Greek philosophy matter was an evil, and life in it a penalty. The myth which was worked up in the old initiation ceremony—a ceremony in itself no more than harvest-magic perhaps—gave the tale of the soul's entanglement in it and the winning of release. Persephone the maiden in Enna is the soul on the original 'spirit-level'; Persephone in Hades is the soul entrapped in matter; and the rite showed how freedom could be won.

The description that we have given may sound little, but there is no doubt that the rite meant much to many great men, and the verdict of one or two of them shows the value of the whole for antiquity, though each speaks naturally according to the cast of his mind. 'These Mysteries restore the soul to its unfallen state' says Plato. 'They tell us nothing new, but they do provide a new and strong motive for living up to known duties' is the verdict of the practical Aristotle. There was little in heaven or earth that was sacred to that master of gibe, Aristophanes, but for these mysteries he has nothing but reverence:

> To us alone, initiated men,
> Who act aright by stranger and by friend,
> The sun shines out to light us after death.

WHAT ELEUSIS MEANT TO INITIATES

Cicero was perhaps the finest mind of his generation, and his verdict is: 'The best we Latins have is what the Greeks have given us, and of all that we have received from them there is nothing to be compared with these Mysteries, wherein we learn not only how to live honourably, but also how to die with a fairer hope.' Myriads went along the Sacred Way to the hallowed Well and the Telesterion, and no doubt many who took nothing found nothing, but many who were seeking for answers to the questions 'Whence and Whither' found much. The inscription that one of them left behind him at Eleusis may be taken as typical of all:

Fair is the Initiate's Secret, that to man
Death is not just no Evil. 'Tis a Good.

V

ATTICA

Eleutherae—Aegosthena—Sunium—Vari—Marathon—Aegina

The casual visitor to Greece usually sees several temples, and some at least of the pre-historic fortresses such as Mycenae and Tiryns. Yet, though he knows that Greek history is full of wars he is apt to be shown none of the fortifications of the historic period, and may get the impression that they do not exist. It is true that they are mostly rather inaccessible for the ordinary tourist— a statement that is true even of the magnificent specimen that is preserved to us at Messene, but there are very fine specimens within the borders of Attica, in the castle of Eleutherae and the little town of Aegosthena. The former of these is quite accessible, and indeed the traveller who goes by car from Athens to Thebes passes just underneath it, though it is true that the best preserved portion of the enceinte is that which faces away from the modern road and it is quite possible to go that way in a motor, and even to stop at that rare landmark of Hellas, a good spring, and not see what is above.

Eleutherae we have already mentioned as the original birth-place of Dionysus, or at least the place where the vine was first cultivated in Attica, and to which old home the god made annual attempts to return at the time of his great festival. Its castle—once the great frontier fort that guarded the way over Mount Cithaeron, and the marches between Athens and Thebes—has singularly little history for such a post. It seems never to have been seriously attacked, and in consequence the long eastern face still stands exactly as its designers left it in the fifth century B.C., and it is a real treasure for the student of the history of military architecture. Aegosthena is also best reached from Eleutherae—though accessible by sea also, for those who can wait the pleasure of a Greek coastal boat—but in our day the road thither followed the amiable habit of its kind in a semi-developed land; that is to say, it started off brilliantly from its point of junction with the *route nationale*, went just 'so far' past one village, and then died rather abruptly on an open hillside, for the saying that roads generally lead somewhere is not to be trusted too absolutely in all lands. Still, the real traveller in Greece does not depend entirely on a motor. Either his own legs, or those of a mule (and there is a village handy) will carry him for a delightful tramp of three hours over moor and through forest, till he sees the towers of the wall of Aegosthena on the blue waters of the Gulf of Corinth below him.

You will probably meet shepherds on the way, who still use crooks like those of our fathers, though not precisely of the same pattern. The shepherds are good folk enough, but their dogs are apt to be formidable, for after all their business is to guard the flock, and that from wolves if need be, for the beasts are by no means unknown here in winter. Thus the Greek sheep-dog is a far more powerful beast than our collie,[1] and may demonstrate against the wayfarer.

However, you may be sure that the shepherd will be absolutely desolated if they bite you, and if they get formidable you can try the expedient adopted by Ulysses, who was bayed at by the dogs of his own homestead when he returned as a beggar. (Good classical precedent is safe to go by in this land.) He sat down, as readers of the Odyssey will remember, and let his staff fall, and the dogs—of course Argus was not among this pack—took it as a declaration of friendliness, and did not attack. We admit that it requires some nerve to try the experiment, and to trust that a big Molossian wolf-hound, with a spiked collar to guard his throat, will really under-stand the gesture, but it must be said that the Greek dog does recognize the obligation of honour.

If the traveller is foolish enough to carry a fire-arm, it is to be hoped that he will not shoot the dogs. Greek custom admits that you may use a knife against one, but to shoot is criminal, as is reasonable enough to those who think the matter out. A dog into whom you can stick a knife has clearly come near enough to bite you, but he is probably at some distance if you use a gun or revolver.

Aegosthena was one of those little City-States of Greece that were

---

[1] Those in Crete form an exception to this rule, as wolves are unknown there. The Cretan sheep-dog is usually a quite small and harmless little beast.

too small to be of any importance, and yet too isolated to be taken into any other. Forest-clad hills, the most impassable of barriers, cut it off from its nearest neighbour, Megara, so that it was never part of that State, and as it had a good harbour on the Corinthian gulf, it was apt to be used as a convenience by anybody. Athens found it a most useful base for her fleet, when it was operating in those waters during the Peloponnesian war, and the slips that the Athenians cut in the rock for their triremes can still be seen at the place, though the level of the sea has risen a bit, and they are now under water. Then a little later, both it and the neighbouring port of Creusis were occupied by the Spartan king, Cleombrotus, with a strategic instinct rare in that nation, when he was sent out to put the impertinent Thebans in their place once for all in 373, and decided that easy communication with the Peloponnesus would be advisable. Hence it was, a few weeks later, that a flabbergasted Spartan force was able to fall back on this refuge, when the utterly impossible had happened; for a Spartan army, with their king to lead them, had been undeniably broken and beaten in a pitched battle for the first time in history. Thermopylae was a glory, and Sphacteria an accident; but Leuctra a fact that could not be denied.

The fortifications of both Aegosthena and of Eleutherae are of the fifth century B.C. and they show how very little the mediaeval engineer had been able to improve on what the Greek had evolved at that date. The upright curtain wall, of good hewn stone with square towers at bow-shot intervals, and a narrow battlemented allure for bowmen, went on till gunpowder had become a really effective force, and the Knights of Rhodes were still relying on it at the end of the fifteenth century of our era.

The two points that a visitor to Athens who spends more than one day there will want to go to are, Marathon and Sunium. One road from Athens leads out toward both, Sunium being about thirty-seven miles from the city, and the road to it branching off from that to Marathon about seven miles out. To get from that point to Sunium, return, go out the fifteen miles more to Marathon and so get back to Athens, is a long day but a feasible one—something over one hundred miles in all.

The Cape of the Columns is a sort of recognized door-post at the portal of Greece, and Pausanias can find no better point at which to begin his description. Its defect is that with all its acknowledged beauty—and there is no finer position in the land—it lacks all human interest. Even Pausanias, with all his opportunities and love of a good story, could find none here, save the fact that Phrontis, Menelaus' ship-captain, died and was buried there in the course of his return from Troy. There is nothing to tell about the place.

The famous temple, which was dedicated to Athena, stands on the brink of what is a steep slope rather than a precipice, down which one could walk, if necessary, given good nails on one's boots. Byron's description of the place as a 'marbled steep' is even meticulously accurate. The surviving columns of the temple strike the visitor as almost painfully white. They have none of that golden tinge which a trace of iron in the marble and the passage of centuries have given to those of the Parthenon and which adds so much to their beauty. The Sunium columns come from a local quarry, at the village of Agrilesa, and the absolute purity of the material constitutes a positive defect in their appearance. The present building is a little later than the Parthenon in date, and both it and the smaller sanctuary of Poseidon that stands at its side represent older fabrics, built of stone in pre-Persian days, and destroyed in the invasion. The curious can find the name of Byron carved on the temple, and we fear that there is no doubt by his own letters that he did perpetrate that sacrilege; indeed the appearance of the inscription even suggests that, like a modern memento-hunter, he carried a small hammer and chisel about with him for the purpose.

The sanctuary had to be fortified in the Peloponnesian war, for there was a standing danger that the slaves in the neighbouring mines of Laurium—a township through which the visitor has to pass on his way hither—would revolt under the leadership of the Spartan garrison at Decelea, to which individuals were constantly escaping. As for the mines at the present day, only a very enthusiastic archaeologist will feel bound to visit even one of the two thousand ancient shafts that have been discovered. They were a most valuable State asset for Athens, for Greece is badly off for the precious metals, and the 'Lauriot owl' on her coinage was as important for her empire as was 'the English horseman' [1] in days when we still used golden sovereigns. He was so useful that the type could never be altered, for semi-civilized tribes would only take the coin that they knew by experience was always good. Hence a die of a rather archaic and not very artistic character marks the Athenian coinage to the very end of her independent life. It would seem that

[1] 'England has invaded Arabia—with two million of her yellow horsemen' said the Turks during the war of 1914–18.

the owl even survived his original source, for the mines of Laurium had ceased to pay, as silver mines, in the days of Pausanias, and though they are worked today by two companies, both of them have to seek for lead and not for silver.

All this country-side, with its good asphalted roads and modernized houses, looks modern enough as your car takes you through it but if you can stop and enter into real talk with the peasants, you may find there beliefs and practices that are almost as old as the hills under which you go. Of course, folk will not talk to a stranger, but it was once our luck to wander there with a Greek friend who had been bred in the district, and the shepherds spoke readily to one whom they had known as a boy. One of them, when asked how the sheep were getting on, replied quite naturally, 'Very poorly. Pan has not been at all kind to us this year,' for the old shepherd god is still a power, not ten miles from Athens as the crow flies. Sometimes indeed he is 'the Black one' for when his tail grew longer in mediaeval days he got identified with the Devil himself, though it is rather in his older character that he still calls to lone women, and if they do not put their fingers in their ears and flee, they may have to obey his summons.[1]

Many of his old sanctuaries are in the land, such as one at Phyle, underneath the ancient fortress on the hill, and an even finer one at Marathon, where the quaint stalagmite formations still bear the name of his goats. Finest of all however is one particular cave that is not so far from the road we have been traversing, though the car must be left if you mean to get to it, and a local guide found, for the Cave of Vari is not easy to discover by yourself.

Holy from all time, this place was solemnly dedicated to Pan and the Nymphs in the year 440 B.C., by a certain Archidemos, whose figure, rudely carved in relief, still peers through stalagmite overcasting in the interior. It was a regular place of resort for those who sought Pan's aid, though the reliefs from it in the Athens Museum suggest that the girls who were the god's most regular clients had better come, for safety's sake, in parties of three at least. Hence it was quite in the fitness of things that when the infant Plato suffered from some infantile complaint his parents should bring him here for the god Pan to cure. They got the best of omens, for the swarm of bees that settled upon the infant's mouth showed that it would produce what should be sweet as honey. Pan is not unhonoured in

[1] A lady of the writer's acquaintance met a woman fleeing in just this way. She had heard 'the Black One' calling her by name on the hills.

6. Sunium: Temple of Athena

7. Temple of Aphaea: Aegina. (From South West)

this sanctuary yet, though here it is not his tail but his name that has got longer, and with confusing results, for he is now called 'Pan-Agia' (the Blessed Virgin) of all inappropriate titles! The offerings however are still the same, for what you ought to bring to this ancient place of worship is the bean porridge and honey that Pan loved of old, though it is true that, on occasion, you add another of quite different provenance and signification. If you are really out for revenge on an enemy, and are willing to make such an offering as the Power here must accept for very shame's sake, and act on as well, you proceed hither and deposit—a rag that you have stolen from a priest's robes. Exactly what power that is addressed to is not known, and perhaps it is better not to ask, but a connoisseur of queer rites must be grateful for ceremonies that are gathered from as many as three different sources. Confusion of two we know, but three is a real rarity, and we get it here. Pan of course is Hellenic, or properly pre-Hellenic, and the Panagia naturally Christian; this rag ritual however is neither of the two, but is rather Anatolian and Asiatic.

Marathon is about 22 miles from Athens, on a beautiful road that leads over the pass between Pentelicus and Hymettus, through olive groves and pine forests, till at last it makes it way through the narrow passage between Mount Agreliki and the sea—a passage made narrower by one of the marshes that played their part in the battle—and emerges into the plain where 'the mountains look on Marathon and Marathon looks on the sea'. One may be certain too that the modern road follows the general line of the older track, by which the Athenian army marched out and returned in triumph, and on which Pheidippides staggered home with the glorious news.

It is certain then that this is the place where, for the first time, the Greeks dared to face the dreaded Persian, and found him not invincible. Further, thanks to Herodotus, we know the tactics used, and can picture the line advancing for 'at least a mile' at the quick-step before the final assault and the hand to hand fighting. Quick-step and not literally a 'run' it must surely have been, for no heavy-armed men could have kept rank at the double over the rough ground, and through thorns which must have given the 'well-greaved Greeks' full need for that defence. The actual site of the toughest fighting is clear enough also, for the *Soros*, the mound where the Athenian dead lie to this day, is there to testify to it, though the *stele* that stands on the spot now is no more than a re-production of the monument of one of 'the men of Marathon', the original of which is in the Athens Museum. Examination of the place has proved the fact that the men of Marathon lie there,[1] and proved also the statement of Pausanias that they were regarded as local heroes, and worshipped with sacrifices up to his time. The tomb of Miltiades, which Pausanias saw here, has vanished, as has that of the men of Plataea also, and you can no longer go there by night and see, as you could so often on old battle-fields, the spirits of the dead fighting the great struggle over again. Perhaps this is as well, for our trusty authority assures us that, though no harm came to chance visitors, yet to go there to see this supernatural sight 'never yet brought good to any man'.

If, however, the spirits of the warriors are at rest, the critics fight the battle still. Herodotus gives us the tactics, as described by men who fought there, but leaves the positions occupied before the fight, and the preliminary manoeuvres, rather uncertain, and there are not wanting people, who know what happened much better than he did, to tell us all about it now. However, it is admitted by all that both armies stood looking at one another for some days before the battle actually joined, the Athenians because they were waiting for the dilatory Spartans (who actually arrived before the dead were buried), and the Persians, seemingly, because the Athenian position was so strong that they did not care to undertake a frontal attack, or possibly because they expected to be joined by the detachment from plundered Eretria. It was only when the Persians, realizing that the Athenians would not leave their strong position and attack them, started on their move to Athens—either by sea or by land—that Miltiades made his desperate charge and succeeded. Where that position was has now been definitely identified, for the shrine of Heracles and Pan that marked it has come to light, so that it is known to have been in the valley now occupied by the little village of Vrana, which is due west from that *Soros* mound to which the visitor is sure to go, and about the distance given by Herodotus. There they would have a position that could hardly be turned, and a stream to give them a water supply, while a path led from their rear to Athens and to villages that would supply them with food.

Mere passing tourists do not often get to Aegina from Athens. A visit by the ordinary steamers from Piraeus to the island harbour takes at least two days; the sea passage is less than three hours, but the temple that one wishes to see is a good two hours further from

---

[1] Vases of the date, from that mound, are now in the Athens Museum.

the town, and away on the other side of the island. A special launch may be chartered to take the traveller to St. Marina bay, or a cruising ship may arrange to anchor off that inlet and allow its passengers to walk up the hill to the temple, an easy half-hour's tramp from that beach, but the solitary wanderer will have to take a horse from the capital, or walk if he prefers it, to his destination, and then get back to such accommodation as the fishing port can give him for the night. It will not be a first class hotel, but he will not have much to complain of. The temple has no village near it.

By tradition, the original name of the island was Oenone, and its only inhabitants were ants. When father Zeus however carried off Aegina, the daughter of the river-god Asopus, and established her here, he gave the isle her name, and there was born their son Aeacus, afterwards judge of Hades and father of Telamon and Peleus. Asopus made some natural enquiries as to what had become of his daughter, and it appears that it was Sisyphus who imprudently 'gave Zeus away', 'wherefore in hell he now pays the penalty for his wagging tongue.' It seems that this was the sum of his offences. Unkind grammarians, who know nothing of these matters, say that the name is no more than a derivative of Aegaeos, an old name for Poseidon.

In pre-historic days, when the population was Helladic, and later when a second migration of Hellenes from Thessaly of Dorian stock had come in with their god Zeus Hellenius, Aegina was the great trading centre of the period,[1] finding its position in the middle of the Saronic gulf good for the commerce of the moment. Its bronze was of value in Egypt, and its weights became for long the standard system for all Greece. It had the finest sculptors of the age—Myron was said to hold that there was no such bronze as the Aeginetan, for that of Corinth had yet to make its name—and according to Aristotle it carried an amazingly large population. The triangular island contains less than three hundred square miles, yet we are told that the slave population alone was 470,000, and that they were such keen traders that 'Cretan versus Aeginetan' was the equivalent of our 'Greek meets Greek'.

All this greatness however had too narrow a base for it to endure long, when other and larger States were able to form themselves. Athens, as soon as she was one power, was bound by her position to be a rival of Aegina, and one that carried far heavier guns than the

---

[1] Hence its 'tortoise' is the oldest coin of Greece: older than the Lauriot owl.

island State. Thus when the first signs of the Persian struggle began Aegina carries her hatred of Athens so far, that she even sends 'earth and water', the signs of submission, to Darius, just because he is the enemy of her rival. We see, however, that her greatness has not left her yet, when in the great war with Xerxes the little State puts a fleet into the water in the common cause that is second only in numbers and efficiency to that of Athens, and that squadron by common consent wins the first prize for skill and valour at Salamis. At that date however the quarrel between the two neighbours had already gone too far for any permanent reconciliation. The nominal cause of it was an old dispute over the holy Images of Damia and Auxesia, two deities of whom nobody knew anything at all, but of whom men told this tale, suggesting that they were fertility-powers. There had been a drought in Epidauros, and the oracle of Delphi had bidden the people of the land put up two figures of 'holy olive-wood' in honour of those names, and the Epidaurans had done accordingly, taking Attic olive-wood as the holiest they knew and paying a 'pepper-corn rent' for the privilege. Then the men of Aegina, in some raid on the coast, had captured those images, and when the Athenians demanded their rent from the original owners, they had been told 'ask the Aegina folk. They stole our gods'. Athens had then tried to collect the tiny due by force—a fact that shows that they hardly desired peace—and had failed. The images had been put up at a shrine called Oea, where a queer festival had been instituted in their honour, or adapted to them; the men of the place danced before the temple, and were specially allowed to sing all the most scurrilous songs that they could compose against the local women, an observance that would seem to be older in its origin than the beginning of the fifth century. A kissing contest, like that of Megara, also took place. When the Athenian expedition came, they tried to drag off the images, which instantly knelt in supplication at the violence. There came an earthquake and a panic; either there was an attack by the men of the place, or by somebody else, or the Athenians in their scare beat down one another. Nobody knew exactly what happened, but it is certain that the expedition was destroyed, and it is said that only one survivor returned to Athens. There he met a worse fate than any, for all the women gathered round him and each asked him what he had done with her husband, accompanying the enquiry with a jab from the long pin of her brooch, so that the poor wretch was pricked to death in the market.

All the world was scandalized then, and a law was passed ordering the wearing of less formidable brooches, while an embassy to Delphi asked what ought to be done about the whole affair. A sanctuary to Aeacus, the hero of Aegina, was erected at Apollo's order in the Agora, and any further war with Aegina forbidden for a space of a full generation, thirty years. The Persian invasion took place in that interval, and one might have hoped that pan-Hellenic feeling, and the memory of common glory at Salamis, might have healed the quarrel; yet when men pleaded those matters before Pericles all the reply they got was: 'Everybody knows that Aegina is the eye-sore of the Piraeus;' and the war began again. For four years the little island held out against the Athenian fleet, but was brought to its knees at last in 456, and the terms of surrender included demolition of its walls and the payment of tribute to the old rival. Twenty-five years later, the Peloponnesian war began, and Athens 'took precautions' against her old enemy, without troubling, it would seem, to seek for even a pretext beyond that. All the inhabitants of the island were expelled—some say even that the thumbs of all the men were cut off, to disable them for war—and the place made into an Athenian colony. Even the refuge which Spartan charity gave the men of Aegina was raided by the Athenian fleet. All the glories of Athens ought not to make us forget the existence of this dark side to her national character, expressed in the fates of Melos, Aegina, and Mytilene. When Sparta triumphed, at least she did not forget her small ally (perhaps because her position might make her so useful as a bridle to an enemy) and restored the Aeginetans to their home. However, their day was done and as a State they were never important again.

Aeginetan religion contained two distinct strains. The Hellenes who came in from the north had brought Zeus Pan-Hellenius with them, and the Sky-God was provided with a sanctuary on the top of the high central peak of the island (where now the little white church of St. Elias can be seen), a precinct that in classic days never gained a temple. Here Aeacus ended drought by prayer to Zeus, and here St. Elias still gives rain when invoked. The town of Aegina had temples of its own, dedicated to Athena and Aphrodite, the latter of which is still marked by:

A marble shaft that stands alone,
Above a wreck of sculptured stone
With grey-green aloes overgrown[1]

[1] Rennell Rodd, *Charm of Greece.*

The strange rites of Auxesia were probably celebrated at the 'ancient place', Palaeochori, in the centre of the isle, where a nunnery that no man can ever enter claims to have 366 little separate chapels scattered among the rugged rocks of the black hill.

More important than these rites however was the worship of Aphaea, to whom the great temple that is the main attraction of the island for the modern visitor was dedicated. Aphaea, according to Pausanias, was the same as the Cretan Britomartis, whom legend called a daughter of Zeus, with whom her half-brother Minos fell in love. He chased her, and she ran away and tumbled over and into a set of nets laid out to dry, whence her Cretan nickname Dictynna. Actually, Spenser's Britomart is not more changed from the original than is this lady of Hellenic myth. We know her now as the great Earth-Mother of Crete, where we shall meet her again, and Zeus is in this earlier form of the story the very inferior male being by her side, at once husband and son, who later grows greater than his mother and eclipses her.

As the Earth-Mother, it was quite right and proper that Aphaea of Aegina should be rated by Pausanias as a form of Hecate, and that her mysteries, celebrated here, should seem to this experienced initiate a form of Orphism, and claim that great figure as their founder. She represents the underworld aspect of that *Diva triformis* who was still recognized as such in the days of Horace, the power who was the lady of the wild wood on earth, the moon in heaven, and the queen in the mysterious underworld below. Her beautiful temple, which still survives as one of the finest specimens of Doric architecture outside Athens, has a special interest to students as being the Aeginetan trophy and thank-offering for Salamis, the battle in which Aegina played so noble a part. Hence it is natural that its sculptures should have represented the first of the great conflicts of Greece with the barbarian of Asia, the Trojan war. Here Athena—of course supposedly invisible to the combatants—is the central figure, and it was this that gave rise to what is now recognized as a very natural mistake, the attribution of the temple to Athena. Inscriptions however prove that the modern identification is not correct. As for the figures, casts of them can be seen in the British Museum, and the originals are in Munich.

Few temples, even in Greece, have so wonderful a position as that of Aegina, standing as this does high on the promontory that looks over to Attica and Piraeus. With a good field-glass one can easily see the Parthenon on its rock, the white marble standing out against the dark foliage of Lycabettus behind. We have never, we must own, been able to pick out the temple of Aphaea from the Acropolis, as the grey of its columns in their present state melts into the pine woods with which it is surrounded; when it gleamed white with the stucco that once covered it, no doubt it was as conspicuous as the Parthenon today. Aegina is one of many places that make it hard to believe the statement so often made, that the Greeks cared nothing for natural scenery. If that was so, at least they put their temples in marvellously chosen sites, and in the case of Aegina, which was never a fortress, the reason of defensibility can hardly be urged.

Of course, the present fabric was not the first to stand here. Under the foundations of the temple, at its western end, can be seen the foundations of the apse with which its older and rougher predecessor terminated. It is an interesting piece of evidence that this style of building—so universal among Greek churches today—may really be a throw-back to very ancient practice, and it does not stand alone.

VI

THEBES AND DELPHI

Cithaeron—Thebes City—Parapoungia—Plataea—The Sphinx—
Lake of Copais—The Vlachs—Scripu—Livadia—The Oracle of
Trophonius—The Centaurs—Delphi—Its Oracle, Precinct and
Temples

The castle of Eleutherae is the practical boundary of Attica, though the road goes on up the pass, and over the hills of Cithaeron. These were forest clad once, as we see from the scenic setting of such stories as those of Pentheus and Actaeon, but they are for the most part bare enough now. The villages of the plain used to gather at fixed intervals to build a grand ceremonial bonfire in honour of the Daedala (wooden images that were solemnly burned in it), but in these days it would be hard to get wood enough for a blaze that 'burned so very high and was seen so very far' as our never-failing guide Pausanias tells us was the case with this. It is the Turks that get most of the discredit of this destruction, which has had, no doubt, its evil effect on the climate of the country. The wanderer in Attica thinks regretfully of days when 'the heat of the sun was never too hot beneath the thick shade of our forest trees'. No doubt it was the Ottoman who did a good deal. He never established a really effective government in the mountains of the land, for the Turco-vouni that are now almost inside Athens are said to be so called because they were the only hills where the Turk did rule; and it was open to anybody always to adopt the honourable trade of brigand:

> *Mother, I cannot stand these Turkish bullies.*
> *I will take a gun and go and be a Klepht,*

runs the song. Hence, it was natural that the government should take steps, at times, to destroy the brigands' cover. Still, in later days it has been the reckless cutting and burning of the peasant that has done most to prevent recovery, and now the winter rains have washed the hillsides till the bare bones of the rock often show on the surface, and hardly anything but a cactus can be expected to grow. It is the goat, men of knowledge say, that is the real problem, for he will eat anything anywhere, and never allows a growing tree to have a chance of getting under way; and yet, who will take the responsibility of regulating or abolishing 'the poor man's cow'? When forests are started, they have to be pine of some form if they are to grow at all, and the shepherds are only too apt to burn them of set intent; for if you destroy twenty years of growth in one night, you will get one year's decent growth of grass for your goats from the ashes. Yet, when it has been done, how are officials to prove that it was not accidental? We have the same difficulty in Cyprus, where our efforts at increasing the ultimate wealth of the island by scientific afforestation have done more to make us unpopular than anything else.

Passing the crest of Cithaeron, you begin the descent into Boeotia proper, the dwelling place of those Greeks of all others who were said to be stupid and dull. The atmosphere seems to have had its effects on the imagination of the modern dwellers in it, for why else should they have given such names to new villages in this storied land as 'Cold Beans' and 'Boiled Noses' (Krio-kouki and Vrasto-metsi) and that on the very battlefield of Plataea? Yet if the Boeotian be so stupid, how does it come about that this district should have produced the finest myths of Greek story, the tales of Oedipus, of Antigone, and of the Bacchae, and in fact the material of half the great tragedies? Have all the rest of the old myths been lost with the lost tragedies of the 'great three'?

We are supposing the traveller to have taken the Cithaeron road from Athens, but as a matter of fact there is another, which follows the line of the railway to Thebes. This takes you by Acharnae (where the oaks for the charcoal-burner are few indeed now) and up past Decelea, between the hills of Pentelicus and Parnes. Here, at the modern Tatoi, was the old country house of the Kings of Greece, and the passer-by can judge how thoroughly the fort that the Spartans put here dominates the whole of Attica.

Eleutherae is about thirty miles from Athens, and Thebes some twenty further, but the only reason for going there is that the road goes through the place. Historic city though it is, it is now just a country town on a rounded hill that as a matter of fact was once the

Acropolis of Thebes, the Cadmea, but where nothing of classic interest appears above the surface. The ancient city walls and gates have been traced, and there is a big spring that must have been Dirke, but the Thebes, not only of Oedipus, but of Epaminondas and Alexander, is buried some eighteen feet under very fertile soil, and is not likely ever to be brought to the surface again. The only building that is not absolutely modern is a square tower of mediaeval date, now used as part of the local museum, and originally a portion of the Palace of the Latin Dukes. We have already referred, in dealing with Athens, to the strange Latin dynasty of adventurers that, coming too late to share in the plunder of Constantinople in 1204, took Greece as their part of the Byzantine Empire that was then the prey of any adventurer that wished to carve out a principality for himself; and we shall touch upon their fortunes once more when we come to Sparta. Here we may note that, in northern Greece, it was Thebes, 'Estivae' as they called it, that was their capital rather than 'Sithenas', and here that the house of De la Roche had their main stronghold.

It will be noted that in their pronunciation of Greek, they followed the corruption that made 'Stamboul' out of Constantinople by prefixing the 'es', meaning 'to'; and also that at that date the 'B' had already become 'V', in the mouths of common men. Otherwise it would be hard to recognize 'Thebes' and 'Athens' in the two names given.

If however there is little for the archaeologist in Thebes, there is plenty near it. Up on an outlier of the Helicon range and just above the field of Leuctra lies the village of Parapoungia, famous as the site of one of the finest neolithic settlements of Greece. This however hardly attracts the normal tourist, and also, it is a little outside ordinary civilization and law.

Plataea, famous both as the site of the great battle in the Persian War, 479 B.C., and for the siege 429–27, is about four miles to the west of the road over Cithaeron, starting from the village of Kriokouki through which the line of the old road goes. It lies near to the modern village of Koukla, and towards the bottom of the northern slope of the range. Its name implies that it lies on a level, and that level, in winter, produces the most adhesive mud of our experience, as well as the most slippery, so that we do not wonder that those who had to traverse it then—e.g. in making their escape from the beleaguered town during the siege early in the Peloponnesian War —preferred to go with bare feet. In summer (the great battle was fought in September) it is only somewhat dusty.

The city walls may be traced, and stand a few feet above ground in places. It is quite probable that above that level they were always of mud brick, as in classic days was certainly the case: the mud is of first-class quality for brick making. But we fear that nothing of what we see goes back to the time of the Persian War, or even formed the rampart that the townsfolk held against the Spartans for two years. The present circuit is about two miles and a half, or nearly 4,500 yards, which is an impossible length for a garrison that only numbered 450 men, to say nothing of the length implied for the Spartan 'walls of circumvallation'. That which was defended in the Peloponnesian War must have been a much smaller circuit, and we know that there were at least two rebuildings of the town, after as many destructions by the ever-hostile Thebans, and much of what is left is probably not even Greek.

The battlefield in the Persian War must have extended pretty well from the site of Plataea to the present village of Krio-kouki, which stands on the approach to the pass over Cithaeron which the Greeks had to cover; still, none of the details that Herodotus tells of can be identified satisfactorily. The Spring of Gargaphîa was the focus for the manoeuvres that preceded the battle, but there are now two groups of springs, either of which might be the spot. The island formed by the River Oeroe, which divided and joined again, and so formed the stronghold to which the Greeks fell back from Gargaphîa to get cover from the Persian cavalry attacks, seems to have vanished with a change in the river's course, and the Sanctuary of Demeter round which some of the hardest fighting took place has not been identified. Inscribed blocks that may have come from it are known— but they do get carried such perplexing distances by a peasant who wants building material. All that we can say is, that the battle must have been fought on the lower slopes of Cithaeron, between the modern Krio-kouki and the ancient Plataea, and that the numerous forces engaged may well have covered a large proportion of that space of four miles.

From Thebes the road goes on, over open plains and a low pass, to the great level of the Copaic Plain, once the lake of that name. The whole mountain on your right (that is, to the north) as you traverse this road is the Mountain of the Sphinx, the beast which we know used to haunt this district and put her riddles to travellers, till Oedipus so annoyed her by guessing right that she leapt down from the rock on which she sat and broke her neck. Here at least nobody can complain that the legend lacks substantiation, for the Sphinx herself is there to see! The whole sky-line of the hill that bears her name, as you

look back on it from Haliartos, gives you the outline of the monster,
You can see the outstretched lion-like paws, the projecting breasts.
and finally the woman's face of the creature, with the head thrown
back so as to rest on her animal spine. When she was the terror of the
road, she would seem to have been smaller, for her seat was a rock
that rises just above the line of the present highway, and it must
always have followed that line, just between the lake it skirts and the
rough hills that rise to your left as you go.

A 'Catalan tower'—and why Catalan we explain later—rises on
the rock now, and makes it unmistakable. Of course, when Oedipus
came and had his famous colloquy with her, he was coming in
the opposite direction, for he was coming from Delphi towards
Thebes, and was musing over the terrible lot that the oracle had just
told him was his—that he should kill his father and wed with his
own mother.

The Copais Plain, once the Copais Lake, is a most interesting
district in itself. A huge mountain girdled basin, some fourteen miles
by ten, it has no outlet above ground to the sea. Hence the streams
descending from Helicon and Parnassus made it into a lake, from
which the water drained away by a series of 'Swallows', or *kata-
vothra*, and made its way by underground channels to sea level,
there to come out in great springs, either at the marge of or sometimes under the salt water. The whole plain was an expanse of water
in the winter, but 'swallows' and evaporation reduced it to a marsh
in summer, producing the Copaic eels so beloved of the Athenian of
old. Many attempts have been made in history to drain it, and so to
add a fertile province to Greece, and the first effort was that made by
the prehistoric Minyae of the district, whose great citadel at the
lake-island of Gla, coupled with the magnificent 'Tholos tomb' for
their royal family at Orchomenos, prove that they were on a level
as builders with their contemporaries at Mycenae. (Pausanias says of
the tomb 'there is no greater marvel, either in Greece or elsewhere'.) The Minyan scheme was magnificent, for they proposed
actually to cut through the hill where it is lowest, and make a
passage for the water down to the lower lake of Likeri, and the deep
channel that they began is a landmark to this day. The work proved
too much for them, as might have been expected, but either before
or after the larger scheme was undertaken, they constructed a series
of 'polders' round the edges of the lake, so as to increase their
cultivable area of dry ground. Alexander was the next to make the
attempt, and the shafts that he sunk, which were to be connected

in due course by the drainage tunnel for which the bottoms of them would be so many working points, still remain to bear witness to his scheme. It was not until the nineteenth century that a French company brought modern science and power to bear on the problem, and they did succeed in driving the drainage tunnel through the hill and running off the water, so that only a great area of swamp was left. Then a misfortune that they may be pardoned for not foreseeing befell them, for the lake caught fire! The great mass of damp vegetable matter that lay at the bottom of what had been the lake heated like a gigantic wet stack and began to smoulder—a process which continued for years, and may not be quite over yet.[1] Of course, it burnt itself out in time in all the main central areas, but the great mass of ash left was naturally much smaller in bulk than the vegetable stuff that it had replaced, and the whole lake bottom sank to a lower level, so that the drainage tunnel remained high and dry, and the lake began to form anew.

The unfortunate French company was now at the end of its resources and sold its rights to an English one, who proceeded to carry on the work. The level of the tunnel was lowered and the whole expanse drained and left as fertile and irrigable land, though of a character that requires occasional deep ploughing with machinery far beyond the compass of the ordinary Greek peasant's plough. It is therefore let out to tenants, who find it the most fertile land in Greece, and, as is the wont of their kind all the world over, do not always appreciate how much brains and capital have done, and how much they still have to keep doing, to keep their land in a cultivable condition.

The company had to deal, of course, with the trouble of brigands in old days, a problem which they solved effectively by making most of the men concerned into watchmen; and they have also to keep a working understanding with the Vlachs. This very interesting people are not Greek at all—though they are presumably Greek subjects now—but a race of nomads, who come down from the Balkan lands in the winter with their flocks, and pass the cold months in the comparatively warm climate of Greece. Though gipsy-like, they are not gipsies. They are shepherds by business, and their tribal name has become a sort of synonym for that ancient profession. They come down into a district where they have a traditional right to camp, build huts for themselves and for their flocks the odd circular folds

[1] Parts of it were still smoking in 1926.

109

that will protect their sheep in any weather,[1] and so remain till the late spring calls them to their northern camping ground again. Some of them have taken and are taking to village life in these days. Generally, they are a people as kindly as they are picturesque, patriarchally hospitable and good sportsmen, as many an English Consul knows, and by no means ill-favoured.

At the western end of the plain—which is so absolutely level as to show the curvature of the earth—there is to be found not only the tomb mentioned above, but also the great spring that a classic age called 'the Fountain of the Graces'. This magnificent source, which is fed from the snows of Parnassus and never fails, sends a river ready-made across the plain, but is alas less romantic now than its name should imply. It is no more than the general washing place for the ladies of the neighbouring town of Scripu, and neither in person nor in costume can they be said to resemble the eponymous spirits of the place.

The river flows only for a few miles, and then sinks into the largest of the 'Swallows' referred to above, 'the Great Katavothron', which was anciently considered one of the mouths of Hades, and which certainly lived up to its reputation once in the experience of the writer. He chanced to enter it with the glow of a fine sunset behind him, and in the dusk of the great cavern there were seen everywhere, in all possible and impossible places, heads of multitudinous little horned devils, each with a pair of red and fiery eyes. For one moment we found ourselves believing almost anything, but presently enlightenment came, and revealed the demons as no more than a flock of goats, whose faces supply the standard devil of mediaeval art. They had clambered up, as they will, everywhere about the cave where they were to shelter that night, and the fiery eyes were no more than the reflection of the afterglow of the sun behind.

It was near Scripu that the picturesque Frankish rule in Greece underwent a terrible shock that modified it altogether. The Burgundian adventurers who had occupied the land were having all of them a splendid time, when trouble intervened in the shape of a big 'Free Company' of Catalan mercenaries, who were out of an engagement because there was no war on at that moment, and who thought that they had as good a right to carve out a principality as had their betters. Such insolence had of course to be checked, and the Frankish nobility of northern Greece all gathered to put the

[1] The high bush fences used are sloped inwards all round the circle of the fold, and thus always give a good 'lee' in any wind.

commonalty in their place, with the Dukes of Thebes and Athens at their head. The most splendid feudal chivalry of the day, they rode out to war, to find their despised foes drawn up in line, footmen all, on the open plain of Scripu. Creçy and such battles were far in the future then, and infantry had never been known to stand before the rush of the mailed horsemen; so it was clear that heaven had delivered the insolents into their hands, and the knights of Greece formed in line, helms on,[1] and rode down to sweep these contemptibles from the face of the earth.

The Catalans had turned the irrigating channels over the soft ground in their front, and that mass of cavalry galloped straight into an unsuspected morass, where in an instant every horse was mired to the girths, and every knight who could 'avoid his selle' was helpless, while the light-armed foot rushed in with the long Catalan knife; and of that army of feudal chivalry two men survived that day, both captives. The Frankish governing class was destroyed and the rough adventurers had only to walk into the land and take possession.

It was the towers which these adventurers built or are credited with building, as their holds, that are the 'Catalan castles' of today. The success was more than they knew what to do with, and the victors could only turn to their prisoners, who were gentlefolks, and ask them to take command. One, a knight, refused; it was too much shame for him. The other, a squire, was more pliable, and took control of the position. A lad with his fortune to make on the Monday, he had been a ruined prisoner on the Tuesday—and was ruler of all the land on Wednesday! Still, the matter was beyond him, and he could only advise his captor-subjects to call in a real prince—one of the house of Anjou—while he accepted the big fief and castle of Amphissa or Salona for himself.

Two roads lead from Copais to Delphi. One goes on to the north through the Plain of Chaeronaea, where the Macedonian Philip crushed the independence of Greece once for all, and where the marble lion that was raised over the fallen—the Sacred Band of Thebes, that fought to the death that day—still looks over the plain. This road goes on to Vralo, hard by Thermopylae, and then doubles back over the western shoulders of Parnassus to find the sea at Itea below Delphi. The round is about sixty miles from Livadia, which is

---

[1] These had grown so heavy at this date that they were only donned at the actual moment of action. This appears at the battle of Bouvines in King John's day.

some thirty from Thebes. This is the military road, which we built during the 1914–18 war, when we had to feed the Salonika front and it was well to avoid such a nest of submarines as the Ægean as far as we could. (You can also reach Vralo by train from Athens, and take a car there to Delphi.) The other road, the old track, turns off west at Livadia from the main road, and so direct to Delphi, only twenty miles as the crow flies. This road, which was only opened in 1931, passes by the *Schiste*, or *Triodos*, the narrow pass in the rocks where Oedipus slew Laius, and leaving the famous monastery of Hosios Lukas to the south, reaches Delphi over the southern shoulder of Parnassus, on which lies the town of Arâchova. Delphi is about twelve miles from its port, Itea, by the winding road; about two and a half hours' walk by the uncompromising old track.

Either of these routes takes you through Livadia, which proudly calls itself the Manchester of Greece, on the strength of (we think) two small cotton mills, for the Copais Plain grows some cotton. To the student, it is more important as the site of the Oracle of Trophonius, a place that we may call an undeveloped, but always revered, edition of Delphi. The point of the comparison will be seen when we reach the greater shrine. The place at all events provides contrast. You go straight in a few yards from the unattractive streets of the 'Greek Manchester' to the tremendous gorge of the Hercyna, where a magnificent spring gives water to the town. Here are the obvious remains of a shrine of the powers of the Underworld (the surviving inscription declares it) and a small church of mediaeval date which contains classic fragments enough to show that here was once the temple of the God, known reverently as 'the good Demon'. The spring is one now, but was originally two, those of Memory and of Forgetfulness, for here we have the waters of Lethe themselves for us to drink, the springs that in later days coloured the imagery of the Orphic mysteries, and of the sixth book of the Aeneid that derives from them. The actual site of the oracle was on the rocky crag above, in what was once a sacred grove, but where everything is now obscured and confused by a Catalan castle of late date, in which the place of the oracle seems to have served as a cistern for the water supply, after enduring some grievous mutilation.

Fortunately, we know the procedure of consultation as practised here, from the accounts given to us by two trustworthy initiates, who were not bound to any secrecy in this instance, Pausanias and Plutarch. You began, as usual, with several days of 'retreat' which had to be spent mostly 'in the house of the good Demon', which was

8a. Eleusis: Callichorus Well 'Where Demeter
sat in her sorrow'

8b. Delphi: Temple of Apollo from East

9. Delphi: Temple of Apollo from North

the temple itself. There were rules of ritual purity, and constant baths in the River Hercyna, on which occasion you were attended by two acolytes from the temple; also there was a whole series of sacrifices to offer, the omens from which would tell the priests whether it was worth your while to go on, and whether you would get any answer from the oracle at all. At least you were not bound to fasting, for you were allowed, and even recommended, to eat abundantly of the sacrifices for which it was your privilege also to pay.

At last, after a final bathe, and anointing, by your two attendants, you were allowed to approach the sacred grove. First you must drink of the waters of Lethe, to clear your mind of all that it contained, that it might present a *tabula rasa* for the oracle; and you must also drink of the Spring of Remembrance, that what the god wrote upon your mind might remain in it. Then, robed in white, and after reverence to the archaic image of the deity that stood by the oracle, you were provided with the two honey cakes that each worshipper must bring, and you were conducted to the Pit or Chasm in which the answer would be given.

This was, says Pausanias, an artificial or partly artificial pit in a marble-paved area, 'rather like an oven' in shape, some four cubits across at the top, and a little more below, while it was about eight cubits, or twelve feet, in depth. When our author says 'oven', we presume him to have in mind, not the bee-hive shaped structure of mud that one sees outside many a cottage now, but something more like the *tanura* or *tandur* of Anatolia, which is just such a pit, bigger at bottom than at top, and lined with fire-brick; when it is used, a big fire is lit on the level floor at the bottom, which is supplied with air by a passage from without, opening at that level, and the dough is clapped, in small cakes, on to the heated sides to bake there. Into this pit—which was of course on a larger scale than the ordinary *tanura*, for that is only about four feet deep—you descended by a light ladder, honey-cakes in hand, and were told to lie down flat at the bottom. For this there was adequate space, seeing that you were expected to thrust your feet into 'a small opening, two spans by one', that you could then see at the bottom of the oven wall, and which it will be seen corresponded to the air-flue spoken of above. Then, a strange sensation beset you, for you felt as if you were being sucked down into that little hole, and whirled round as in an eddy of water, till you lost consciousness, and strange visions, varying with the individual character, seemed to come to you. Plutarch—or the friend for whom he speaks—felt that he was drifting on a cloud in the heavens, and seeing the islands where men dwelt in a blue ocean below. Gradually, consciousness returned, and you might find yourself still lying in the pit with a racking headache, in which case you were picked up by the priests and allowed to rest 'in the Chair of Memory' hard by till you had collected your ideas; or you might be carried back by them still unconscious, and only come to yourself when again in the 'House of the Good Demon'. In any case, it was an awesome experience to the believer, and we are expressly told that it was usually some time before the power of laughter returned to the shaken man. The suggestion is that here as at Delphi some intoxicating gas collected in the little chasm (or welled up from it, as there), and that those exposed to its influence were 'out of themselves' for a while, and firmly believed that it was the god of the place that had inspired them. Perhaps the flow was, as at Delphi, intermittent, for we have seen that it was not always worth while to go down into the pit.

It is a wild country with few villages that you pass over between Livadia and Delphi, and even the more frequented road by Vralo is of much the same type. So wild is Parnassus still, that it is even possible to meet a Centaur in these his native haunts, for he is at least believed to be still there, and not there only. In modern speech, he is known properly as the *Kalo-Kentauros*, the prefix being of course euphemistic, and veiling the conviction that he is really far from being either good or beautiful. The same is true of a very near relative of his whom we shall meet later, the *Kalo-Kantzâros*. Here, so far as we are informed, the Centaur that you may meet (though of course you avoid him if you can) is the ordinary type that we know on the Elgin marbles. Actually this form, if the most artistic and most common, is only one of many, and is properly known as the Hippo-Centaur; for there are many compounds of the more or less human with the brute, and folk-lore knows of the Ono-Centaur (Man and Ass), and also the Aigo-Centaur and Ichthyo-Centaur, which we call more commonly Satyr and Merman, compounds of goat or fish with man. The morals of the Hippo-Centaur have not improved with the passing of centuries (the virtuous Chiron was quite an exception), and when the winter storms blow he comes and hammers with his hoofs on the doors of isolated cottages on the mountains, demanding as of old that a woman shall be sent out and given up to him. Fortunately, there is a simple means of self-protection, for you only have to put out a sieve on the doorstep. Then the Centaur is filled with curiosity to know how many holes there are in this mysterious object, and starts to count; but, as his primitive mind cannot count above two, the poor creature goes on all night counting 'one—two, one—two, one—two', till the cock crows and thereby dismisses him with all other creatures of the night-world, to their proper place.

Delphi is a place which you may reach by one of three roads, either down the valley from Arâchova, which is the original 'pilgrims' way', or up the hill from Amphissa-Salona, where the great 'Frank' castle reminds us of the adventure of the young squire of Scripu, or by climbing the hill from the ancient port of Cirrha, now Itea, on the Corinthian Gulf. In any case the scholar will not forget his first impression when he sees the place that he has heard of from childhood lying on its steep beneath the twin crags of the glistening Phaedriades.

We suppose that to most visitors Delphi means just the famous oracle of Apollo; but while to a Greek it was that, it was also much more beside, seeing that there he could find a Pan-Hellenic sanctuary, containing one of the great temples of his lands, and a collection of monuments without a superior even in Greece, that commemorated all the great events of history, whether wars with the Barbarian or against brother Greek, or great sporting events, or portraits of famous men and women. Further, here there was held one of the great sets of Games which meant so much to him; there was a grand theatre; and at the proper time one of the mysterious miracle plays that went back to the beginning of his story. Suppose that there was, somewhere in Europe—let us say at Rome, but in the finest scenery of Switzerland—a grand precinct that contained as its centre a cathedral that all men revered, in which was an infallible oracle that would always answer when questioned. Place in this precinct magnificent buildings that can house the United Nations and the International Court of Justice as their members feel that they ought to be housed, and scatter about it a series of groups of statuary, that shall commemorate, one the victory of Charles Martel over the Saracen, and another the Crusades. Add groups for Hastings, Bannockburn, Creçy and Agincourt, with others for Joan of Arc, Austerlitz, Waterloo and Sedan. One memorial for the union of Italy, and another for Majuba Hill. Then for Sport, put in the Australians' cricket tours, the Prince of Wales' shooting trips in India, a Derby winner or so, and two or three boxing champions; add a St. Bernard dog, a lady Channel swimmer, and portrait statues of Ninon de l'Enclos and one or two other ladies more renowned for beauty than propriety. Every one of these statues, be it understood, is the offering of the leading hero commemorated, and is a masterpiece of the art of its date. Throw in a theatre, a race-course, and a Passion Play, and you have something of what Delphi stood for to the Greek.

Every one of those is paralleled by something that was at Delphi once, for apart from the Temple and Oracle, there were the halls where the Amphictyonic Council met, groups or monuments for Marathon, Salamis, Plataea, Himera, for wars against the Barbarian. Monuments for Sphacteria, Aegospotami, Syracuse, and Leuctra represent inter-Hellenic wars. Alexander's hunt, the famous Charioteer, and a Pancratiast or two, stand for sport. A figure of the pious wolf, that first killed the thief and then revealed where he had hidden his plunder, corresponds to the dog. Phryne, Rhodopis and Lais all had portrait statues here, while the swimmer is represented by the diver Scyllias, who swam out in the gale and cut the cables of the Persian ships off Artemisium, so that they were wrecked. The Panorama must have been a marvel, even if there were scenes in Greece that equalled it, and it was not the only precinct at Delphi.

But, if this is what Delphi was in her glory, how did it all begin? How was it that all this centred here, far from any city, under the crags of a mountain glen? As we have been told, if we go back far enough we always find the roots of civilization knotted round some sacred stone or holy well, and so it was here. In old 'Helladic' days, long before Dorian Apollo was heard of, and indeed before there were any Hellenes, Delphi was a sacred place, the shrine of 'Pelasgian' Pytho. In those days, it was just the local shrine of this glen, with a precinct perhaps, but no buildings, bounded by a Cyclopean wall under the Phaedriades, and containing two fetish stones, sacred the one of them to Mother Earth, and the other to Poseidon. This Poseidon, however, was not so much the god of the sea as of the earthquakes so common here; he is the true 'Earth-shaker' whose symbol and holy animal was the mole.[1] Then there was the cleft in the rock in the precinct, from which issued the vapour that at times

---

[1] This is an aspect of Poseidon that we have forgotten, but it was familiar to Athenians, as we see in Dicaeopolis' defence of himself in the *Acharnians*.

> *First, understand this, that I hate the Spartans,*
> *And wish Poseidon, God of Taenarus*
> *Would bury men and city with an earthquake.*

A little Church of St. Nicholas in the hills shows that this saint, often heir to Poseidon of the sea, can connect himself at Delphi with the earthquake deity also.

inspired the priestess, being in fact the breath of Mother Earth inspiring her child. There was a threshing floor handy for dance and drama, the readiest place for solemnities of the sort as we have seen at Athens, and that was all. The place was annexed by Apollo and the old rites went on under his shadow, in slightly altered form. Thus the actual fetish stones are there still though Greeks did say that one of them was the *Omphalos* that marked the centre of the earth (Zeus set two eagles to fly from the two ends in his desire to solve that geographical problem and they met at Delphi) and the other the sacred stone that Rhea gave to Saturn as a substitute for Zeus, when the god was devouring his own children. The cleft in the rock from which the vapour issued seems to have been closed now, by some shift of the strata, as is natural enough with what was no more than a crack at best; but it has opened elsewhere and the vapour still comes up, at intervals. Its intermittent action (for at times it will blow out a candle repeatedly, and at others will do nothing at all) can be annoying to one who wishes to show it to visitors. As for the worship of Mother Earth and of the Earth-Shaker, it went on as long as did that of Apollo himself, for the shrines of both deities were by the side of his great temple, and they had their own priests, the *Pyrkones*.

These were the first deities upon the spot, before history began, and by the side of them Apollo appears as a mere parvenu. As a god may, he comes to Delphi by two ways at once, of which the first is that of the Dorian Apollo, the tribal god of that rather late-coming type in Greece, whose wanderings his history reflects. It is from the north that he comes with them, leaving behind him the Hyperboreans, with whom he nevertheless keeps up a connexion, going back to spend each winter with them, and leaving Delphi vacant for others in the winter months.[1] Somehow he can also maintain—or acquire—identity with an Anatolian deity. Apollo in Homer is pro-Trojan, and not Greek at all, and his name 'Lycian-born' (*Lycogenes*) proclaims his nationality. Still, having been somehow taken up by the Dorians he comes south with them, and his temples at Tempe, Iolcos and Thebes mark the steps of the migration. Indeed he nearly stops at the last place and only comes to Delphi by a very

[1] The virtuous dwellers at the back of the North Wind were by no means the mere fiction we are apt to think them, but are probably the part of the original Dorian stock that did not migrate and remained in the old home. They kept touch with their kinsfolk who had gone south, not only by means of Apollo's annual visit, but also by the periodical offerings that they used to send to the god's other great shrine, at Delos. *Herod.*, iv. 36.

characteristic accident, for he chases the nymph Telphusa over Parnassus, and only sits down where he catches the poor girl.

There, he annexes both shrine and oracle, after a great battle with Mother Earth, personified in the dragon Pytho, whom he slays. This it was that was commemorated every four years by the great Miracle Play, the drama of the *Stepterion*, in which the youth comes from Tempe, fights and slays the dragon and then, after burning his hut, flees back to Tempe for purification and comes again in triumph with Apollo's laurel.

There was much in the drama that was performed regularly because it was the proper thing, but which had already become unintelligible to Greeks in classic days, so that we may be excused from guessing at the meaning of it now; but it clearly symbolizes the triumph of a new religion and god over the old one. Later, there is a reconciliation, and the priestess who gave the oracle becomes Apollo's lady, and she uses the laurel or bay which may (or may not) have been his sacred bough from the beginning. The Games are introduced later, and were originally only a musical contest—but the bringing in of athletics does not need much explanation where Greeks are concerned.

But there is also a Cretan side to the legend, which men of old did not trouble even to try to reconcile with the other. According to this tale, it was a ship from Knossus in Crete that came to Cirrha, the harbour of Delphi, being led by the dolphin that showed the way and secured a perpetual fair wind, and that transformed himself into a noble youth when the ship reached harbour, and led the strangers from Minoa up the steep to the Phaedriades. There he proclaimed himself as a god and declared that his sanctuary should be forever on that spot, and when the Cretans objected that no worshippers would ever come to so inaccessible a place, and that there would be nothing for poor priests to eat, he assured them that if only they would be faithful and obey him 'the sacrificial knife should never have rest' in so favoured a temple.

That there is some very ancient Cretan influence at Delphi is certain. In the lowest stratum to which the French excavators penetrated—and they went down either to rock or virgin soil everywhere —they found objects that are plainly of Cretan provenance (a Minoan *Rhyton* or funnel among them), while we know now that the odd Delphic calendar, which was incomprehensible to classic Greeks, is of Cretan origin. There is influence of the same type in the ritual; before asking questions of the oracle at all it was felt

118

expedient here, as at the sanctuary of Trophonius, to ask whether it was worth while asking, and to get an augury about that. The safest way of deciding that question was to throw a bucket of cold water over a goat, and draw omens from his behaviour; and that is distinctly a Cretan method of augury.[1]

Apollo, then, whichever way you prefer him to come, is a foreigner confessed in this great sanctuary of his, and he is by no means the only invader in the territory of Mother Earth. Heracles, when mad with the blood-guilt incurred by the slaughter of Iphitus, came and tried to enter the precinct while still unpurified, and was indignantly repulsed. In his anger he got drunk, which was always a habit of his, and tried to force his way in and steal the sacred tripod of Apollo, on which there followed a battle royal between the gods—a favourite subject for local artists in later days. Some say that Heracles was beaten out, others that Athena came down, made the peace, and got the riotous fellow to behave, and anyhow the episode made a useful lesson to impress on any visitor who might seem inclined to disregard ritual rules in the precinct.

Dionysus also comes in, somehow. How he arrives is not certain, but he is found in possession during the three winter months while Apollo is away with the Hyperboreans and there are no oracles given, and his tomb—for he was one of those semi-human gods who die and revive annually—was always shown in the temple. In the winter—and Delphi is a snowy place then—he and his Maenads used to go up to the cave of Alonia or Corycia on Parnassus, which is some hours' climb from Delphi, and carry out their rites there. Of course he had his own corps of priests, the *Hosioi*, as all gods had here.

Other deities there were too, such as Neoptolemus and—in a later age—Antinous, for the place in its glory must have been as full of differing sanctuaries as a mediaeval cathedral of chapels, each of which, as in the cathedral too, might have its own endowed priesthood; but we must touch on each of these as we come to them. At its greatest, the precinct was about five acres in extent (200 yards by 125 yards), which is about the size of the enclosure of our Houses of Parliament, and was so full of marble statues in its cypress grove and its shrines, that Nero could take away seven hundred when he came here to collect works of art, and yet leave three thousand behind him.

We have seen that the Oracle belonged to Mother Earth in the

---

[1] Not only Cretan, however: some Himalayan tribes use it to this day nor is this the sole coincidence with Delphi.

beginning, and was annexed by Apollo, who is not an oracle-giver
always, and does not, for instance, take over the ancient one at Delos.
Beginning as a merely local matter, and answering such practical
questions from its own folk as 'Who stole my sheep?' it gradually
wins prestige, but is always business-like. Xenophon asks how he
shall secure safe return from the *Anabasis* that he contemplates, and
gets the shrewd reply: 'You have not asked if it is wise to go.' Cicero
when here, asks how he shall obtain the fame to which he feels that
his genius entitles him, and is told 'Take your own character as guide,
and do not be forever thinking what other folks are thinking of
you'— a reply that shows that Apollo's priests either knew their man
or could judge character.

The procedure of consultation was as follows. After a bathe in
Castalia spring, you offered your victim to Apollo, being allowed to
select a cheap one if you liked. Then in turn—lots settled precedence
—you entered the *adyton* of the temple and put your question to the
Pythia, the priestess of Apollo, women having to do so by deputy.
The Pythia was in fact a slave of the temple, and only formally a
priestess, and had to be always an uneducated woman and—vase-
pictures to the contrary notwithstanding—was old and *not* beautiful.
She had to bathe, to fast, and then chew the laurel or bay leaves and
sit on the tripod over the little crack from which the gas rose. Under
these influences she raved furiously and was often violent, and was
(according to Lucan) exhausted by the paroxysm.[1] There were
always three on duty, in turn. The woman's ravings were written
down by the attendant priest, who put them into hexameters that
were not always of the best ('I've known Apollo's poetry laughed at'
says Hermes in one of Lucan's dialogues), and the applicant had to
make what he could of the answer.

Beginning locally and with mere individual consultants, the
influence of the oracle extended gradually by means of the Colonies,

---

[1] We have seen how very unpleasant was the result of one exposure to
inhalation of what seems to have been a very similar gas in the Cave of
Trophonius. The Dainyals of the Himalayas put their 'Pythia' or prophetess
into a frenzy by making her inhale the fumes of burning cedar 'needles',
to this day: an interesting parallel. May we suggest that the experience of
spiritualistic circles seems also to supply an analogy to what happened at
Delphi.

There the Medium (the Pythia) when in trance, seems sometimes to
read the minds of the 'Circle' and to give out what is in them with the conviction that it has been dictated to her by her control. It seems possible that
something like this happened sometimes at Delphi, though the Pythia
might reflect what was in the mind of either the enquirer or the priest.

for the custom arose of coming to ask its counsel before a party of emigrants went out; and by keeping touch with and drawing tithes from cities thus founded, it gathered both wealth and information, and became a 'general intelligence bureau'. For instance, those who founded Byzantium came thither, and were told 'go and build opposite the blind men'. Their scouts asked far and wide for a city of sightless folk and found none; but when their wanderings brought them to the spot where men had built a city at harbour-less Chalcedon and neglected the Golden Horn just opposite, they felt that they had found their blind men without doubt, and Byzantium was founded. The Dorians who founded Tarentum were ordered to put a city where they should get 'rain from a clear sky', 'ex aethra'. They wandered far enough without success, till Phalanthus, their leader, threw himself down in despair on the shore one day, and his good wife took his head into her lap and wept in sympathy over him while performing her conjugal duty of cleaning the lice out of his hair. Her name was Aethra, and as her tears fell, the man had a brainwave. 'Rain from Aethra! It is not the clear sky but the woman that the oracle meant!' And Tarentum was founded.

The answer that Delphi gave to the enquiry of Croesus won it much prestige, as well as magnificent offerings, and it really does suggest something like clairvoyance on the part of that particular Pythia. The King, anxious to get a reliable reply to the question he wanted to put—'Shall I go up against Persia to battle or shall I forbear?'—sent round his messengers to all the oracles of repute in every land, charging them each to ask the same test question on the same day, a question to which they themselves did not know the answer. It was: 'What is Croesus doing at this moment?' Various replies were given at various places, but that of Delphi was: 'The woolly offspring of the flock: the shell-clad daughter of earth: together in a house with walls and roof of brass: a murmur, as of water boiling.' Croesus sprang up when he heard this, and said, 'That is the oracle for me;' for he had been doing the most extraordinary thing he could imagine—boiling a lamb and a tortoise together, in a brazen cauldron. Accordingly, it was of the Delphic oracle that he asked his great question—and alas that we must confess that on this second occasion the god hedged, and took refuge in the old trick of a *double entendre*. If the king were to cross the River Halys, 'he would destroy a great empire.' He did so in fact, but it was his own.

In the Persian War, the oracle hedged again past question. It feared to offend Persia, and when the Athenian ambassadors came to ask what they should do, it only gave a message of doom, and had to be brought to reason by a hunger-strike. 'We will starve here in your precinct', said the ambassadors, 'but go back with that message to Athens we will not.' Did Themistocles have anything to do with the revised word, that said that fair Athens' stay should be the 'wooden wall'? One is inclined to say that Apollo had unmerited luck in the whole episode, particularly when he said that he would himself defend his shrine against Persia after the disaster at Thermopylae, and the earthquake that hurled rocks on the advancing detachment of Barbarians made them flee in the belief that the divine guardian of the place had himself come out to fight against them. One can still trace the shrine of the *Phylax*, and see the rocks that he threw, in the small precinct of Athena Pronaea.[1]

Yet on the whole, though the oracle could sink below itself occasionally, as when it called the ruffian Cleomedes 'the last of the Heroes', or was unwise enough to try to bluff such a man as Sulla,[2] it is an influence for honesty and unity in Greece, and one that improves and develops with time. Ignorance and innocence is no excuse for Oedipus, but later when mere lustration is said to purge sin, the god declares:

> *Whoso is foul of heart, let him depart;*
> *To wash the body does not cleanse the soul.*

When the fraud Glaucus asks if he may take an oath that he means to break:

> *Aye, swear—but oaths have nameless, handless sons,*

is what the oracle says to him. There is something of the doctrine of the widow's mite in the saying: 'Better the poor man's cake than the rich man's hecatomb,' and Delphi can declare that there is no sin where there can have been no sinful intent, in the case of the

[1] 'Before the Temple.' It is so called because this precinct is that which the pilgrim comes to first, if he comes as he ought to do, but seldom does in these days, by the road down from Arâchova. This precinct also contains the 'Penal Shrine' which the Phocians had to build as penance as will be stated below; and also the twin 'Sanctuaries of the Litigants'. These commemorate two families who made themselves such a nuisance to their neighbours by their never-ending lawsuits that the good folk of Delphi confiscated all the property of both, and built two little temples with it, side by side.

[2] He came to 'borrow' Apollo's treasure in war, and a harpist was set playing in the shrine. 'It is the God, take the gold if you dare,' said the priest.

'Yes, the God, playing to show how glad he is to oblige a friend,' said Sulla.

'Children of Caphyae', who were said to have hanged an image of Artemis and so committed sacrilege.

One must have a kindly feeling for the oracle that when asked 'Who is the wisest man on earth?' said, 'No son of man so wise as Socrates,' and can understand how it was that such men as Plato, Aeschylus and Pythagoras could reverence it, and that Aristotle can say of its claim to be inspired, ' 'Tis hard to believe—and harder still to deny.' At the worst, one forgives much for the sake of the last recorded answer given, to the Emperor Julian, after something like two thousand years of life. It is one of the most pathetic episodes in story, when the man who was intensely religious and devotional by instinct, and yet could not be Christian because of what Christians had done to him and his, came to the ancient shrine, still in all its old beauty, to ask nothing for himself, though he had been fighting the lost cause like a hero, but merely to beg to know this: 'how could he give back his old glory to the Sun-god' whom, alone of his entourage, he truly revered? A lie would have cost little enough then, and Julian would have paid for one like a prince, but the last oracle of the temple speaks the truth:

The glorious house is fallen, tell the King.
Apollo has no longer any shelter;
The water-springs that spake are quenched and dead.

What wonder that, in the day that was only a few months distant then, the wounded Julian tossed up his own blood in the face of the Sun-god who had abandoned him in his need; *'Vicisti, Galilaee!'*
So ends the long story: Ω Γαλιλαιε νενικηκας

Apollo from his shrine
Can no more divine
With hollow shriek the steep of Delphos leaving.

But a few years pass, and Arcadius pulls down the great temple that he dare not leave standing, and the foundations of a Christian church dating from the fifth century show that Another has come to claim the worship of the Greek.

The temple of which we see the foundations at Delphi is the last of a series of six—supposing, that is, that we take as historical the hut of laurel from Tempe, which the Hyperboreans came to build, and the shrine of feathers and beeswax that took its place. A 'Brazen House', or temple of wood covered with bronze plates, may

quite possibly be historic, for we know that such a one existed at
Sparta, and this is said to have stood at Delphi till Homer's day. The
first that was built of stone with a tiled roof was the fourth of the
series, and tradition had it that Trophonius the deity of Livadia came
over Parnassus in neighbourly kindness to help in the construction
of this. Actually, the only two that are of any importance are the last
two of the series. The fifth, which was built in the period 550–500
B.C. by the house of the Alcmaeonidae, was newly finished in the
days of the Persian War, and is said to have been the first building in
which marble was used for the sculptures. The great retaining wall
of the foundations is *in situ* still, and it shows Apollo in the new light
of a manumitter of slaves, for the whole face of it is covered with the
inscriptions of those who owed their freedom to him.[1] This temple
was destroyed, probably by an earthquake, in the year 373 B.C., and
rather oddly some of its sculptures have been preserved by the fact
that they were used as filling in the foundations of the new one, and
are in the local museum still. Not a trace of those that adorned the
later temple has come to us. It is presumed that when the Emperor Arcadius destroyed the temple he dared not leave, he took them
to Rome or Constantinople.

As for the last building, number six, it was of the ordinary Greek
type, and built of Sikyon limestone, at a cost of 700 talents, or about
£250,000 in gold.[2] This was about half the cost of the Parthenon,
and was raised by subscriptions from all the Greek cities from
Trebizond to Marseilles—save only Olympia and Miletus, which
refused to subscribe, a fact which was carefully inscribed on a tablet
for all the world to see. It is not quite obvious why the architect
should have gone to the tremendous labour of transporting the huge
blocks of stone across the gulf and up the long steep ascent to Delphi,
when the Phaedriades were so near at hand, but we must presume
that he did not consider their light grey limestone, that gave

[1] There was more business than philanthropy in the matter, one must
own. The slave, who in theory could own no property, could not perform
the legal act of buying his own freedom. If however he could scrape up a
sufficient sum for the purpose, he could dedicate that to Apollo, who would
then buy the slave from his owner, and of his charity set him free. Sometimes we find conditions attached. One inscription records the manumission
of the girl Dioclea, who must nevertheless remain for some time with her
former owner. If she should bear a child, her right to strangle it if she will
is reserved to her, but if she elects to keep it and bring it up, the child is
to be free. There was an underside to Greek civilization, when such inscriptions were put in a 'cathedral'.

[2] The architect's fee was two drachmas per day—just double that of a
labourer.

them their name of 'the shining ones', to be good enough for his purpose.

In its interior, the *adyton* where the oracles were given was a mere cell twelve feet square, at the side of the actual sanctuary where the 'cult statue' probably stood, and it contained nothing but a bench for the enquirer and a grating in the floor, over which stood the tripod where the priestess sat, and through which the vapour presumably welled up. In the great *cella* or 'nave' of the temple stood the iron chair of Pindar, the 'Hearth of Apollo', on which the perpetual fire was kept burning, and the two great 'fetish stones' from the original sanctuary that we have mentioned above. Here, too, was the Tomb of Dionysus. No doubt there were many other offerings of greater intrinsic value. It was outside, however, in the little level court before the temple, that the most famous offerings were kept. Here was the great bowl of silver, holding 16,000 litres (at a rough calculation a cube of eight feet), that Croesus gave to the shrine he reverenced. Here was the gold tripod the whole of Greece dedicated after Plataea, the bronze base of which may still be seen in the Hippodrome at Constantinople. Here, too, were the great golden tripods and bowls that Gelon of Syracuse gave for his contemporary triumph over Carthage at Himera, and the silver covered altar that Chios gave for the last great victory over Persia that crowned the work, Mycale. However, by 347 B.C. all of these had vanished, and only the marble bases were left, that we may see there to this day. Their places had been taken by statues that must have seemed unspeakably shocking to the reverent of an older generation, beautiful gilded bronze portraits of such ladies as Phryne and Rhodopis, portraits that did full justice to the figure that won the former her acquittal in court.[1] It was the Sacred War that did the mischief, the result of a quarrel that Thebes picked with the men of Phocis. Though Thebes was undoubtedly in the wrong to begin with, she was able to arrange 'matters' with the Amphictyonic Council of Delphi, so that that 'League of Nations' pronounced a solemn curse with terrible penalties on the comparatively innocent men of Phocis. On that the little State resolved to be hanged for a sheep rather than a lamb, and seized the actual shrine of Apollo and melted down its treasures to hire mercenaries with the cash. With rather grim humour, they gave a substitute for the

[1] There was one Roman memorial here—and for once we feel it has the right. Prusias or Perseus, last king of Macedon, challenged Rome in 168 B.C. and put up a large anticipatory monument to bear the inscription commemorating his triumph. Aemilius Paulus defeated him at Pydna— and put his own name on the vacant space.

irreplaceable glories they had taken, in the shape of a marble group representing the battle between Heracles and Apollo for the Delphic tripod. The Phocians went down at last, and were sentenced—the whole procedure sounds quite worthy of the twentieth century—to pay an indemnity of an absurd and impossible amount, some of the first instalments of which built a beautiful *tholos*, or domed shrine, in the precinct of Athena Pronaea. Finally the whole proceeding gave to Philip of Macedon the excuse he wanted for 'intervening to restore order' in Hellas, and Greek independence came to its end.

The whole precinct of Delphi is, as we have said, a museum of Greek history, with the objects flung together as there happened to be room for them or opportunity to put one up, when somebody who might have objected had for the moment no power to interfere. Westminster Abbey is not more confused. As one goes up the winding course of the Sacred Way—that processional route to the temple that remained unchanged even when the whole site was covered by the village of Castri—one finds the great monument of the Spartan triumph over Athens, the trophy of Aegospotami, standing opposite to the memorial that Miltiades was allowed to put up for Marathon, while absolutely on the toes of the Spartan memorial—for the base has been cut away to make room for it—was the Arcadian thank-offering for the construction of Megalopolis and the recovery of their national independence from Lacedaemonian tyranny.

Two very pompous groups of Argive kings and Argive heroes recalled some very small triumphs of theirs over Sparta, and a very modest little recess was put up by the man who really did the work, for this is the offering of Epaminondas for the day of Leuctra.

The Treasuries[1] of Siphnos and Sikyon have less historic interest, though the carvings that adorned the former are among the chief marvels of the museum; but those of Athens and Syracuse, commemorating the one city's gratitude for the great day of Marathon and the other the triumph of Syracuse over Nicias and his hapless army, stand looking at one another like the tombs of Elizabeth and Mary Queen of Scots in Westminster Abbey.

[1] Treasuries (or Houses as the similar buildings are called at Delos) are little temple-shaped buildings, which any State could get leave to erect at one of the great Pan-Hellenic shrines of the country. In them were kept the 'properties', often very valuable, which the city in question required for its peculiar ceremonies in the place, or on great international occasions in it, and it served as a sort of 'club-house' for the nationals of the State owning it. It was on this road that there was found, buried, in 1939, the one instance of a statue of the 'chryselephantine' technique that has survived. The figure (an Artemis) was sent to Athens on discovery, for treatment.

126

The Athenian Treasury, one of the most beautiful buildings in the precinct, is a triumph of reconstruction. It was destroyed by an earthquake, which not only threw the building down completely, but sent the carved slabs of the metopes flying through the air as if they had taken wings. They have been recovered from incredible distances down the hill, and sometimes from graveyards where they served as tombstones. Yet the reconstruction has been possible, for the walls diminish in thickness as they rise, so that each block goes readily into its course, while long inscriptions on the walls facilitate the whole process, and now the beautiful building is today what it was of old. The carvings, representing the Labours of Theseus, have been voted too precious and fragile to expose to the weather again, and rest in the museum, being represented by casts in hard cement in the original place. The style forms a valuable link between 'the Aunts' of the archaic period and the finished work of Pheidias and his school. To read that Xenophon dedicated here his thankoffering for his safe return from the great Retreat of the Ten Thousand, gives a touch of human interest to the whole.

A look at the lower side of the building will show where there has been some unauthorized trespassing on the 'Athenian site' at some time when Athens was in no state to interfere, and chains and pillars have been erected to stop the process. This we know took place in 250 B.C. when the anti-Athenian Aetolian League was in command here. Athenian influence was restored fifty years later, when a big embassy to Delphi put up the chains, and by a most interesting coincidence, the Ode used on this occasion remains, still with its musical notation, on a slab of marble that is in the museum. It is our one authority for Greek musical symbols.

The Athenian Stoa, the monument of Salamis, stands just by the great retaining wall of the Temple, and in front of it is the *Halôs*, the open threshing-floor where the miracle play of the *Stepterion* was performed. Hereabouts a Messenian memorial commemorated the stinging day of Sphacteria. As for minor precincts included within the great one, we have already mentioned how those of Earth and Poseidon stood just below the Temple, which Dionysus occupied in the absence of Apollo. Just above the Temple at its eastern end was the important enclosure of Neoptolemus, or Pyrrhus, son of Achilles. He was certainly buried here, by very old tradition, which said that he came to Delphi soon after the fall of Troy, with intent to solemnize his marriage with Hermione, daughter of

Menelaus, and had the ill fortune to meet her old lover and his old
enemy in the place:

And soon Orestes, mad with crime
And wroth to lose his promised bride,
Smote Pyrrhus in unguarded time,
And at the Altar-fire he died.

Aen. III, 330 (Conington).

His tomb had but little honour till as late as 270 B.C. when the great
inroad of the Gauls under Brennus seemed to have brought back the
old danger of the Persian once more, in an even more barbarous
form. Thermopylae was lost again, and again Apollo said that he
would guard his own shrine, 'if only you leave it to me and the white
maidens, Artemis and Athene.' On this occasion their agent was
Neoptolemus, who came out of his tomb and defeated the Gauls, and
was rewarded with a precinct and offerings. Previously he had been
regarded almost as a foe. This invasion, and the wave of emotion
that its repulse produced in the minds of men, certainly had its full
artistic effect, as of old: it gave us 'The Dying Gaul' and all the
sculptures of the Pergamene school; and men say also such figures
as the Artemis of Versailles and the Apollo Belvedere, figures which
may be paying just now for having been overpraised in an earlier
age, but may come back to their own yet.

Another, but much less interesting cult that had a shrine here was
that of Antinous, the favourite of Hadrian, and his statue, one of
many representations of that effeminate and uninteresting beauty,
has been preserved by one of those freaks of fate that sometimes give
us what we care little about, when much that is really precious is
lost past recall.

One can wander for days about Delphi, for the great Precinct of
which we have only described a few of the more important contents
is only one of the many things to study there. We have barely
referred to the *Temenos* of Athena Pronaea (which bears the ominous
name of *Marmaria,* 'the marble quarry', to show to what base uses
it descended) and have not touched at all on the gymnasium, on the
ground where Ulysses once hunted the boar, and received the wound
of which his old nurse recognized the scar long after. The Theatre
with its surroundings is a subject for study by itself (with its trap-
door for the appearance of ghosts and gods in its choric area),
especially since it was the scene in recent years of some of the most
successful revivals both of Greek tragedy and Greek dancing. The

128

10. Delphi: Phaedriâdes Rocks from the
Portico of the Athenian Treasury

11a. The Cyclopean gallery
Tiryns

11b. Mantinea: Walls

Stadium, if rather late in date—for it is the gift of Herodes Atticus—is one of the most complete and fine in the land, standing as it does on the site where the Pythian Games were held in the later period of their history. It has a course of rather special length, for it seems that it was held desirable to provide a certain amount of automatic protection to the home product among athletes.

Castalia spring still wells up in its gorge between the two great rocks, and once more provides good, drinkable water for the thirsty, if not inspiration for the poet. It ceased to run in mediaeval days, the flow being stopped by an earthquake, but another shock some sixty years ago removed the obstacle and set the spring going once more. One can see plainly, hewn out in the imperishable rock, the arrangements made to enable the pilgrim to take his needful bath before approaching the oracle.

Altogether, Delphi stands by itself even in Greece, both for its beauty and its surpassing interest; it seems that light-hearted Apollo, when he wandered here over Parnassus, gave a special charm and beauty to the ancient shrine on which the older and greater gods had already bestowed their heritage of reverential awe.

VII

CORINTH AND THE ARGOS DISTRICT

*Approach from Megara—Modern Corinth—Legends—Temples of
Apollo and Aphrodite—Sack—Roman Corinth—Nemea—Tiryns—
Mycenae—Tombs—Argive Heraeum—Nauplia—Epidaurus—Argos*

Fifty miles divides Athens from Corinth, and another thirty-five
from Corinth will take you *via* Argos to Nauplia. The roads
are motorable, of course, but a 'motor road' in Greece is a
rather uncertain quantity, and may be either very good or very bad.
Roads that were constructed for light mule-carts in which the driver
could sleep his homeward journey comfortably away were suddenly
called upon to bear heavy motor traffic, and naturally collapsed under
the strain. Then the country began to re-make its system like all
others, at a time of special strain and poverty, and was not more
exempt from the temptation to false economy than others. Many of
the highways are quite good, but are like the Greek restaurants in
this—they are apt to vary rather quickly in character from year
to year.

The Athens-Corinth road takes you past Eleusis to Megara, a
historic place which has no modern interest, save on Easter Tuesday,
when the populace still keep up one of the old folk-dances of the
land. Though we quite believe that this goes back to classic days, we
must admit that it has lost one of its original charms. The old kissing
contest that so intrigued Theocritus is no more.

One of the most beautiful stretches in the land is that portion of
the road between Megara and the Isthmus, which an older generation named the Evil Stair, the *Kake Skala*. It was here that Theseus,
coming from Troezen to Athens, encountered the robber Sciron and
slew him. That pest made everyone who passed wash his feet, and
then kicked his servitor over the cliff for the tortoise to feed on.

Theseus vanquished him in fair fight, and then kicked him to the tortoise, which was turned into stone afterwards and is there to this day to testify to the truth of the tale. That at least is the Athenian tale, and at any rate the tortoise is there. Folk of Megara had a different version, saying that the virtuous Sciron had made a good road over the dangerous rocks, and only charged a small toll to passers-by. All went well till 'that Athenian robber' (Athenians always were robbers) came along and refused to pay, and in the squabble that followed murdered the public benefactor. Thus the road remained perilous till Hadrian repaired it when he passed this way, but the modern tourist does not go by the Roman's road. A newer and well engineered one will take him past the Evil Stair, and so on to the Isthmus. This is, of course, pierced now by the Canal, a passage which many have attempted to make, though it was only finished about 1890. Alexander, Caesar and Nero each tried their hands at it, and the memorial plaque that the last named left on the rock, to show how far he got with the work that he started with a golden pick and shovel, can still be traced near the western end of the cut, on its southern side. The line of the canal roughly represents that of the old *diolkos*, by which light craft in old days were dragged from sea to sea, and it traverses the ground of the sanctuary of Poseidon, the site of the Isthmian Games.

Even now that the canal is finished, it is, we fear, hardly a commercial success. Only comparatively small ships (up say to 8,000 tons) can pass it, and the saving in distance that it affords is not much in these days, nor is the Cape of Taenarum the name of fear that it once was to mariners. Further, for economy's sake, and to save excavation, the walls of the Canal were made rather dangerously steep, in the hope that the soft rock of which they are composed would stand up of itself—a hope that has been most grievously disappointed. Hence navigation is often interrupted, and that for long periods together, by untimely landslips.

Corinth is an absolutely modern town. The fact is that it was moved bodily from its ancient site—some five miles beyond it—in the nineteenth century. The idea was, both to avoid earthquakes which had ruined the place more than once, and to secure nearness to the port. The latter has, of course, been won; for the former, in 1928 a shock brought every building in the town to the ground, with the single exception of the Cathedral. How it came about that this, a structure that is both lofty and, truth to tell, rather jerry-built, should survive such an experience, no man can say. Some said

131

miracle, and no wonder. Others suggested that its foundation must rest on some subterranean rock that had resisted the 'wave' of the earth's surface. No lives were lost, for a slight preliminary tremor had sent all people flying out of their houses to the safety of the open air, and in consequence the buildings that fell a few minutes later were empty. Of course the destruction of property was tremendous, and the whole town left shelterless. This will show the reader that he must not seek antiquity in New Corinth, and he may be thankful that all that is standing in the old city resisted the shock.

The part that Corinth plays in classic periods is not the worthiest possible. Athens and Sparta may fight, but they stand for great principles, and are 'the eyes of Greece'. Corinth is always important, for her position on 'the two seas' secures her that, but she stands for no great cause, and plays a minor part in the Persian and Peloponnesian wars. When her great citadel does become a strategic centre, in the period about 300 B.C., as one of 'the three keys of Hellas' (Volo and Chalcis are the other two) they are only the keys with which Demetrius the City-taker locks her chains. She is great at art and trade, and has to undergo one notorious sack at the hands of Roman invaders, but she never leads any thought, or any great movement.

The history of the city is long enough, for when cities began to be at all, such a site would never fail to attract settlers. Her very name, with its termination 'nth', is pre-Greek, and the abundant prehistoric remains in the neighbourhood have more of human interest than is always the case. Thus at the village of Zigourion in the neighbourhood, a perfect house and hearth of about 3,000 B.C. came to light, with the platters for the family meal all in order, and the bones for that rare delicacy, beef broth, still in the tureen. The household must have been just assembling for some family festival when the raiders broke in, and one sympathizes with their fate. Another excavation, some 1,500 years later, but prehistoric still, revealed a potter's stock-in-trade. Nearly a thousand pots and goblets, some quite unbroken, came to light, and it would be possible to drink wine today from a 'new' cup, in the local museum, made by a man whose sons may have followed Agamemnon to Troy.

Corinthian myths, when the Hellenes proper had come into the land to make them, were abundant. Was it not Sisyphus, King of Corinth, who first rolled up the great blocks of stone to make the Acropolis, and when his fort needed a water supply he was able to do a good turn to Asopus the river-god and get the spring of Pirene on the Citadel as reward? The good turn in question was that he gave away the secret of Zeus, telling Asopus how the god had carried off his daughter, Aegina, 'wherefore in hell he pays the penalty for his wagging tongue.' Whether Asopus really did give him a spring on his citadel is doubtful. We at least have never been able to detect any natural flow into the big cistern on the hill, which is one of many up there, and it certainly gets much of its water from an artificial catchment area. However, the family kept an interest in the site, for it was here that Athena handed over Pegasus, bridled, to Sisyphus' grandson, Bellerophon.

Here too came Jason, when he was anxious to settle down respectably, get out of his entanglement with the enchantress Medea, and marry Creusa, heiress of the King of Corinth. So it was here that Medea sent her rival the poisoned marriage robe by the hands of her own children, and poor tortured Creusa drowned herself in the fountain of Glauce, 'which is alive to this day to testify to it, wherefore deny it not.' The oldest form of the legend said that the men of Corinth killed the innocent children in revenge, not that they were slaughtered by Medea. In fact, until the time of the Roman sack, Corinthians were still accustomed to offer a yearly sacrifice of propitiation, and the ritual of the act (the goat that was to be sacrificed had to find the knife itself, and so be made guilty of its own death) shows how ancient the custom was. The story that it was Medea, and not the citizens, who killed the children, was put about by the Corinthians themselves, and when Euripides made the tale into his tragedy, they persuaded him to alter the text for the sake of their own reputation. Even so, traces of the older story survive in his choruses.

The shape of the countryside dictated the site of Old Corinth. Acrocorinthus, the Acropolis of the place, lay for a refuge to the south of it; where the hill fell in a long stepped slope to the sea, a series of springs gave a site for a town to grow. Here stood the town, and some three miles away—which is far enough for a primitive settlement to get warning of the coming of an attack by sea—a shelving beach on the shore of the great gulf gave a landing that was sufficient for such ships as they had. A later age dug out a double harbour here (which is now a salt marsh) and connected it by 'long walls' with the town on the slope above.

The temple, the seven surviving columns of which are the most conspicuous object in the ruins, is the most ancient now existing in Greece (580 B.C.), though of course very far from being the first to be built. It is of a Doric style that almost corresponds to Norman in our architecture, so squat and heavy are the stone pillars of the peristyle. Twelve of them were still standing, less than a century ago, but as the old Turkish owner of the site explained to an English traveller who asked about them, 'I was in want of building stone.' On the under side of one of the two that lie prostrate, there can still be seen the coats of white stucco that once covered the grey limestone—that Greeks should have plastered their temples seems to be most improper, but it is undoubtedly the fact—the thicker and coarser coat of Roman date overlying the finer Greek one.

The temple, as was often the case in Greece, was a double one, so that if Apollo was the owner of half of it, as is generally said, he had to share his house with some other deity, and it still contains the old Treasure Chest of the sanctuary; for temples were classic banks. Some wish to identify this with the chest in which Cypselus, the supposed founder of the temple, was hidden by his mother, and from which he took his name. (An oracle had said that the son of Eetion should end the rule of the Bacchid, royal house of Corinth, and soldiers were sent to put the infant out of the way.) However, another chest, said to have been dedicated by Cypselus when he fulfilled the oracle and became Tyrant of Corinth, was shown at Olympia.

Tyranni generally were devoted to great public works, for which they got but little gratitude from their subjects. Periander, son and successor of Cypselus, went in for improving the water supply of the city, as did also Peisistratus at Athens, and Polycrates of Samos. The springs of Pirene in the city (there were two of the name, and that on the citadel was held to communicate with the one below) and of Glauce came out at the foot of one of the low precipices about which the city was built. Periander tried to increase their flow, by driving long 'catch tunnels' into the rock behind them. In due course, the precipices were quarried away and vanished into mere slopes, save where they stand up as isolated rocks, looking like houses, over the springs today.

This ruler, though counted one of the Seven Sages of Greece, was really most famous as the hero of the most successful spiritualistic seance of antiquity.[1] Someone had entrusted treasure to him to keep, and he put it 'in a safe place'—and then forgot where. Like a wise man, he asked the help of his wife. Unfortunately, the lady was dead, so he had to call up her shade for the purpose, and the spirit took advantage of the opportunity to tell him that, where she then

---

[1] *Herodotus*, V. xcii.

was, she had nothing whatever to wear. 'But I buried all your wardrobe in your tomb', urged the husband. 'Buried it! And wouldn't anybody but you have known that you ought to have burnt it?' said the indignant spirit. The king went straight back to his palace and invited all the ladies of Corinth to a reception. They came, naturally in their best attire, and then the king called in his guards and relieved every one of her apparel, which he then burnt to satisfy the needs of the lady Melissa.[1]

When the American archaeologists were excavating Corinth the fountain of Pirene in the City was naturally one of the things they most wished to find. It was said to have a magnificent front, begun by Periander and finished by Herodes Atticus; Pausanias describes both it and the marble tanks adjoining, with much care. All search had failed to reveal it, till a young member of the staff was lowered for the fun of it down a well in the garden of the house the party occupied. Arrived at the bottom, he found himself in *running* water, and was able to crawl along the passage whence it came. Presently, the passage widened, and he saw portions of two arches in front of him. Instantly he recalled the 'chambers made like grottoes' of Pausanias' description, and made his way to the surface to announce that he had found Pirene. Excavation proved that he was right. The object of their search had been just under their feet all the time!

Corinthian history in the classic period is that of an ally of Sparta, prosperous and corrupt, who always plays for safety. There was an oriental or Phoenician strain in the local type, that came out in their religion, for the principal deity of the State was not Apollo, but the 'armed Aphrodite' whose temple stood on the summit of the Acrocorinthus, and was the really great shrine of the place. She was a type that puzzled the Greeks, who could not connect Aphrodite and war, so that Praxiteles could only get over the difficulty in his famous statue that stood in the Temple by representing the goddess using the stolen buckler of Ares as a mirror. The paradox was a stock theme for schoolboys' essays in Cicero's day. We know her prototype, however, the Ishtar or Ashtoreth of the East, goddess of love and war, and her cult in Corinth had its usual accompaniment—a troupe of sacred courtesans or *Deva-dasis*. One of these women rose to fame, the girl Lais. She was a captive from Sicily, sent back to Corinth from the camp of Nicias, and probably the only spoil that the Athenians ever sent back from that ill-fated expedition. The Corinthians gave her freedom and rank in their city from sheer joy

[1] The row that followed cost him his throne!

135

in her beauty, and when that beauty began to leave her, she dedicated her looking-glass in the temple she had served:

> *Now I, Lais, vow my mirror, Queen of Paphos, unto thee;*
> *What I was of old I cannot, what I am I will not see.*

Corinth prospered in her safe game till she was tempted to join the Achaean League. That is an episode of Greek history that was left out of the standard text-books of the writer's schooldays, which were apt to end with Alexander, but is nevertheless an interesting instance of the way the Greeks tackled the problems of imperialism and federalism. When the League was foolish enough to make war on Rome (146 B.C.), Corinth, the latest member and the richest prize, was left to pay the bill for all. She was not only looted, but destroyed and left desolate, for she passed through the hands of that rough old ranker general, Mummius. He did know enough, however, to collect the works of art, though we may gauge his appreciation of them from his famous order to the 'removal contractors' of his day, that if they damaged any in the course of removal, he would expect them to make others as good to replace them. The modern excavations still contain statue-bases that bear the name of Lysippus, to give evidence of what was taken then.

The place was absolutely abandoned—even worship at the temples ceasing—and the town left to mere squatters for a century,[1] so that when Julius Caesar restored it, men had forgotten the right way of performing such odd local cults as the Atonement for the Children of Medea, and they lapsed in consequence. With its destruction there also perished the little subordinate city of Perachora, that then stood on the head of the peninsula of that name that divides the head of the Gulf of Corinth into the two bays of Corinth and Aegosthena, and is about eighteen miles distant from the mother city. This was never rebuilt, so that its site on what is now Cape St. Nicholas remains for excavation today. Here, the little temple of Hera was of the primitive apsidal type, of which we have instances elsewhere, and it had, as was usual, a sort of 'Votive Depot' (or dump) in which votive offerings that had met with accident and could no longer be used were cast.

---

[1] A poet of the day, Antipater of Zidon, makes the sea-gulls pronounce her dirge.

> *Not a trace, not a trace, unhappy,*
> *Hast thou left behind in falling;*
> *All has been devoured by the glutton throat of war,*
> *We only, Ocean's children, still hover, calling, calling.*
> *The sea-birds wail thy sorrow, along the lonely shore.*

These discards of the temple authorities are of course priceless to the student, and the place has yielded for us the first real 'Corinthian' bronzes known dating from the eighth century B.C. The pottery discovered gives, what the mother site does not, a comprehensive picture of artistic and commercial Corinth, in days when she was the dominating influence of Greece in the cultural sense, the seventh and sixth centuries. It also supplies proof that the city had her commercial connexions, not only with Greece at large, but also with Phoenicia and Egypt to the east, and Etruria to the west. She was, what her position marked her out to be: the *entrepôt* of the commerce of the day.

So good a site could not be left forever, and Caesar restored the city, though the plan he cherished of a canal through the isthmus was too great a work for his generation. His restored Corinth was built on an entirely new plan, and he left, in consequence, a very fine set of problems for future archaeologists. The great Processional Way that Pausanias describes and that the Americans have discovered, was the spinal cord of the whole, and new roads were laid down as was convenient, in the ruins. Thus street fountains were buried in debris, and not discovered till they come to light in this twentieth century, ten feet below the Roman street level—which is itself some fifteen below the surface of today—with the water still flowing from the original lion-heads of bronze. Buildings were erected on old roadways, and temple sites buried, unless, like that of Apollo, they stood on elevated rocks. One can picture the joy of the archaeologist in disinterring a tiny classical oracle-shrine, holy no doubt to some local deity, where the secret entrance for the priest who was to utter the oracle and the stone trumpet mouth that was to give his voice a seemly sonorousness, were still *in situ* and usable. Even the warning on the marble barrier, that kept the approach private ('No admittance. Fine for trespass, five drachmas') was there to be read, and adorns the Museum today.

It was this Graeco-Roman Corinth, of course, that was the town visited by the apostle Paul, though one can hardly hope to find Aquila's tent factory, which would be down in the poorer quarters by the harbour.[1] One spot, however, where the apostle undoubtedly stood, has been identified; the Tribune or Court of Justice where Gallio delivered that admirable exposition of the duty of government

---

[1] The inscribed lintel of the doorway of the Jewish synagogue has been found, but in surroundings that give no hope of its providing a clue to the position of the building.

to religious disputes that we read in *Acts*, xviii, and refused to trouble 'Paulus' for his defence. Here it was that 'the Greeks took Sosthenes, the ruler of the Synagogue, and beat him before the judgement seat'—a bit of 'lynch law' that authority did not object to and that seems to have had the admirable result of converting its victim to Christianity, as he next appears as a warm adherent of St. Paul (1 Cor. i. 1). The statues of Augustus, Tiberius and Germanicus, now in the Museum, were found in a basilica in this area. They stand side by side, as when St. Paul looked at them in Gallio's court.

Corinth in Roman and Byzantine days had no history, and through all the Middle Ages only one episode, and one legend. Historically, it was one of the very few places in Greece that resisted the Frank Invasion that overran Greece after the capture of Constantinople by the Fourth Crusade. Here, one Leon Sgouros did hold out on Acrocorinthus, defending the walls that are there now, a mixture of Mycenaean, classic and mediaeval work. He was a rough customer, and when the Archbishop of Corinth came as ambassador from the besiegers to urge him to surrender, he blinded the prelate and kicked him over the precipices of the citadel. Patriots who have their backs to the wall have little courtesy to spare for fellow-countrymen who have made terms with the enemy. Blockaded by forts on that Mons Acutus, Montague or Mont Aigu that now masquerades under an odd corruption of its old name, as Penteskoufia or 'Five Caps', he saw at last that all was over, and so sought an end like that of Kingsley's Knight of Altenahr. Mounting his charger,

> *He spurred the old horse, and held him tight,*
> *And leapt him out over the wall,*
> *Over the battlements, into the night*
> *Five hundred feet of fall.*

Still one can trace the site of the leap, and can leave him with Kingsley's farewell:

> *A glass or a prayer now, good gentlemen,*
> *For such a bold rider's soul.*

As for the legend, it shows how classic lore survived in a mixed way in mediaeval minds, which still recognized the original mistress of the place. Once, Queen Aphrodite the Beautiful ruled on Acrocorinthus, having also a palace at Daphne by Athens, the two being joined by an underground way. She had two lovers, between whom she could not or dared not choose openly, so she set tasks to both. A was to fortify the Acrocorinthus, B to sink a well in it, and find water. B's task seemed the easier, for she privately favoured him, so they wasted time in one another's arms, till news came that the work of the diligent A was done, all save the keystone of the great gate. Then perfidious Aphrodite took A aside, and sat flirting with him in the shade, while B worked furiously, found water, and won the prize. If you seek proof of the story, climb the citadel—it is a good hour's walk from the city below—and look at the keystone of the portal.

Of all sieges of Corinth, the most famous to our grandfathers was that commemorated by Byron, and though he does not spare the high colour, it did take place, in the year 1714. The Venetians, then in decline, were the defenders against the Turk, who stormed it with all the horrors that Byron depicts, though he omits one point—the melancholy fact that the Oecumenical Patriarch of Constantinople issued sentence of excommunication against any Greek who fought for the Latins against the Sultan.

The road from Corinth to Argos, the main road from the Isthmus into the Morea, runs over the pass of Derbenakia. This is no very formidable climb in itself, but its southern descent was the scene of an important event in the Greek War of Independence, for it was here that the Greeks, under Kolokotronis, cut up the Turkish army that was marching to the relief of Nauplia. The Turks were, as usual, thrown away by bad generalship that played right into the hands of an able leader of *guerilleros,* and the feat is commemorated by a rather ugly statue, that stands in duplicate at Athens and in Nauplia. At the crest of the pass, the road to Nemea diverges from the main highway, leading down into the upland valley where Heracles killed the famous lion, and where the Nemean Games of classic Greece were celebrated. All the countryside was the scene of the famous Labours, for Heracles was Argive by birth; and archaeologists still live in hope of discovering the traditional den of the lion, which was said to be somewhere in the hills of Nemea. It would probably yield as many votive offerings of a Heracles Cult as did the Caves of Zeus in Crete.

As for the games, they are said to have owed their origin to the carelessness of a nursemaid. Oracles had declared that Opheltes, infant son of the local king, must not touch the ground till he could walk, and orders had been given accordingly. Unluckily, the girl in charge of the child met the famous Seven when on their march from Argos to Thebes, and put the child down to stare at the soldiers, when they asked her for water. She showed them the spring, Adrastea, which still marks the site of the episode, and a 'dragon' came out of it and ate the baby. The girl's fate is unknown, though the heroes killed the dragon, but the games were instituted in memory of the event, and the judges always appeared in mourning garb for that reason. It was these games that gave the 'parsley' (or celery, *selinos*) crown as their prize, and the central event of the contests was the race in full armour, or 'heavy marching order', that was afterwards copied at Olympia. The stadium was on the plain near the temple, but only the curved end of it can now be traced. It was here that Alcibiades swept the board at one of the celebrations and then incurred censure for his 'impiety', in that he commemorated his triumph by a picture of himself, seated on the knees of the nymph of Nemea. He had represented himself as better-looking than the nymph!

The temple stood originally in a grove of cypresses, and the American school has made efforts, disappointing in their result, to excavate the buildings of the precinct. Only a Byzantine church was discovered. The temple had Doric columns of singularly slender and graceful type—they would be slim even if they had been of the Corinthian style—which form a fine contrast to the clumsy pillars of the existing fane at Corinth. Only three stand now, for they were overthrown by an earthquake, but the drums of all the rest lie in order on the ground, and seem to cry aloud for the reconstruction that is now possible. The road runs down from Nemea station to the Plain of Argos, to Mycenae, Tiryns, and Nauplia.

This plain is the hearth and origin of the local civilization, the direct parent of the Greek type from which all that is best in Europe springs. Here the colonies from the immemorial civilization of Crete united with the 'Helladic' stock that came down from the north, and the Hellene of history is their offspring. We know of one great feat of theirs, because Homer has told it, when the Achaean tribes joined in one confederacy against their cousins in Troy, and smote that city down. The fact that we can guess now at commercial reasons for the quarrel need not make us disbelieve the great tradition, that said that one woman's beauty was the actual torch that lit the fire. Another great war of theirs was certainly carried out by the *fortes ante Agamemnona*, when for unknown reasons they attacked and ruined the ancient, perhaps decadent, civilization of

Crete. Here, the 'long night' in which they have been forgotten for so many ages, *carent quia vate sacro*, has yielded more or less to the explorer. At least the Achaean House of Atreus, so long great in legend, is taking its place as a historic fact, now that we find the *Atreyadae* and the *Akhaiusha* mentioned on Hittite inscriptions, and know that men of Mycenae fought against Rameses the Great at Kadesh. Later, another migration came in from the north, the iron-using Dorians, and when they established themselves at Argos, Mycenae and Tiryns sank to secondary rank. Still, they could approve themselves true Hellenes, for when Argos shirked her duty, the older cities shared in the Persian War, and could claim to have their names put on the Delphic tripod, the Greek trophy of triumph. Their witness stands to this day, though it has been moved from its own home to Constantinople, proclaiming how men of Mycenae stood to die with Leonidas at Thermopylae. Naturally, Argos could never forgive the older cities for having done the duty that she had conspicuously failed in, and within ten years she had picked a quarrel, and destroyed both. The pretext was the right of presidency at the Nemean Games, and the two most ancient sites in the land have been deserted since. Of Argive conduct, the less said the better, but at least the result of their spite has been that the monuments have been preserved by their desolation from the destruction that continuous inhabitation would have brought upon them.

Tiryns is the older of the two places, and according to the legend was the foundation of Perseus, who settled there with Andromeda after the unfortunate death of Acrisius, and employed Cyclopes, whom he brought in from Lydia, to build the wonderful walls. Another story makes it also his birthplace, and so allows us to see in the gate-tower the 'tower of brass' where Danae was confined, and where she was visited by the Shower of Gold. The work is 'Cyclopean' enough in all conscience! 'Why should we trouble to go to see the pyramids when we have this at home?' says Pausanias. The blocks of which the place is built are many of them 100 cubic feet in measurement (6 ft. by 4 ft. by 4 ft.) and must weigh more than five tons. They are rough-squared with the hammer, and bedded in clay and smaller stones. They appear to have been quarried (such as were not on the site) by the boring of a row of holes with a wimble of some sort, that would bore a circular hole with a core left standing in it. Then the core could be broken and removed, and the block split off by wedges driven into the row of holes. The site of the fortress was a limestone crag projecting from a swampy flat; like the Acropolis at Athens, this was revetted by building up a wall of big blocks, upright, against its sloping side, and then filling the V-shaped space left with smaller stones. Originally, the height of the wall was about fifty feet, and the thickness at the top—naturally the thickest part—about as much. Thus a flat platform was produced for the castle. The main entrance is a long ramp, so arranged that the approaching party exposes the unshielded right side to the defence, entering by the towered gate already described. A tiny postern, approached from within by a vaulted gallery, is the only other means of ingress.[1] The most marvellous feature for the visitor, however, is the set of 'casemated galleries', vaulted with Cyclopean blocks, and giving on to chambers, constructed in the thickness of the walls, and meant either for defence through loopholes or perhaps for stores. From about 470 B.C. (the date of the destruction of the city) till 1880 A.D. or thereabouts, when it was excavated and protected as a monument, this gallery served as a sheepfold. The friction of the sheep's fleeces, through the centuries, has worn the hard marble into smoothness and brought it to a high polish.

Tiryns is a fortress, not a city. It is just the dwelling place of the King and no doubt a refuge for villagers living near, in time of need. As such it is about the size of an English castle, and like it has its three Wards or Baileys, with the dwelling of the Chief in the inner-most. Mycenae is more than a city even, it is a capital. Perched on its hill-top, it commands and overlooks the plain of Argos, the seat of a king, even though Argos may be the better site for a later ruler to put his seat, and its citadel (the Larissa) an even finer position for a fort. It is the centre of a regular system of chariot roads, that extend from it to Corinth, Sikyon, and Epidaurus, and these roads are provided with bridges and guardhouses—a fine specimen of the latter stands close by Mycenae railway station—though a drive along them in a springless chariot would not be luxurious to modern ideas. A great commercial centre, it is described as 'a city of broad ways' and 'rich in gold'. Certainly it was in touch with Crete, and it is still the hope of archaeologists that the bilingual inscription that will give them the key to the Cretan alphabet may yet be discovered here. Thus we can see, now that we have the right to think of Agamemnon as more than a myth, how the capital of the man who was 'king of men' was a real centre for the pan-Hellenic life of his day.

[1] This is also the case at Mycenae.

It is less impressive in its construction than Tiryns. The huge blocks of the latter are lacking. Even so, however, the workmanship here shows a very real advance in the builder's art and the Lion Gate and the Treasury of Atreus both excite the wonder of the modern engineer. In both of them the structure of the doorways—the combination of the lintel and the 'corbelled arch'—is a marvel of skill, for men knew how to raise the 120-ton block to its place above the portal and also how to spare its mass the transverse strain. Further, both the corbelled arches and the dome-like construction of the Treasury show how these proto-Greeks were feeling their way to the discovery of the great builder's secret that men have made independently in so many different lands and ages: the principle of the arch and the vault.[1]

The Lion Gate never fails to be impressive, but the lions (or lionesses) that are its chief visible feature are really subsidiary. The imagery of the composition is Minoan in its provenance, and Cretan seals give us the theme in its entirety. The pillar, against which the animals stand rampant, is a conventional representation of a mountain, and it is the stance of the Great Mother, the central figure of the Minoan pantheon; on Minoan seals she stands upon it in her glory. She is the Lady of the wild wood, the mistress of all creatures, who at once gives life and on occasions requires the sacrifice of it, and the lions who ramp against the sides are no more than her attendants.[2] The Hera of the neighbouring Heraeum, to which we come shortly, is a civilized and softened version of her, and the Heraeum, as we know, was the main sanctuary of Mycenae. She is really also the same as the grim Artemis of Patras, and possibly of Sparta.

The palaces of Tiryns and Mycenae are of the same 'Homeric' period, and the same general plan, both of them illustrating the conditions of life depicted in the *Iliad* and *Odyssey* in a most illuminating way. The plan of the Tiryns palace is far the more complete and clear of the two, for that of Mycenae has suffered both from the fact that a temple of classic date was built upon the crest of the hill, thus cutting up the remains of the previous building, and

[1] It is quite certain that the Greeks went on from the start made at Mycenae and elsewhere, and learned how to make true vaults and arches. The vaulted passage in the theatre at Sicyon (date, about 500 B.C.) is sufficient proof of the fact. If they did not use them in their temples, but stuck to the lintel principle, that was a matter of choice. The reason may have been taste, conservatism in religious matters, or possibly knowledge that the lintel or architrave principle resists earthquake shocks better than the arch.

[2] J. E. Harrison: *Themis.*

also because a landslip has occurred just at that point, so that large portions of the palace and of the original wall below it have gone down together into the torrent bed below.

In both, we have a main gateway opening into a colonnaded court, in which stands the altar of Zeus. (It is on the pillars of this court that Ulysses hangs the servant girls.) The men's hall, the *megaron*, opens from this court, having a porch or entry in front of it. Inside it, the great feature was the family hearth, with the four pillars round it that supported the roof at this point, where the hole by which the smoke escaped called for support additional to the ordinary pillars of the hall. Here was the seat of the lady of the house, and this was the sacred hearth, where any refugee might claim sanctuary. The women's hall, with its separate and smaller court, was at the side of the men's, and the whole was enclosed by the one gate mentioned. There is a postern at Tiryns, as said above, but in the *Odyssey* the fact that there is only one gate, which Ulysses and Telemachus secure before the fight with the suitors begins, is an important point in the battle.

It would seem that the palace had only one storey, and that part of the roof was flat, as it could be used for sleeping on in the heat. The low gable and pediment of the central hall, however, seem to be original features, and inside the hall there was what we see in village houses of Greece today, a sort of loft just under the roof, approached from the floor by a ladder, and used for the storing of goods and, in the *Odyssey*, of weapons. Both men's and women's quarters had their separate bathrooms (the provision of more than one bathroom for a house is a very modern thing with us, but here we find it in say 1300 B.C.), and enough remains of the one at Tiryns to show us pretty clearly what the arrangements of it were: a big slab of marble, with escape for the water, and a big tub in the centre as actual bath. There were screens fitted for propriety. The bathroom of Mycenae is lost, alas, having gone down the hill in the landslip, so that we can no longer stand on the actual spot where Clytemnestra slew her lord, and we must be content to approach by the very steps on which she spread the Tyrian purple to welcome him. At Tiryns, a good and orderly house, there is no direct communication between the men's and women's portion. A wall separates them, and any girl having lawful business with the men must go down a long passage, go out by the guardhouse at the gate, and explain her errand to the porter. So great is the care for the proprieties, that there is even an 'elbow' arranged in the corridor, lest the porter, standing at his end, should be able to flirt with the slave girls in their own court. If we follow the legend that tells us that this was the house of Perseus, Andromeda becomes much more human when we envisage her as a matron who, adventures with sea monsters done with, has due care for the morals of her maids. It may be remembered that when Ulysses, sleeping as a wanderer in his own hall, is given a pallet in the porch of the men's *megaron*, he is disturbed by the fact that the naughty servant girls pass over him, to go and keep company with their lovers among the suitors; a passage has been opened in the barrier wall. In the palace at Mycenae a similar opening has been traced, one pierced after the making of the wall. No doubt it dates from the days of Clytemnestra and Aegisthus, when all propriety was at a sad discount!

The lighting of the *megaron* is rather a problem. To us it seems most probable that the arrangement was what we have seen often enough in the houses of Kurdish Aghas; that is to say, that all the light came in by the door and by the big 'smoke-hole' in the centre of the hall. Little golden models of a Mycenaean mansion, preserved in the Museum at Athens, suggest that there was a big louver over the opening, with openings at the sides of it, and that this was supported by the four pillars of the hearth mentioned, and carried—again in Kurdish fashion—horns to keep off the Evil Eye. Sufficient of the ancient decoration has survived—and has been restored, in the Athens Museum—to enable us to form an idea of what it originally was. The plaster was frescoed, by artists who perpetuated the Cretan tradition, with scenes representing boar-hunting and bullfights. The gold-plated doors with silver jambs that appear in the *Odyssey* in the palace of Alkinoos may be a reminiscence of what was known to have been in the palace at Knossos, or they may be mere poetic licence. It must be noted, however, that though the decoration of the palace was copied from Knossos, the design of it seems to have been original and native to the tribe. It would appear to have far greater architectural possibilities, however rude the early form may have been, than the planless assemblage of rooms that we find in the far more luxurious and magnificent palaces of Crete. The front of the *megaron*, with its pillars, contains the germ of the porticoes of the Parthenon. The private houses, specimens of which remain at Mycenae and on the Acropolis at Athens, seem to have been mud-built, on a high basement storey of big stone blocks. They were floored by tree trunks, between which the débris of the meals could fall into the cellarage and so provide us with a very fair notion of the

Mycenaean menu—which again confirms the *Odyssey* in a most gratifying way. Pork, goat, and mutton are the main articles of diet; beef is a rarity and a luxury; Eumaeus complains that the suitors have eaten all the swine and sheep and are now beginning on the oxen. Fish, seemingly, is *taboo* altogether, and this surely is evidence that the Mycenaeans did not come, as some have held, from a land where men dwelt in 'lake villages' raised on piles. Fish is never *taboo* to such. The furniture no doubt was far simpler than in Crete. Ulysses makes his own marriage bed, beginning with the standing tree; and an axe, as with the Russian peasant of yesterday, was his one tool. The luxury and sheer daintiness of the Minoan was quite unknown, save in legends, in Homer's day. Civilization had gone down several stages.

Tombs in Mycenae are of two types, the 'shaft', from which Schliemann drew the treasures that are now the glory of the Athens Museum, and the 'dome and entrance passage' or *tholos* and *dromos*, of which there are several on the site, and elsewhere in Greece. These are known by fanciful names but the title 'Treasury of Atreus' is at least as old as Pausanias. Attempts have been made to derive them, the shaft from the two-storeyed house in the basement of which, as in Iraq, the departed were put in very close proximity to the living; and the dome from the semi-underground hut of Armenia, which is approached by a passage serving in winter as a fold. Others have referred them to two dynasties, Danaan and Achaean, but the problem remains that neither type corresponds with the Homeric custom of cremation. Now, the dome tombs have been definitely dated, for the door of the Atreus Treasury is identical in style with the decoration of the porch at Knossos, which is 'Middle Minoan II', or about 1600 B.C. Fragments of pottery in the tomb called 'Clytemnestra's' bear this out. There is at least a strong case for holding that the bodies in the shaft tombs of the famous stone circle were removed from the domes to these new quarters to keep them safe in a time of danger, and that then this new royal cemetery was enclosed in an extension of the wall, that implied the erection of the Lion Gate.

A reconstruction in the Athens Museum shows the method of interment in the shaft tombs. The pit was sunk in the rock and a chamber constructed at the bottom of it of great slabs of stone set on edge. The body or bodies—for a tomb might serve more than once—could then be deposited in it, with weapons and provision for the Great Journey. Wooden balks and a roof of horizontal slabs were then put over the chamber and the shaft filled. Naturally, the beams rotted in time, and the slabs then fell into the chamber and crushed all that was in it.

Tholos tombs are of two kinds. The smaller are simply a passage cut in the rock and expanding into a circular chamber at the end of it. Many of these are to be found about Mycenae, but they are not conspicuous. The grander tombs, like the Treasury, were made by sinking a great pit in the hillside and digging out the approach to it. This was then lined with masonry, placed on the 'false dome' method of construction, as was also the *dromos*, and the place was covered in with earth. The little chamber at the side of these tombs may have been the actual place of interment. Human sacrifices generally accompanied the ceremony, and the skeleton of a young woman was actually found just outside the doors of the great Treasury; it was the obvious duty of the slave or the retainer to follow their lord on the Great Journey on which he had started. The king took his rest clothed in the gold 'scales' we see at Athens—but it would seem that when the tomb was opened to put in, e.g., his son, it was lawful to plunder the former occupant. When once his corpse had dissolved, he had no further need of offerings.

The Argive Heraeum, a shrine not visited as often as its interest merits, lies only five miles from Mycenae on a road by which (in late spring and summer) a car can go thence to Tiryns. It was always the religious centre of this district, even when the political capital shifted —the great seat of the goddess who was always 'Argive Hera'. Samos might claim to be her birthplace, yet even Samos owned that the Argonauts brought the sacred image of the goddess hence to them, and her local rank is made clear by the fact that the Argive calendar was dated by the years of the priestesses of the shrine. She was the Pelasgian form of the universal Earth Mother, and the inferior son-husband developed later into Zeus. To him she was wedded annually, and the solemn bathing of the sacred wooden image in the spring of Kanathos at Nauplia by which 'Hera renewed her virginity yearly' was really the ritual marriage bath.[1] She was the goddess of the family life, and of the farm, and so her herd of sacred cattle lived on the hill 'Good-for-Oxen' (Euboea) by her temple and the drinking of water from 'the river of Freedom' (Eleutherius) that rose by her temple was a part of the ritual of the freeing of a slave. To win 'the shield of Argos' (a reproduction of the shield of the hero, Euphorbus, that was kept in the temple) was distinction comparable to Olympia.

---

[1] Later legend transferred the bath to Aphrodite. The spring is now in a nunnery.

Her sanctuary has three periods, corresponding to the three cities that have ruled here, and the oldest of the temples is said, by evidence of orientation, to date from 1830 B.C. Even so, it was not the first shrine upon the site. Here, in the Mycenaean age, the chiefs met to make their confederacy against Troy, and here Agamemnon was chosen to lead the united effort. The sanctuary was far too venerable to move when the Dorians occupied Argos, though it seems that they made the attempt. The episode of Cleobis and Biton (*Herod.* I, xxxi) shows that at that time the priestess had been made to reside in Argos, and only went out to the sanctuary for great occasions.

The year 420 B.C. saw the destruction of the ancient temple. A priestess named Chryseis went to sleep when on vigil, and her lamp set the hangings alight and started a conflagration. Not unnaturally, the girl fled for her life and found refuge in the temple of Athena at Tegea. It says much for the kindness of the Argives, however, that they did not destroy the statue of the girl which was already in the temple (it would seem that the Heraeum had such statues as the famous Aunts at Athens, see p. 23), and it was there for Pausanias to see.

The second temple, of which only the foundations remain, was put upon a lower terrace, and it contained as the 'cult-statue' the famous chryselephantine Hera of Polycleitus, a figure which all ranked with the Athena and the Zeus of Pheidias, and some thought more beautiful than either. The original has perished, of course, but what is believed to be a contemporary copy in marble of the head of it—a head formerly called Apollo—is now in the British Museum, and may be studied there. (See *Journal of Hellenic Studies*, xxi, p. 31.)

Nauplia is pretty certain to be the traveller's next point of call. The Minoan colony of Asine[1] was close by it, but the place itself was at once one of the oldest and most modern of Greek cities. Founded in prehistoric days by 'Nauplius, son of Poseidon' (which we may interpret as 'the Phoenician sailor'), whose son Palamedes built the citadel that goes by his name, it was the port of Argos in all classic history, and the first capital of modern Greece. Like Corinth, it has the credit of having defended itself against the invading Frank, and its position as a port was the reason why it was one of the strategic points that the Venetians elected to hold in the East. The lower fort, Itskala, is obviously Venetian building (for all that it still retains its later Turkish name), and was held by Venice from 1388 to 1540,

---

[1] One of the wonderful gold cups in the Athens Museum comes hence.

and again from 1686 to 1715. The fortifications belong to the latter date, and to build them, the Senate of St. Mark sacrificed without pity all the walls and temples of Aegina. Here, modern Greece really began, for the capture of the seemingly impregnable Palamedeion by a daring *coup-de-main* (it is not the only castle that has fallen victim to its own supposed impregnability) gave the patriot armies the belief in themselves that they needed, and the rout of the Turkish army sent to relieve the lower fortress was their most spectacular victory in the whole war. Hence, when Greece had been granted independence—though 'Greece' then was limited to the Morca—Nauplia became the capital, for the year or so that they had to wait for the recovery of Athens, and it rightly remembers its old rank. Unfortunately, evidence was given here, too, that the history of the revived country would not be too peaceful, for it was here that the first president, Capodistrias, was shot as he was leaving the church of St. Spiridon, where they still show the mark of the fatal bullet on a pillar. The cause of the murder was simply private revenge.[1]

The great shrine of Asclepius at Epidaurus is best visited from Nauplia and a good motor road takes you over the sixteen miles to that point, though it is far nearer in mileage to the northern coast of Troezen. The road passes the fine Cyclopean castle of Lissa, and follows the line of one of the ancient Mycenaean tracks, on which one of the original bridges still survives. Originally, Epidaurus was no more than a local shrine of healing, such as were to be found in many places, each with its own god. How it was that Asclepius, a Dorian importation from the north, superseded all the others, we cannot say. The same thing has happened elsewhere; for what religious reason has Lourdes so completely overshadowed La Salette?

Legend made Asclepius the son of Apollo and the local king's daughter, Coronis. She exposed the child on Mount Titthion (the 'Breast', easily identified by its shape and still a great place for medicinal herbs), and there the usual shepherd took him up. As for Coronis, when she found Apollo had abandoned her, she married a mortal, and the fact was betrayed by a crow. The jealous god killed them both, and the crow (white till then) turned black with shame

---

[1] It was at this time that the custom arose of using the castellated islet in Nauplia bay as the residence of the public executioner. The gentleman who was 'next upon the list' was allowed to volunteer for the job, when it fell vacant.

and disgust; Apollo then put the child under the tuition of Chiron, the good centaur.

Asclepius is never quite Olympian. He is, in fact, far the highest conception of the divine that the Greeks could rise to, for he who had immortality by right of his divine father then refused Olympian luxury, and stayed on earth to help poor mortal men. Jealous Zeus blasted him with lightning for helping them too well! It is only fitting that his statues should be far finer in expression than those of any other god. Indeed the traditional representation of Asclepius has been found to need but little modification to serve early Christians as their idea of the Christ.[1]

A healing shrine in old Hellas was generally of one pattern. There was the spring, usually a hot one that had healing virtues, and a temple and 'cult statue'. Then there was some sort of portico where patients might lie, and in an *Asclepeion* some sort of den for the sacred snakes that played their part in the ceremonial. At Epidaurus, the centre of healing became a watering-place like Bath. The little shrine developed into two magnificent temples, with a *tholos* or domed structure that was specially devoted to the underworld side of the worship. Then there was a racecourse, a club and library, and a theatre that is now the best preserved and the most beautiful in Greece. As in all of them, the acoustics of the place are such that a person speaking in an ordinary voice on the stage is easily audible by all of the 12,000 possible seat-holders. All over the enclosure were scattered *exedrae*, or 'sitting-out places' where visitors could indulge in converse. You could do anything that you wished in the precincts save be born or die! The first was taboo, the second an affront to the *Genius Loci*. The Emperor Antoninus provided a refuge, outside the precincts, for the accommodation of such patients as were discourteous enough to break this rule, and were expelled when they were seen to be likely to commit the offence.

With so many other attractions, the curative side of the life must, as at Bath, have become distinctly secondary to the social. It was there, however, and the ceremonial followed the same course as that described at Athens (see p. 47). The offering to the underworld aspect of the deity seems to have been more conspicuous here, for the *tholos* is not, as at Athens, a mere side-show to the rest. The building that contained the pit down which those offerings were cast was one

---

[1] The 'Gerasa' statue, discovered in 1930, is a statue of Asclepius, and in the Vth or VIth centuries became—with very slight alteration—the first known sculptured representation of our Lord.

of the most elaborate and beautiful in Greece, and it would seem from the foundations that remain that he who would offer was shut into an underground crypt and set to grope his way through a complicated maze of passages till he reached the pit in the centre, down which he would cast his offering.

The records of cures give us the usual medley of good common-sense counsel, faith healing, and auto-hypnosis. One patient, Apellas, is told, 'Wash yourself well, tip the attendant liberally, eat only digestible food, and—keep your temper!' The girl Ambrosion was rash enough to mock at the god and then, having got sore eyes, had to eat humble pie and come to him to be cured. The god was kindly and cured her, but she had to consecrate her offering, a silver pig, with her name on it, 'for her stupidity!' Pandarus, the innocent man who was branded as a thief, is told to sleep on the portico, with a fillet over the scars, and wakes in the morning to find the lettering transferred to the fillet. Echedorus, a real thief who had suffered like penalty, borrows the magic fillet, but finds the lettering transferred from it to his forehead, so that he bears double brands ever after. For sheer delightful human character, however, we give the palm to the *stele* of 'Aristides the Orator', 'whose immortal discourses everyone must have heard of', for he tells us so himself. This gentleman was a *malade imaginaire*, who became a positive nuisance to the management of Epidaurus, as one who refused to be cured and who would talk to everybody about the fact. On the staff of the establishment there was one functionary who must have been most useful at times, 'the official Dreamer.' If you could not get a dream to tell you what to do to be cured, when sleeping on the portico, this obliging gentleman would have one on your behalf. He dreamed thus on behalf of Aristides, and the vision said that he was to go away and visit all the other shrines of the god. The persevering man obeyed—and came back again, uncured still. The Dreamer was set to have another vision, and this time the direction was that the patient was to go away again and not to come back till he had written a good original poem in honour of Asclepius, *and he was to make it a long one!* It would seem that the unfortunate orator is working at it still![1]

An *Asclepeion* was not a regular hospital, but a priest there could hardly fail to acquire a good deal of knowledge of medicine and of human nature, so that it is not surprising to find that many of the great doctors of antiquity, Hippocrates among them, belonged to the confraternity.

[1] See J. E. Harrison: *Themis.*

Argos itself is something of a disappointment. While the place has legends and history about it enough to fill a volume, they do not attach themselves to any one definable spot. Further, the very facts that made it a great city in old days have kept it an important town in the worst of times, and that leads both to the destruction of old monuments and to the existence of obstacles when you hope to excavate their sites.

You cross Inachus as you come down from Mycenae to the capital, and are apt to find his bed as dry as it was of old, and you can hardly miss the hills of the double citadel of the place: the Aspis (so called from its resemblance to a circular shield flung down) and the Larissa, a name that goes back to pre-Hellenic days. Even what has been discovered in the modern town is counted second-rate in such a land as this. The Theatre would be a marvel in most places—but that at Epidaurus is finer by far. The Larissa contains a splendid 'Cyclopean' fortress, though the Venetian work that you see from below masks it till you actually enter the enceinte. Fine though it is, it is not so good as Tiryns or Mycenae. The old places that were left in ruin have secured a belated revenge on their spoiler. So, if you are travelling in Greece in the leisurely way you should, scramble up the steep Larissa by all means and you will be rewarded. If, however, you are tied to time, as is only too likely to be the case in these hurrying days, you may at least feel that you have lost nothing of incalculable value if you give the ancient city a miss.

VIII

SOUTHERN PELOPONNESUS

Lerna—The Nereids—Tegea—Mantinea—Sparta—Mistra—
Monemvasia—Langada—Pylos—Ithome

Agood motor road leads from Argos to Sparta, the distance
being about seventy miles, with the town of Tripolis as a
half-way point. The traveller, to begin with, has to go along
by Lerna on the western side of Nauplia Bay, where he skirts the
swamps that once were the haunt of the 'Lernaean Hydra', and can
see, if he likes, the very den of the noisome creature, now hallowed
by having been made a chapel of St. John. The evangelist, as we
know, was always ready to protect believers against poisonous
serpents.

Another old acquaintance of Heracles is here still in the person of
the Queen of the Nereids. A beautiful lady with sea-green hair (it is
pleasant to see that Horace was quite right when he spoke of the
virides Nereidum comas), who is known not too courteously as the
Lamia, can be seen here on moonlight nights. She stands waist-deep
in the water and invites any passer-by to come to her embrace—
which means death. As for Nymphs and Nereids—it is the latter
name that is used now for all sorts of spirits of this *genre*, whether of
mountain, forest, or water—they have not yet abandoned their old
land, and can anyone really wish to turn them out? Daughters of the
water (it would seem that the modern word for water, *nero*, is really
a good deal older than the classic one that it has displaced), they are
here still, and the gossamer that wreathes the grass in the dawning
is known by the beautiful name of 'Nereids' spinnings'. There are
glades where they may still be seen dancing by moonlight, and anyone who is bold enough to try may win the beautiful leader of them
to wife by capturing 'the kerchief'. To this day, in the country dances

153

that one may see in the villages, the leader of the 'chorus' of boys or girls (for mixed dancing is not encouraged) is linked to the rest by a kerchief, held by him or her and the next in the rank. The rest all hold hands, but this arrangement obviously gives the leader more freedom of movement. It seems that the Nymphs use it too. Is this the origin, one wonders, of the long scarf that Thetis always waves in the numerous pictures in which she appears on vases and which she was using when she was captured by the daring Peleus? One would like to think that it means more than just a pretty line in the composition.

Old men say that they have seen them, and one has even given the writer the story. He was gardener to an Englishman on Princes' Islands, off Constantinople, and the garden ran right down to the marge of the sea. He was there in the grey of the dawn, and he saw the band of Nereids come ashore: they discarded their tails and danced in human guise in all their naked beauty on the sand, while the gardener crouched behind the boat, knowing that if they saw that he saw them, madness at the very least would be his portion, yet as unable to withdraw his eyes from the marvellous spectacle as was Actaeon—or Tam o' Shanter—in like circumstances.

They steal children sometimes, as fairies are always likely to do; they invite them to dance with them in the glades, and wile them away to their own haunts, never to be seen again. One modern poet consoles the parents for their loss in words that have something of the ring of at least the silver age of Hellenic poetry:[1]

Trust ye the fable of yore: 'tis not Death but the Nymphs of the river
Seeing your daughter so sweet, loved her and stole her away.

Tripolis, the 'town of three cities', is quite a modern place, dating only from the days of the Turkish occupation, though it has been made the seat of a Metropolitan Bishop. The three cities to which it has made itself heir are those of Tegea, Mantinea, and Pallantium, but one suspects that the shades of the first two must look down on the third with scorn, for they both had a real history and status in classic days, while Pallantium was no more than a village, raised to rank as a city by some freak of a passing Antonine emperor.

[1] Τοῖς πάρος οὖν μύθοις πιστεύσετε, παῖδα γὰρ ἐσθλήν
Ἥρπασαν ὡς τέρπνην Ναίαδες οὐ Θάνατος.

At Tegea, there is really nothing above ground now, but it was once the site of the great temple of Athena Alea (said to have been so called from the name of Aleus its founder), which was one of the great monuments of the Peloponnesus and a sanctuary for any criminal. It had this peculiarity among temples of the Maiden goddess, that it was always served by a priest and not a priestess, though it is true that he was always a boy, and had to vacate his office as soon as he attained the age of puberty. A church is the only mark of the site now.

At least it was the work of a great artist, no less than Scopas, who was both architect and sculptor, and in the latter capacity was counted as one of the 'great four' of the Golden Age. Pheidias for majesty, Polycleitus for beauty, Scopas for passion, and Praxiteles for grace. Thus, Scopas carved the groups that adorned the pediment that he designed, and though they have perished, of course, with the temple, yet by good fortune excavation has yielded the heads of many of the figures, and these are now in the Museum at Athens, to justify the verdict that was popularly passed on the artist. One whole group represented the hunt of the Calydonian Boar, the pelt of which was one of the relics in the temple, and Pausanias has given a list of the heroes who appeared in it, though of course the identification of most of the heads is merely conjecture. There is one, however, of which we may be fairly sure, and that is the most recent addition to the group, a very fine face of Atalanta. We know that this athletic lady was in the great hunt, and indeed is said to have 'taken first spear' (or rather first shaft, as she used a bow), which should have entitled her to the tushes. The subject is a favourite one on sarcophagi, and these may perhaps give some idea of what the original composition was like; though in that case, Scopas' courtesy seems to have been rather to seek. Atalanta is usually represented in these groups as shooting in a style as dangerous to her companions as the most exacting opponent of female sport could desire as an example.

Tegea was the scene of one of the few Spartan defeats, one inflicted on Charilaus, nephew of Lycurgus, and therefore so early in history that they may at least have been able to urge that their discipline had hardly 'set'. The king had ideas of getting control of Arcadia, a thing which Sparta certainly achieved a little later. The Delphic oracle had declared that Apollo could not give them as much as that, but that 'their feet should measure out the Plain of Tegea'. The Spartans therefore came prepared for victory, bringing fetters with them for the benefit of their Tegean prisoners, but were caught in an ambush and utterly cut up. The *coup de grâce* was given by the women of the city, who took arms and came out to fight under their queen, Marpessa, and had the joy of leading their captives into the city. They had to till the plain in the fetters they had brought, thus fulfilling the prophecy, and the chains were naturally kept as a trophy and shewn to Pausanias on the walls of the temple.

Mantinea has perished as completely as Tegea, but there at least the circuit of her ancient walls can be traced, though only the *socle*, or base portion, remains. This, which is of fine masonry, stands for most of the circuit at a height of about three feet above ground, and probably was never higher, the rest of the wall being mud brick. At least, we know that this was the case when in 385 B.C. the Spartans flooded out the place by damming the river, and forced it to surrender by reducing its walls to wet mud; and it appears that when the town was rebuilt after the fall of Sparta, in 371 B.C., they followed the old system of fortification and only diverted the course of the River Ophis to guard against a repetition of the former disaster.

The 'Praxiteles Sculptures' from here rest in the Athens Museum and are certainly his design, though they may be the actual work of a pupil. The three plaques, which represent the contest of Apollo and Marsyas, formed three sides of the base (the fourth has perished) of a great group which that artist carved and which Pausanias saw here. It represented 'Latona and her children', and was one of the treasures of a double temple here, sacred one half to Asclepius and one half to Apollo and Artemis. The statue has perished, and these slabs were used as the pavement of a church in which they were fortunately put face downward, and so were preserved to be rescued by a French excavator in 1887.

Between Mantinea and Tripolis lies an open plain, narrowing a little about half-way, between the hills of Maenalus to the west and another range to the east. The famous battlefield known as Scopê, *perhaps* from the last 'look' of Epaminondas,[1] was at this point, and

---

[1] Actually, the name Scopê probably belonged to a small watch-tower, the ruins of which stand on the hill Mytika above. The battle was fought on the plain below, and we need not think that his friends carried a mortally wounded man up a steep hill to see an action that we know broke off when he fell. Epaminondas had been warned by one of the ambiguous answers that the Delphic oracle was fond of, that 'Pelagos' would be his bane. In consequence of this, he would never go to sea, and he was killed near an oak-wood of that name.

on the lower slopes of Maenalus. The actual site is not certain, for the oak wood of Pelagos that once marked it has vanished, as has the tomb of the hero also. This is, however, of the less consequence, as the action was one of those decided by tactics rather than position; Epaminondas used the same scheme as at Leuctra—plus an element of surprise in this case—and threw the whole weight of a strong left wing on his opponent's right and broke it, while 'refusing' the rest of his line. It took more than one good beating to make a slow-moving Spartan think out the answer to that attack.

Arcadia was always the backward and primitive part of Greece, the only district that had no sea-coast or port—the upland valleys of the interior. It was inhabited too by an old race, some of the first Hellenes to come into the land in prehistoric days, who were afterwards driven up into the hills of the centre by the invading Dorians. Thus, it was a place where old beliefs and habits would crystallize, and where they may be found even now. It was the home of Pan of old, and the shepherds aver that they hear his pipings still in his own Arcadia. Other primitive beliefs survive too. We once knew a Russian lady who spent a summer in one of these hill villages, and was sitting out, in a white dress as it happened, on the bridge in the dusk as the boys were driving back the goats for the night. She saw them stop and stare suspiciously as they approached, and when they drew nearer with great caution and then began to gather up stones she thought it was time to intervene and did so with a sharp question. The lads dropped the stones with huge relief: 'Oh Kyria, it is only you. We thought it was old Glycerion who died last week. She was so loath to leave the village that we made sure she had come back again.' There was no reason why she should have come back, they explained, for she had been properly laid out, with the death-penny on her tongue, though the idea is now that the use of it is not to pay the grim ferryman but to provide the inevitable *bakhshish* to Telonia, who controls the custom-house of heaven, and will not otherwise let you in.[1]

Charon, though he is not the ferryman, appears in a different character, and one that is quite probably far older in origin than the more familiar aspect. He is the collector and guide of souls that have departed; and when the rain clouds lie low on the hills in the winter, all know that it is Charon who is leading souls to their grim bourne, and that they may never rest any more than the clouds that

[1] The thought that metal has virtue to keep off evil spirits may not be absent, but the other explanation is the one folk give.

they resemble, for if Charon once let them scatter to their familiar homes even his power might find it hard to collect them again.

When minds are working on these lines, it is comprehensible that the common mind should believe in the Centaur whom we have described above, and in his even uglier cousin, the *Kalo-Kantzaros*. This horror is a hobgoblin even more formidable and gruesome than the Centaur, for he may appear in almost any monstrous form, and not only in that of man mixed with some more or less familiar beast. He may come and terrify, he may carry off children or women, but fortunately like other bogeys he is easily deceived, and if only you keep your head you may be able to dodge him. The farmer whom these goblins beset when he was driving home the mule laden with flour from the mill escaped them by getting on to the back of the mule and lying there face down. 'A sack on each side', he heard the leading Kantzaros say to his fellows, 'and one on the top too. But where is the man?' They hunted around and about for him but did not discover him between the sacks till such time as he had got safe to his home, where they might not follow. The mill, however, is a place where they always haunt.

Most of the year, fortunately, these goblins are confined underground, where they gnaw forever at the roots of the great tree that bears up heaven and earth,[1] but in 'the Twelve Days' between Christmas and Epiphany, they are out. It is a reversal of our fathers' belief—for once the more beautiful—that in that blessed season no evil spirit stirs abroad, 'So hallowed and so gracious is the time', but perhaps it is as well, for in those twelve days the root of the Great Tree grows again and the world is safe for another year. Those days, however, are dangerous, and the danger is even greater for babies, for those who make their first appearance then are only too likely to become changelings of the most objectionable description so that Christmastide is a most inauspicious time to be born in.

Of course, there is protection to be secured—there always is. These hobgoblins can only go in straight lines, so that if you put obstacles in their way—a log across the path up to the door is enough to bar that way of access—you are secure from them. In the room, it is best to keep up a blazing fire in the grate, for the chimney gives a straight way down that they are sure to try, and that must be secured.

[1] This tree is not a classic idea at all, but our own ancestors in the north had the same notion, and believed also in a foul monster that gnawed for ever at the root of the 'Ash Ygg-drasil'. Seemingly, the Cretans of the Minoan age had the same superstition, so that it would seem that we have here a survival of something older than anything Hellenic.

On the Feast of New Waters, which is Epiphany, when the remembrance of the Baptism of Our Lord hallows all waters for the year and the *Papaz* comes around with incense and holy water to sanctify every room, then these devils have of course to go to their own place, and vanish, chanting:

> *Quick, begone, let us away;*
> *Here comes the Pot-bellied Priest*
> *With his censer in his hand*
> *And his sprinkling vessel, too.*
> *He has purified the streams,*
> *And the Holy Water will scald us.*

Not that Arcadian superstitions are all of this grim nature. We remember an English lady who was wandering there and found that she had been the means of crediting the Blessed Virgin Mary with a new and quite delightful miracle. On her walks she had noticed a stray goat, and soon after found a small girl in the depths of woe. Asking the reason, she was told that the child had lost her goat and feared that she would be punished accordingly. The English lady promised help, and the goat was found and all was well. Then she asked, 'What is your name, dear?' 'Maria, Kyria.' 'Oh, do you know that is my name too?' (Her name happened to be Mary.) 'Oh yes, Kyria Panagîa, of course I know that is your name. You found my goat.'

In Arcadia, the kindly deities are still felt to be walking among men, so with that thought we can proceed on our wanderings, over the low ridge that bounds the old province to the south, and away down long hills into a warmer climate, as we enter 'Hollow Lacedaemon' and see the snows of Taygetus rise ever higher above our heads.

The Spartan is a proverb for stern courage and hard living, the Prussian of ancient Greece, but yet his home in the land is exactly what it ought not to be, a wide fertile valley under the shelter of a mountain with a climate as soft as that of Granada; far more beautiful and less rugged than Attica, and of a type that one would say was sure to be a 'Capua' for any race that came down from the north and settled there. We know what an 'Acropolis' ought to be, from Athens and Corinth, but at Sparta we find a low and gentle hill in the middle of a fat, flat plain, some fifty feet high, that never was fortified even till mediaeval times.

In her great days, Sparta was not even a city, but as Thucydides says, a group of villages with no noteworthy buildings and no walls. 'Her ramparts are her men, but were she ruined nobody who saw her would ever believe her to have been great.' Of course she was fortified in a later age, hurriedly in 295 B.C. against Demetrius Poliorcetes and Pyrrhus, more scientifically later by the Tyrant Nabis, and it was only when she was fortified that she was taken by an enemy—by the Achaean League. Then they abandoned the ancient and obsolete system of Lycurgus save in so far as it concerned the training of the boys.

Thus, we must not expect, at Sparta, buildings such as we have seen at Athens, or even look for another Corinth. She is a country town now, and never was more than a group of villages with a large space in between them which constituted her Agora, or as her sons called it, her Chorus. Hereabouts were such buildings as the Senate House and here took place the great dances which formed such a feature of Spartan life, the Gymnopaedia of boys and (in their turn) of the girls which not even the news of Leuctra was allowed to interrupt. The Plane Tree Grove, 'on an island in the Eurotas,' was the scene of the great annual fight between two picked troops of lads, the bands 'of Lycurgus' and 'of Heracles', 'in which', says Cicero, 'I have seen these parties of lads fighting with incredible fury, dying rather than confess themselves beaten.'

The Acropolis, which is just above a rather late and uninteresting Theatre, contained two shrines. One of these was that of the principal deity of Sparta, Carnian Apollo, who seems to have existed here from of old as an agricultural divinity but to have been of such a character that the invading Spartans could adopt him as identical with their own tribal god. The other deity was that Athena of the Brazen House whose very rough sanctuary was covered with plates of brass, or rather bronze, and appears in history as the scene of the deaths of the two kings who were suspected of tampering with the sacrosanct constitution of Lycurgus, Pausanias and Agis. The former, it may be remembered, took sanctuary in the place when his schemes were detected, and the Constitutionalists, led by his own mother, blocked up the doors and kept him a prisoner till he was starving, when he could be carried out without violence and brought to judgement. Agis, who tried to reform the system at a moment when every decent man felt that reform was long overdue, also took refuge here, but was decoyed out of the sacred precinct by his opponents and made prisoner. One famous statue has recently been brought to light here also, the magnificent portrait of Leonidas, which is now one of the treasures of the Athens Museum. His Heroon, or what is believed to be such, is elsewhere in Sparta township.

There are two shrines that we know existed in Sparta which the conscientious Pausanias seems to have missed in his round of sight-seeing: that of Lycurgus and that of 'the Great Twin Brethren, to whom the Dorians pray'. Of course it may be, particularly in the light of the discovery of the Statue, that the Heroon called the Leonidaeon is really that of Lycurgus, and that the shrine of Leonidas was on the Acropolis; but of the other, no trace has been found. That it existed is certain, for in one of the wars of Magna Graecia, between Locri and Croton, we hear that the *Sacra* of the Twin Brethren were brought from Sparta to help the former city, and that a special cabin was provided for them in the ship. It was no more than a *temenos* with no temple, and the Dioscuri were repre-sented by T-like fetish-poles.

Of all Spartan shrines, however, the most famous is that of Artemis Orthia with its cruel ritual, and fortunately this is by far the best preserved in the place, having been excavated by the British School, in the period 1906–10. The general idea of the worship practised there is known, and it was this: Orestes brought the famous image of 'the upright Artemis' who so delighted in human sacrifice, from Tauris when he rescued Iphigeneia. It is true that 'those Athenians' said that they had the real image at Brauron, in Attica, but that was not genuine. There was evidence sufficient of that in the rock down by Gythion, on which Orestes sat and where he was cured of his madness. The little archaic image, a wooden one as is usual with these old types, demanded that its altar should be wet with blood, and according to the Spartan tradition this was done by means of human sacrifice at first, though in the days of Lycurgus the scourging of the boys as a contest of endurance was substituted, and if the executioners did not 'play the game' and endeavoured to spare the lads, the image testified its anger by growing heavy in the arms of the priestess who superintended the whole proceeding.

The question arises, what was this rite in its origin? Was it a human sacrifice to the Great Mother with whom Artemis was so often identified, and of which we certainly find evidence elsewhere in the Peloponnesus, as at Ithome and Patras for instance? Or was it a thing peculiar to Sparta in its origin, a contest of endurance such as we find among other primitive tribes[1] e.g. the Bechuanas, whose lads

---

[1] There was a shrine of Dionysus where girls were whipped—at Aleus in Arcadia.

would often, like the Spartans, endure even unto death without flinching?

The evidence of excavation suggests the second explanation. At Limnae, 'the swamp', where the sanctuary stood (it was always marshy, till the water was dammed out by the Romans), the *temenos* contains a 'succession' of four altars, one under the other. Of these, the uppermost one is Roman, and therefore late, and one classic, of about 600 B.C. The two others are, the one archaic, dating from perhaps 800 B.C., and the other primitive, from perhaps 200 years earlier.

There are also two temples, again one under the other. The one of classic date is contemporary with the altar of that type, though it has been repaired in Roman days, but the older is archaic, of mud brick, and giving evidence that it was destroyed by a flood and replaced, without there being any breach in the cult of the place. At the very bottom, under everything, a rough pavement has been found, made of 'cobbles' from the bed of the Eurotas.

In other words, we find nothing on the site that is earlier than what we have now learned to call the comparatively modern date of the original Dorian invasion, a mere 1000 B.C., though that is two centuries or so anterior to what we used to call the beginning of all history. We may take it that the sanctuary was founded then, and that Artemis Orthia is purely Dorian and not older; she is not the same as the Cretan Great Mother, though a religious type that might be quite easily identified with her. This makes it likely that the rite was always a savage initiation to manhood though one does not wish to abandon the Spartan tradition that it was, also, a human sacrifice softened down a little.

There are plenty of other points of interest in the *temenos*, which was just inside the city wall as constructed by Nabis in 200 B.C. The Romans were so delighted with a spectacle that exactly suited their tastes that they built a theatre round about the altar, so that the temple stands to it in the same relative position as the stage, with the altar in the middle of the *orchestra!* Here, too, are the bases of several of the statues that were erected in honour of the *Bomo-nikes*, the lad who was victorious in the grim contest. It shows how long it continued, that we find one here that actually dates from the fourth century A.D. in honour of the 'conspicuous endurance' of the boy commemorated.

A feature of this shrine is, the number of the votive offerings that were discovered in it, of so ancient a period for Hellenic objects as that between the ninth and seventh centuries before Christ. As is known, the precious metals were taboo in Sparta by Lycurgus' law, and even the currency was iron. However often that might be disregarded in practice, it would seem that it had to be honoured in theory at the temples, and votive offerings were not therefore of silver or gold, but of lead. This has had the happy result that the little figurines that it was the custom to offer here were not worth the trouble of taking away, and accumulated in such amounts that they had literally to be swept off the path from altar to temple; the excavators found them here by the basketful, and plenty of choice specimens can be seen in the museum, and some even found on the spot to this day.[1]

Of course, the whipping was not the only festival held in this precinct. There was a contest of song and 'declamation', though eloquence was not an ordinary Spartan gift, and there was a great harvest festival in which the girls were the principal actors. It is suggested that the bronze sickles that were also found here were votive offerings from that solemnity. A very characteristic Spartan observance that took place here was 'The Stealing Contest'. Cheeses were put upon the altar and closely guarded, while competitors had to come by night and steal them thence. It will be readily guessed that the penalty for failing was a sound whipping.

If classical Sparta offers comparatively little above ground, its neighbourhood contains two memorials of exceptional interest from that mediaeval history of Greece that is really part of her story, as well as of the general tale of European civilization. When the Franks came down into Greece in 1204, as already stated, and made it prize of war, it was the fertile Morea that specially attracted these men of Burgundy, and they made Sparta their capital. Not that they called it by that name; those whose tongues made 'Dieu d'Amour' out of 'Didymus' and said that the castle on the twin-peaked rock of that name in Cyprus was the spot to which Cupid took Psyche, were not likely to pronounce Lacedaemon aright. They made it into the good French 'La Cremonie', and when they had taken it, then (according to the testimony of the sympathetic English Bishop William of Faversham who has written their story) 'les damoiseaux et les demoiselles menoient la plus belle vie possible'. It was then that

---

[1] All *antikas* found on an excavated site are Greek national property, but Greek courtesy invariably asks the excavator to select some objects among those found—besides duplicates—for himself.

their duke, Guillaume de Villehardouin, felt that it would be well to have a stronghold, and erected Mistra, 'Cream-cheese Castle,' on a hill some four to five miles from his capital, a spur of Taygetus which had that name from its shape. Unluckily, 'la plus belle vie' did not last very long. The nobles went adventuring in 1260 against the Greeks in Macedonia, and met at Pelagonia a disaster almost as complete as that which befell their northern kindred at Scripu. They were caught in an ambush and practically the whole of the nobility were captured and held. They began to speak of decent ransom, expecting the usual easy terms, but found to their horror that the Greek was not in this for sport, but to recover lost territory to which he thought he had a right. 'Mistra, Maina, Monemvasia' were the three castles the cession of which he demanded before the gentlemen could be let go, and these were the three keys of the southern Morea. Maina guarded the entrance to that untaken peninsula of Taenaron, where grim men of the old Spartan blood (they still proudly call themselves Lakones or Zakones) were not to be turned out of their rugged land by any force the Frankish knights could bring. Monemvasia we shall deal with later, and Mistra was as we have seen Villehardouin's own 'Saucy Castle', that looked down from its rock on his very capital. A great *parlement* was held at Nikli to discuss the matter, and it was the first ladies' parliament in history, for all the tenants-in-chief who had the right to come were in durance vile with the Greek, and the ladies represented their lords. The practically-minded English bishop was for letting the nobles remain in the pit they had digged for themselves, but the ladies all wanted their husbands back, and the terms were agreed to.

After that, the keys of the Morea were in Greek hands that never let them go again, and a Greek city, with Byzantine churches, monasteries and nunneries, gathered at the foot of Mistra and remained there. Gradually, though there was no fighting, the Latin rule weakened. The type became Graecized by intermarriage, the church became Greek, and in fact that came to pass which we see in Cyprus also, where the Greek stock, though to all appearance weaker and less disciplined than the Latin, yet prevails against it in the long run. Unhappily, as the Latin grip slipped, it was the Turk that began to rise above the horizon, and though the Latin might have been able to keep him at bay the common people would have none of such help, for 'better Turk than Latin' is a cry that was not raised for the first time when the Conqueror was outside Constantinople. When efforts were made to get help at the price of selling such fortresses as

12. Pantanassa nunnery, Mistra

13. Cliffs of Sphacteria: East side, North end of the island. Showing the gully up which the Messenians ascended to the crest and gained a point in the rear of the Spartans

Acrocorinth and Mistra to the best fighting force of the day, the Knights of St. John, the people would have none of the bargain.

The intellectual Greek life still went on at Mistra, and the place even produced the last of the Platonic philosophers, Gemistos Plethon, in the year 1400. He was a great lecturer on the works of his master, and his pupils taught at Oxford; but he was a prophet of but little honour in his own country, on account of his views on church questions. He was before his time, and urged that all Greeks ought to unite against a common foe, and even use the treasures of the church, if need be, as a war fund to keep out the Moslem, and that they ought to make such 'parasites on the body politic' as the younger monks do more for the country. This heretical doctrine brought the professor into the hottest of hot water in those circles, and he fell into disrepute.

The Peloponnesus was, of course, a province of the Empire of Constantinople, falling naturally into its old position as the Latin rule faded away. The ruler of it was generally a 'despot' of the royal family, and the last of them was that Constantine Palaeologus who was the last emperor there, so the man whose heroic death throws a final gleam of lustre on his long line of predecessors, was crowned as Despot and Emperor in Mistra. Of course, after the disaster of 1453, the land of Greece was ready for the conqueror to take when he willed, though it was not till 1460 that he did actually put an end to the last of the tributary Greek rulers. Mistra then died away, but the churches remain to this day, monuments of a singularly romantic episode in the long story of Greece.

Monemvasia, which is another expedition worth making from Sparta—for those who happen to be interested in the mediaeval portion of Greek history—is a full fifty miles from the city, and on the eastern side of the Malea promontory, about twenty miles north of its cape. The road to it goes near to Gythion, the old port of Sparta, which is some thirty miles distant from it. Spartans never pretended to be sailors.

This 'Gibraltar of Greece', a great rock that is only connected with the mainland by a causeway (whence its name, *Mone Embasis*, 'Only one way in'), was a self-governing town in the year 1200, and its little harbours made it a big depot for the Greek wine trade that then had almost the monopoly of Europe. Indeed, the sweet Greek wine, which actually came mostly from Crete, where it still flourishes, was even known by a corruption of the name of its distributing centre, *malvoisie* or malmsey, for *pace* 'Simon the Cellarer' these are one and the same wine.[1] At Venice, it was so popular that a *malfasia* came to mean a wine shop, and still gives its name to a *fondamenta* there; the Archbishop even declared in Latin, which was as deplorable as some will judge his sentiments to be, that 'Vinum de Malvasia nihil de malfasia habet sed nomen', so that His Grace at least appreciated it.

This town, nearly impregnable as it was upon its rock, was left alone at first when the Franks occupied Greece, and the Byzantine Eagle flew there till 1246 unchallenged. Then Villehardouin did undertake the siege, but the solitary fortress held out till 1249 and only surrendered then on the condition that Monemvasia was to be a free town still, taxing itself, and rendering feudal service only, and that at sea and for good pay.

We have seen how the return of this fortress was the first thing that the Emperor of Constantinople demanded when he got the opportunity, and it became Greek once more, building a cathedral of St. Sophia, a fine church that still stands there, in the year 1280, and having the salutary rule that if any man should die intestate, his estate went at once to pay for repairs to the fortifications.

When the Turks were in the Morea, even the Conqueror himself did not like the look of this place, and once again for some years, the flag flew there alone, over the last relic of the empire of the Palaeologi. It was a scion of the royal house that defended it, and when he realized that there was no longer an empire left to fight for and that the little fort must have a lord, he ceded himself and it in 1463 to the only imperial power that seemed left—the Pope. We fear that the Holy Father was rather embarrassed by the gift, for he took an early opportunity of passing it on to Venice, so that for eighty years more the castle still remained a Christian stronghold, even if it was now under the Lion of St. Mark. When Venice was beaten in war in 1540, then, to the horror of all the defenders, they actually agreed to cede the unbeaten and untaken fort, and it passed under the Crescent for the first time. Still, the 'Serene Republic' did not forget and when in 1686 she put her hands on the Morea again—it was under her general, Morosini, who had just been capturing Athens and destroying the Parthenon—she attacked this point, and again, and for the third time, Monemvasia held out in her own strength for four long years, to yield to sheer starvation at last. In 1714, when Venice lost her Greek possessions again, and finally, a very feeble show was made. The whole of the Morea was lost in 100 days, and

[1] 'Old Simon the cellarer hath good store of Malmsey and Malvoisie.'

this castle with it, though no man was more profoundly astonished at its surrender than the Ottoman commander-in-chief. 'I couldn't possibly have taken the place' was his consoling remark to its commander, after he had bluffed him into surrender.

In 1825 Monemvasia made its last appearance in history—for as a fortress, modern science has rendered it obsolete—and that was in the Greek War of Independence. Then once more the Turks held out, at least until the last rat (some said the last child) had been eaten, and one fears that one of the massacres that stained that war of bitter revenge followed on the surrender.

For four times in its history of 600 years that little place has held out alone, for four years and more, keeping the flag to which it owed allegiance (whether Byzantine Eagle, Venetian Lion or Ottoman Crescent) flying after all hope of relief had gone. No place has a prouder history than Monemvasia.

Many who are down as far as Sparta have a most laudable ambition to get over the Taygetus into Messenia, and for those who do not mind a rather long day upon a mule (the distance is not more than twenty miles as a crow flies but the track winds and mules do not hurry) the trip gives magnificent scenery and absolutely no danger. At the date of writing there is only a mule-track through the grand Langada Gorge but as mule-tracks go quite a good one, and you can find all the accommodation that a traveller needs in Kalamata, though that is no more than a modern port, with no antiquities to show beyond a Frankish castle above it. From that centre you can easily go by car to two places each of which have left their mark deeply on Greek history: Pylos and Ithome, distant respectively about thirty and twenty miles.

Pylos first appears in history in Homer, as the home of Nestor, that most venerable and respectable bore who is forever wearing out the patience of his hearers with his reminiscences of 'the very strongest of all the men I have ever killed' (*Iliad* vii, 145) and (iv, 303-09) 'the way we used to draw up battles in the good old days'. He certainly lived at Pylos, but there has always been a dispute whether his home is the headland near Sphacteria, or a site of the same name some twenty miles north, which has the authority of Strabo behind it. Professor Blegen's excavations made in 1939, though not yet complete, may be said to have settled the question in favour of the Sphacterian Pylos. There, at the modern village of Englianos, four miles north of the Lagoon called that of Osman Agha, he has found an acropolis of late Mycenean date, with walls, plan, and decoration much resembling that of Tiryns, and an archive room that may yet give us the key to the Cretan inscriptions (see ch. xi, note). There are also the remains of a very fine *tholos* tomb, not yet thoroughly examined, but unquestionably once the last home of a revered ruler. As no discovery of anything near this date has been made at the rival Pylos, we may be content to accept this site as that of the capital of the Pylian kingdom, and the place where (*Odyssey* III) the aged Nestor has the satisfaction of entertaining Telemachus, son of his old comrade Odysseus. One may even venture to describe the great *tholos* as the tomb of Nestor himself. Nestor apart, Pylos, or rather the Island of Sphacteria, is no more than the scene of an insignificant episode in a forgotten war. But, as it has happened that a historian of genius has taken the fancy to tell us about it in detail, while men read the fourth book of Thucydides, they will want to go and study the scene on the spot. It has this rare advantage. The little campaign was very complicated, and in it everything depends on the understanding of the ground. It all took place some 2,400 years ago, but the spot was normally uninhabited then and has been so ever since, with the result that it is so entirely unaltered that one can trace with certainty every move in that complicated game. There are few campaigns separated from us by one tenth of that time of which that can be said.

The occupation was almost an accident. The Athenian fleet was on cruising duty when a mere trireme-captain, Demosthenes (the episode illustrates the very loose discipline of the day), decided to occupy this point with his own little squadron, and was left there to 'play his own hand' by a very unwilling admiral, who told him that there were 'plenty of waste headlands on that coast, if he wanted to waste State resources in occupying them'. The place was only fortified because the men had nothing better to do!

Yet, the occupation of this point was like the 'kidney punch' of a skilled boxer—a mere tap on the back with no power behind it, which yet paralyses the main attack. The thought of an enemy in Messene, a focusing point for that ever-seething hatred of serfs 'who would like to eat the Spartans raw' (as Xenophon says of their feeling at a later date) brought the Spartan army back at once from the Athenian front to attack that little fort from the sea. We can see the exact point—the one possible point of landing, and that a very bad one, on the sea front of Pylos Peninsula—where Brasidas made his attack, and was repulsed. They could blockade the fort, and for

168

that purpose occupy the Island of Sphacteria 'with 420 Spartans and their Helots' (who would amount to at least one per man), but could do no more. Soon, the Athenian fleet was on the spot once more, and Demosthenes, whose obvious success seems to have put him in practical command now, could defeat the Spartan fleet in Sphacteria Bay and blockade the island in his turn. There was now almost a panic at Sparta, for here was a large Athenian force 'dug in' on their weakest side, and a force of 'Spartiatae' cut off on the island. They sought an armistice, and were even ready to make peace on a basis of *status quo*, a peace that would have enabled Athens to finish her Acropolis as she meant and to do her work fully for the world, but the project was howled down by Cleon the Tanner. The armistice ended and the immediate surrender of Sphacteria was expected, particularly as the Spartan fleet (surrendered on terms during the truce) was detained by a rather mean trick, and food was very short upon the island.[1] Still, blockade runners fed the garrison, and matters dragged on till Athens grew impatient and the ugly side of her democracy showed up. Cleon voiced it as usual: 'Were the generals *men* they would finish the job and he would do it in a fortnight himself.' He was sent himself, and by either marvellous luck or a hint from the front, took the very light troops that were wanted, and arrived to find his luck holding still, and the Spartan cover on the island, the forest, destroyed by a fire.

He and Demosthenes at least decided to make sure work of it. The garrison was down to 420—for it would seem that the Helots had either slipped away singly or else declined to fight for their masters now that they were in a hole—yet Cleon landed at least 4,500 men (some explanations would make it 10,000) to deal with that handful. We can see where that landing was effected on the island. Even so, the Athenians dared not close with so dreaded an enemy. All day the fight went on, the Spartans remaining unbroken, and gradually falling back to the hill-top at the north end of the island, where what was left of them stood at bay behind a ruined old wall, that we can see there still; and even then, men would not come to grips with the wounded lion. Spartan discipline was of a very high order. Thucydides describes the last act tersely, and an English scholar has traced things out on the field. A Messenian who knew the ground said that he could get men round the Spartan rear,

---

[1] The one slip in the account of Thucydides is his understatement of the width of the southern channel that divides Sphacteria from the shore. That deep-water channel must have been then about its present width.

the landward side of the isle. On that side, this part of Sphacteria falls in steep cliffs to the sea, but active men can get down to sea level at one point, unseen from the crest, and make their way along the sea-marge to a place exactly below the old fort which the Spartans were holding, 700 feet above. At that very point, a small ravine, steep enough but climbable, runs up the hill; it does not reach the actual crest, but dies out in a shelf or notch but a few feet below it. Messenians who were out for revenge could get up there unseen, in single file, could gather on the shelf, and appear 'suddenly' as we are told, immediately above the heads of the Spartans at the ruined wall, and make further resistance hopeless. The long day's work was done. The result is as high a testimony to the prestige of Spartans in Greece as could well be imagined, for these men had fought all day against ten times (if not twenty times) their number; they were utterly exhausted by thirst for they had been fighting in the dust and ashes of the recently burnt woodland, and a full third of the force was down, including all their officers. Now, after consulting their general and getting his permission, they laid down their arms[1] —and all Greece was amazed that they did not fight to the very end! It was the Messenians' day of revenge for much, and their trophy at Olympia is a thing we wonder at to this day.

Sphacteria Bay, under its modern name of Navarino, makes one more appearance in history in the Greek War of Independence. The patriots' cause had been going down steadily, and though European interest in their fate was increasing it was just a question whether it would come to anything before the Greeks were destroyed; and Ibrahim Pasha, the Egyptian Turk, had brought his fleet and army to end things. He had landed his army in Navarino Bay and his fleet was there still, when the allied squadron of English, French and Russians entered the bay as well, with Edward Codrington in command. Somehow, as does happen when nerves are so tense, the guns went off and the action began, and by morning the Turkish fleet had ceased to exist. Ibrahim Pasha, a fierce old soldier, grinned as he looked out over the bay next day. 'No retreat for my fellows now. Win we must,' he said. Officials in England were scared to their very marrow, and sent out letters to Codrington deploring 'this untoward incident'; but the Duke of Clarence who was Lord of the Admiralty—then known unofficially as Silly Billy, and afterwards

[1] Their shields were kept as trophies in Athens, and seen by Pausanias 160 A.D. One was found—in a cistern—by the Americans in 1936: it is marked 'Athens from Spartans. Pylos'.

as William IV—took the edge off the rebuke that he had to sign, and incidentally expressed the opinion of the man-in-the-street, by scrawling a message to his old fellow-midshipman at the foot of it. It ran thus: 'Well done Ned! Bill.'

In effect, the thing was now done, for the guns of Navarino pushed the timid cabinets into action, and Greek independence was secured. Ibrahim and his army were removed to Egypt again in British ships, and that old fighter (for the Turk to do him justice never bears malice over a fight fairly fought, whether it be won or lost) thought that the best thing he could do would be to take a British girl to wife! And he married a Scots lass.

Ithome, 'ladder-like Ithome' (no one who has tried to climb it will ask why the name was given to it), is about twenty miles from Kalamata, and can be easily reached by motor, either as an excursion from that centre or on the way north from that point. It has always been the great sanctuary and stronghold of the Messenian tribe, the natural Acropolis of the Stenyclarus Plain, the most fertile land of Greece. Now the only monument on the summit is a monastery, inhabited by but one hermit, though the ancient threshing-floor is the site of the old sanctuary, the scene of the events we now describe.

Religiously, this mountain has always been a centre of the cult of Zeus, the sky-god whom the Hellenes brought in with them and whose sanctuaries extend in a line down all this coast of Greece: Dodona, Olympia, Lycaeon, and this hill as the fourth. There are traces of human sacrifice having been practised at each of them, a habit that, as we have seen, went on longer in Hellas than we sometimes think. (Still, we need not wonder, for it took a miracle and nothing less to convince Abraham that the Most High did not require it of him, and the custom was really dying out in Greece before the lesson had been learnt by his descendants. Indeed, the rite was practised at Jerusalem almost as late as at Ithome.) Jer. xxxii. 35.

But, though these sanctuaries of Zeus the sky-god mark the line of advance of the migrating Hellenic stock, on Ithome Zeus meets a cult older than himself, if one with which his worship could be identified. This is the worship of Zagreus, son-husband of the Great Mother in Crete, a figure with whom we deal in a later chapter. Here we must only note that most of the Cretan legends and *dramatis personae* are transferred hither, and we find Zeus born on Ithome instead of Ida, nurtured by the nymph of that name and hidden by the Curetes as there, though it is from Saturn that they conceal him

171

rather than from the Titans. The Megaron of the Curetes on Ithome was the only instance in Greece of that characteristically Cretan cult. While it is a Cretan as well as a Hellenic Zeus who is revered here, the Artemis who also has her sanctuary on Ithome is not the moon-goddess or the huntress, but in origin the grimmest form of the Great Mother of Crete, the Kali-like figure who demands tribute of the life she gives.

The Messenians, whose sanctuary this was, were the old neighbour-enemies of Sparta, and not, we think, of Dorian race at all, for even their legends, as well as their worship, are positively anti-Dorian. The principal deity of Sparta as we have seen, was Apollo, and the favourite legend of Messene was of Marpessa, the only girl who ever turned Apollo down! He fell in love with this maiden—of course a distinct person from her namesake of Tegea—and so did a human lover, Idas. Apollo contemptuously bade her choose between god and mortal, and to his astonishment Marpessa chose the lover who would grow old along with her, and who at least would not be sure to abandon her when her beauty began to fade.

In the great wars between Sparta and Messene—which begin 600 B.C.—Aristodemus is the hero of the first, and inflicts on Sparta, on the very mountain of Ithome, a defeat that she admitted to be one of the heaviest of her career. Even at that date, equipment in Greece had become stereotyped in the two forms of heavy and light infantry, the Hoplite and the Peltast; and the Spartan relied upon the first. Any visitor to Mount Ithome, however, will understand that the heavy-armed man was badly handicapped on ground such as that, while the ordinary Peltast only carried weapons that were too light for any real effect. Aristodemus had introduced a new equipment, giving the Peltast a better armament without sacrificing his mobility; and in consequence he scored heavily on this occasion, as did the Athenian Iphicrates in a later age, by the same methods and over the same enemy. How was it that so effective a reform could be introduced twice and twice forgotten? Still, Sparta was too heavy metal for Messene, and a grim local oracle bade them make the sacrifice that would compel the favour of heaven; let them 'sacrifice a pure maiden to the gods below'. Aristodemus was willing to give his own daughter to the cause, and it seems that she, like Jephthah's daughter, was not unwilling to die for her people, so that all was made ready to renew the ancient rites on Mount Ithome. However, the girl's lover intervened, and when his wild protests were disregarded, he tried to preserve the girl's life by the sacrifice of her

14. Tower on the Wall, Messene. The photograph is taken from a point within the wall, for the tower naturally projects from its line to give a flanking fire. The path on the battlements (the 'allure') is continuous for the whole circuit, passing through the towers, as the doorway shows. Occasional stairways lead down from it

15. Messene: Megalopolis gate

good name, and declared her to be no maiden and so no meet sacrifice to the gods. Aristodemus in fury slew the girl with his own hand on the holy mountain, but not as a sacrifice, and the rite was void.

The nation now applied to Delphi, and received the reply that the one that first placed a hundred tripods on Mount Ithome in honour of Zeus, would be the victor. Spartan wits were sharpened by the emergency for once, and while the Messenian bronze-workers toiled night and day, they sent an adherent to the sanctuary, and next morning the owners of it found a hundred miniature three-legged stools standing there in rows! The Messenians lost all heart then and evacuated their stronghold, while Aristodemus slew himself on the tomb of the daughter whom he had now recognized was innocent, and the nation sank into definite subordination to Sparta.

There was, however, another rising sixty years later, under Aristomenes as the leader. It is true that this revolt had another centre, at Eira in the north, but Ithome was recognized as the shrine and a solemn sacrifice of three hecatombs on the Holy Mount marked the beginning of the war. Again, big victories were won, notably at 'the Boar's Grave' on the slopes of Eira, and Sparta was so disheartened that she thought of peace, and was only spurred to further effort by the songs of Tyrtaeus. Again, she proved too strong for Messene, and Aristomenes, defeated and captured, was thrown into a pit somewhere in the great Langada Gorge. A fox, according to the tale that used to be familiar to every child, guided him thence, but the cause was lost. He could only dedicate his shield in the sanctuary of Trophonius and vanish, and men showed his tomb on Mount Ithome, where they also buried the *Sacra* of their enslaved country. Messenians became serfs to Sparta, and were set to cultivate their own lands for the benefit of their Spartiate lords. Most of the men abandoned their home and found a refuge at Naupactus on the Corinthian Gulf, where a temporary shrine of Zeus of Mount Ithome contained Ageladas' statue of him, and proclaimed that they had not forgotten the old sanctuary, though they had to wait for three centuries before it became theirs once more. At last the day of revival came, when Sparta was broken at Leuctra, and the word went round that, on the eve of that day, the ancient shield of Aristomene vanished from the temple at Livadia, and that a gigantic and mysterious figure fought in the Theban ranks on that field. Whether that were so or not, Theban policy and the statesmanship of Epaminondas decreed the restoration of Messenia, if it was only to

173

plant a bitter enemy on the flank of a foe that they could hardly believe that they had overcome. The State rose from the dead once more, and Ithome became her capital, a great city-site that was probably meant to be a fortified refuge from the inevitable Spartan invasions rather than an actual town. Of course, all the serfs of Sparta, or at least all who could escape over Taygetus, claimed Messenian citizenship and all were accepted without question for hatred of Sparta was the best passport to citizenship there. The *Sacra* were disinterred from the tomb on Ithome and duly housed, the statue of Zeus solemnly brought thither from Naupactus, and the whole place magnificently fortified to Epaminondas' own design. The walls, stretches of which stand perfect as on the day they were built, with even the 'capping-stones' on the battlements in position still, were said to be 'finer than those of Rhodes or Byzantium' (of course, the reference is not to anything standing at those cities now) and are, in effect, the finest specimen of classical fortification of the period extant. The Megalopolis Gate, with its circular 'barbican-court' to entrap attackers, and the huge monolithic lintel (which legend says that a Messenian woman bore up from the sea-coast on her shoulders) 'is specially worthy of study', to quote Pausanias, our guide.

Of course, other sanctuaries were rebuilt, in particular the Temenos of the Andanian Mysteries, which were celebrated in 'the Carnasian Grove, near the Megalopolis Gate not far from the Clepsydra Spring'. We can therefore trace this site easily, for the gate is there to see, as is the spring also, though it is now known as *Mavro-mati*, the 'Black Eye'. The rites are declared to have been of the same type as those of Eleusis, and were in all probability the original initiation ceremony of this particular tribe, though for years they had been forbidden by the Spartans and only practised in secret. Other rites, too, were revived, such for instance as a hero cult at the tomb of Aristomenes, in the threshing-floor on Ithome. A pillar was erected on the tomb and the bull for sacrifice was bound to it. If he pulled and shook it, the omen was good. For the rest, the ceremony was almost exactly that practised by Odysseus in the *Nekuia;* a trench was dug and the blood poured into it, that the spirits might approach and materialize from the fumes, sufficiently to give an answer to the worshipper. Obviously it was a revival, if not a continuance, of a very ancient rite. It was felt, however, that what put the crown on the whole was this: Messenians competed once more at Olympia, and one of their number won the foot-race, the blue ribbon of the Games.

It was felt that Zeus had put his seal publicly on what had been done, and Greece had officially welcomed a sister-State back once more. Sparta, it may be said, did not compete on that occasion; her sons, she explained, were not in the habit of running races with their own run-away slaves!

Of course, Sparta did not give up what she had held so long without a struggle, but when Mantinea was fought in 362 and peace made then on the basis of the *status quo*, that implied the recognition of such undeniable facts as the independence of Messene, and her sister-State Arcadia. Sparta protested and refused to sign, but even her own allies did not follow her in this, proof of her changed position in Greece. She never seems to have had the strength really to attack Messene, and there was no more than a petty squabble about some forts on Mount Taygetus, and the right of pasture on the Gerenian Lands, or *Ager Dentheliates*, on that range. That dispute at any rate endured. It was still open in the days of Augustus, whose commissioners decided in favour of Messene, a fact that was regarded by them as a second victory over their ancient foe, so that the decree was inscribed on the base of their great trophy, the Victory that we shall have to study at Olympia.

Another instance of the way in which old things endure in Greece may be found in the fact that this dispute is an open sore yet, and that the right to the Gerenian pasture lands—where the Roman boundary stones still bear witness to Augustus' decree, and were quoted as evidence in court—caused a dispute that produced broken heads, if not broken necks, as late as the year of grace 1925!

IX

CENTRAL PELOPONNESUS

Megalopolis—Bassae—Phigaleia—Olympia

No one who has penetrated so far down in Greece as Kalamata ought to return Athens-wards without paying a visit to Bassae, though it is one of the monuments of Greece which it is still not quite easy to get to. A good motor road leads from Kalamata to Megalopolis (thirty-five miles) and that runs fifteen miles further to the mountain township of Andritsaena, but at that point you must take either to your own feet or to the back of a mule for the remaining three hours. *En route,* it will be well to make a brief halt at Megalopolis, the only town in Greece that was founded deliberately with a political design, to be capital of a nation. The 'great city' was intended to be the head of the new State of Arcadia (which had never had a political existence before) and the site was carefully chosen for that end by the best judges—and it failed completely. Very few men in history have had the knack—like Alexander and Constantine—of choosing sites for the cities that they intended should bear their names so that those places should remain great for more than a century. Hence, 'freak-cities' are common enough in oriental history, but they usually perish within a generation or two at the least.

In this case, it was in the year following Leuctra that Epaminondas led one of the greatest armies that a Greek had ever commanded, down into Laconia. It was the first time for centuries that a hostile army had desecrated that sacred land, but the Theban meant to capture Sparta herself. He had seventy thousand men behind him, and his own unrivalled skill in the use of them; the unfortified city of Sparta could raise a bare ten thousand, and half of them were armed Helots and other auxiliaries, who were themselves a danger

176

rather than a help. Yet when they approached the open town and saw the real ramparts of Sparta, her men standing at bay under their veteran king, Agesilaus, the Theban hearts failed, and both on that day and on a later occasion they 'remembered an engagement elsewhere'.

It was true that they had work to do; they had to revive the dead State of Messenia as has been said, and also to unite the scattered towns of Arcadia (each one of which had hitherto been an 'independent' city, and so a subordinate ally of Sparta) into one united State, of which the capital was to be 'the Great City', Megalopolis.

The bulk of the Arcadians were enthusiastic for the idea, at the moment. Forty-one cities came forward to form the new league, and those who hesitated, like the men of Trapezus, found themselves either massacred or told that they had best be off without delay to join that other Trapezus, the daughter city that we call Trebizond, which they had founded at the other end of the Euxine Sea. Those who came brought even their gods with them, for the new city was to embody all the life of those from whom it was founded. The cult statue of Apollo 'the Succourer' was brought down from Bassae though it does seem that an older and holier statue was left in the temple. Pan was brought in from Scolitas to make his home, poor rover, in a city, though that was what he never liked! There was a special sanctuary of 'The Mother and the Maiden', Demeter and Persephone, and even a brand new *Telesterion*, that their mysteries, by leave of Eleusis, might be celebrated here. It would have been wiser to leave them in their old home at Lycosoura. Naturally every other god was brought in and housed, and the largest theatre in all Greece and the grandest of public buildings were all included in a circuit of walls, six miles round and seven feet thick, that were far finer than those of Athens.

The government of this new power was to be a new and experimental form, and one that might have done much for political science if the premature experiment had succeeded, for it was a representative assembly. Each one of the forty-one cities in the confederacy was to send so many delegates, numbering ten thousand in all, and they were to legislate for the whole. Somehow, the scheme did not work, though the world was certainly the poorer for its failure. The body perhaps was too big, certainly the centrifugal force of the separate cities was too strong, for the plan to work effectively, and as a result the city died down and died out almost as soon as the enthusiasm of its founders. The 'Great City' had become a 'Great

Desert' before the days of Strabo, three hundred years after its foundation with such hopes, and Pausanias in the year 160 A.D. finds nothing but ruins.

It was his careful description of those ruins that enabled the British School of Archaeology to find them in 1890/91, though nothing but foundations buried underground were there for them to unearth, save in two instances. These were: the big theatre—which is just a good specimen of its kind, of which there are plenty more—and the more interesting 'Hall of Assembly', the *Thersilion*, where an area of 220 feet by 180 feet gives space for the whole of the ten thousand delegates to assemble, provided that they were content to stand, or maybe squat upon the floor.

The whole building is 'a covered Pnyx', i.e. it is like the famous place of assembly of Athens, but roofed over. It was arranged theatre-wise, that is to say with a wooden floor (of course gone now) that sloped upwards on all sides from the orchestra-like area by the south wall, in which the authorities and speakers were expected to sit. The roof was borne by pillars, which were cleverly arranged; they were in rows or ranks longitudinally, yet so placed that their 'files' radiated in all directions from the speakers' area, and presented the minimum of obstacle between speaker and audience. If we only had the place complete, we might be able to see whether the Greek could secure in a covered building those absolutely perfect acoustics that he never fails to attain in an open theatre, and which we can only secure by lucky chance now.

Megalopolis lies in the upland plain which is the basin where the River Alpheios takes his rise, and the road to Andritsaena runs along its length. As you reach the lower end of it, however, the two great hills of Lykaeon and Roudia draw close together, and the stream descends into a narrow gorge, where the exit from the plain is guarded by the ruins of the Frankish castle of Karytaena. There the road leaves river and valley, to wind up the slopes of Lykaeon to Andritsaena, a town which its name proclaims to be Avar rather than Hellenic, and which will not give you any antiquities to study, though it will provide a very decent hotel. Here you must leave the car for a mule if you wish to get to one of the great temples of all Greece, and the one that Pausanias, in times when there was much more choice visible than at present, counted the second finest in the Peloponnesus.

It must be owned however that our gossiping Baedeker has one of the qualities of the perfect sight-seer—he always has a most proper admiration for the beauty of the place in which he happens to be at the moment. 'He is to be envied, to whom the apple that he has is always the best on the tree!' Bassae lies in a nook of high mountains, up at a level of nearly 5,000 feet on Mount Cotilius, in a corner of the Peloponnesus that is thoroughly out of the way and until lately really hard to get at. So isolated is it, that it fortunately never stood in any danger of being used as a quarry, and its very existence was forgotten. In 1765, a Frenchman of the name of Bochor turned up somehow at Andritsaena, and heard one shepherd remark to another that he had folded the goats 'up by the pillars'; and after asking what was meant, he had curiosity enough to get his friend to guide him over the hills to the place. It was forty years later before the Englishman Leake, who was brought to the spot by reading Bochor's account, made careful drawings and plans of one of the finest and most original of Greek temples.

There was 'always' a tiny shrine of Apollo at the place, up on the crest of the ridge, oriented as usual with its entrance to the East, and far from any human habitation. It must have much resembled the little white churches that we see on many a hill-top today, that have service in them once a year when their festal day or *Panegyris* comes round. Then, either in 430 or in 420, for accounts vary, there was a terrible outbreak of plague in the Peloponnesus, as at Athens also, which was stayed locally after a special pilgrimage to this hill-shrine of the god. Hence it was that a grander temple was built as a thankoffering to 'the Succourer', and the services of the best architect of the day, that Ictinos whose work on the Parthenon had become famous, were engaged for the job. His material was the local one that Greeks used whenever possible, in this case a hard grey limestone that could almost be called a marble, for it is amply hard enough to take a polish; his plan was obliged to be an unusual one by circumstances, for Greek architects had no unhealthy craving after originality. The original position of the shrine had become so sacred after the great deliverance wrought, that there could be no question of altering that, but the ridge on which it stood is so narrow that the building of an oriented temple there would imply impossibly big substructures. So the temple had to stand north and south, but the sanctuary, with the cult statue, had to keep its old position, with an opening as large as an ordinary temple doorway to the east.

The peristyle or external colonnade is Doric as usual, but the *naos* or nave—which was open to the sky and roofless, or as architects

179

call it 'hypaethral'—had a row of five beautiful Ionic pilasters[1] on either side, and these, projecting into the *naos,* divided its interior into four 'bays'. It was these that carried the frieze, which in this case was inside the *naos* or *cella,* and not outside as at Athens, and which was protected from the weather by a projecting cornice. There was an opening, of course, from the 'nave' into the *adyton* or sanctuary, and here the big architrave that spanned it above was supported by a Corinthian column, which if it be part of the original design of Ictinos, is the earliest specimen of the style we know. The *adyton* was roofed, and we have already told how the 'cult statue' was carried off to Megalopolis in 371, but the temple authorities had another, and seemingly an older and holier one, to take its place.

This was what is known as 'acro-lithic' in structure, whereas the other was bronze. That is to say, only the face, hands and feet of the figure were of marble, and the trunk—which was clothed and not meant to be seen—was of wood, and therefore probably much older than the temple itself. A wooden figure, that required ceremonial attire, was usually very ancient. Most of this has perished, of course, but a foot and a hand are in the British Museum. As for the frieze, it was found among the ruins where it had fallen from its place, when the English scholar Cockerell was here in 1812, and he easily got leave to remove it to the British Museum, where it now is. It gives us the favourite design of Centaurs and Lapithae on one side and Greeks and Amazons on the other, and it is certainly later in date than the temple. An artist of the time of Pheidias would hardly have put so much of passion and emotion into his figures, even if he allowed himself, as this unknown man has done, to insert figures of nude women. Without venturing on any attempt to fix a date, it may be said that the design is distinctly superior to the execution, and it is quite possible that we have here the work of local craftsmen, carrying out another's plan. There is internal evidence that each slab was carved separately, and in a studio;[2] not, as we believe to have been done in the Parthenon, when it was actually in its place in the building it was designed to adorn. But to say that it is not quite equal to the miracle on the Parthenon is not to deny that it is a very noble work.

[1] The term is not quite correct, but the Ionic columns were attached to the wall behind.
[2] In no case does the composition overlap the junction between one slab and the next.

Apollo is an intruder, even here, for we have seen that the Dorian god came late to Greece, and there are other and older deities in the land, of whom it may be said that the older they are the less they seem to die out. Pan's presence we have noted already. Right opposite to us as we stand at Bassae is the square-headed mountain of Lykaeon, whose crest carried one of the oldest and most awesome of the precincts—as elsewhere, never a temple—of Zeus. Like the shrine of the same deity on Aegina, the house of the Sky-god was a great place for rain-making, and this particular *temenos* was so holy that none dare enter it, save only the priest. It was noted with awe that he cast no shadow while he was within it, nor for that matter did any other man or beast who passed its barrier—a thing that it was rash indeed to do, for any unauthorized creature who did enter it died within the year. Here, said local legend, Zeus was born of Rhea, and here she gave the stone to Saturn in his stead.

On the lower slopes of the same mountain, at Lycosoura, is an older temple yet, a shrine of the Great Mother and the Maiden, Demeter and Kore, the sculptures from which are in the Museum at Athens. The three great heads, Demeter, Kore, and Anytus the Titan—who plays some part in the legend peculiar to this place—are a trifle commonplace as works of art, and one turns from them with relief to the strange symbolism of the 'robe of Demeter' preserved with them. This is the cloak of the Mother that is the surface of the earth, of which the folds are mountains, and the embroidery, trees, plants and animals. The exact meaning of the figures carved, half-human, half-beast, is a point that each student may interpret for himself, for at least no man can take it on him to say that any interpretation is wrong.

All this district is one of the great haunts of the Mother, in legend. Here, said the Arcadian story, she came in the course of that long search for Persephone, having assumed the form of a mare for purposes of travel. In this district, at the place now called Phigaleia, and in a cave on the Mountain of Elaius, she underwent outrage from Poseidon, who took the form of a stallion for the purpose. Therefore in shame and grief, she hid herself in the cave for months, in mourning garb, till she was found by kindly Pan as he roved, and her hiding place reported to Zeus, who was seeking for the power that could give back fruitfulness to the earth. Hence it was that this land always worshipped 'the Black, Horse-headed Demeter', and though later art revolted at the barbarism of the concept, it had to keep the horse's (or rather, the mare's) head somewhere on the base of her statue in her temple at Phigaleia, some eight miles from Bassae.

The cave where she hid herself is still known, on a mountain whose modern name of St. Elias is a very small alteration of the old one. Demeter, however, has locally got confused with the Mother-figure of a later faith, and they call her the Panagia now, and her sanctuary is in the cavern still, but the old memory goes on. To this day, so Greek friends have assured us, the belief persists that once in days now long ago, some awful and unspeakable sacrilege, of what precise nature they know not, was perpetrated against the Holy Mother there, and an annual service of penitence and propitiation is celebrated in that cave on Demeter's ancient festal day!

Most travellers who get to Bassae will be travelling north from that point to Olympia, and such will be anxious only to get back to Andritsaena and proceed direct upon their way. Those who wander more leisurely however, and who get as far as Phigaleia, may make the mule that has carried them so far take them further, and get down the valley till they strike sea and railway together at Neda. There is at least one train in the day that will take you north to Pyrgos and Olympia, and you may meditate on the ancient home of Nestor—for here you are at the rival site of 'Sandy Pylos'—in the hours of waiting for it.

Those who go more direct will find it easier to perform the next stage of their journey now than was the case not so long ago. Five years ago, a mule had to take you to Olympia from Andritsaena, and he might do the journey in eleven hours, though thirteen was a more usual time, and no halting place was available *en route*. Now, there is a motorable road over at least six of those hours, as far as the village of Zaka at any rate, and it is progressing towards Olympia itself, and extending from that point also. However, at the date of writing, there is still the River Alpheios to ford, and as we know by the experience of Arethusa that the god of that stream has always been wanting in self-control and his river liable to flooding, adventure is always possible at that passage. Let us be thankful that travel in Greece is not yet entirely cut and dried!

The central festival of all Greece was emphatically the Games of Olympia, to which men gathered from points as far apart as Marseilles and Trebizond, because they felt their union as Hellenes. How regular a custom this was appears from the fact that, of all the States of Greece, the two who provided most winners in this contest were those of Rhodes and Crotona. It was the great Pan-Hellenic solemnity, and it made both for peace and civilization in the Greek world, in that when it was really great, it could bring the force of public opinion to bear upon any offender against its principles, in a way that it is now the highest aspiration of the United Nations to achieve. States like Sparta and Macedon, when they offended against Olympian laws, were glad to pay any fine imposed upon them rather than find themselves excluded from that great feast.

Olympia's legend told how Oenomaus, King of Pisa, ruled here in the days shortly after Deucalion's flood. In obedience to an oracle, he proclaimed that the hand of his fair daughter Hippodameia would be the prize of anyone who could beat him in a chariot race, but death was the penalty of failure. The course was a long one, from Pisa to Corinth, or a good fifty miles. The candidate was allowed a start, as Oenomaus had to offer sacrifice before he got into his chariot, but the suitor had to carry weight in the person of Hippodameia herself, and Oenomaus had the great advantage of magic horses given him by Poseidon. Many tried, failed, and paid the penalty, but at last Pelops, son of Tantalus and ancestor of all the house of Atreus, arrived and sent in his challenge. Being warned by the sight of a long row of the skulls of his predecessors over the King's stable door, he took the precaution of bribing Myrtilus, the royal charioteer, and that faithless man pulled out the linch-pins of his master's chariot wheels, so that he came by a fall and broken neck. Pelops married Hippodameia, but when Myrtilus proved too exigent in his demands for reward, disposed of him too, and instituted the chariot race in memory of the event; with a rule, not uncalled for under the circumstances, that there should be no cheating.

Another account made Heracles the founder, saying that when he had cleansed the stables of King Augeas hereabouts he sacrificed all the oxen, building an altar from their ashes, and inviting all the gods to come down to compete in his games. Apollo raced with Hermes and boxed against Ares; Zeus wrestled with his father Saturn and threw him; while Heracles, who always provides the low comedy on these occasions, had an eating match with a local hero, Lepreus. When each had eaten one whole ox, the match was declared a draw!

Iphitus and Lycurgus met here in later days, and drew up the rules for the contests on a copper discus that was shewn to Pausanias, and there was a good tradition of a dispute between the local cities of Elis and Pisa for the right to control the games, but legend went no further.

Excavation brings its facts to check the tradition. The spade makes it certain that there was an ancient 'Helladic' settlement here by 1500 B.C. and that such gods as Cronos, Artemis—or the Great Mother—and the local hero Pelops were worshipped here then. After a distinct break, Hellenic immigrants come in from the north, with their Sky-god, Zeus, and it is probable that the struggle of these two elements is the struggle between Elis and Pisa. The name of the hill Cronion which rises above the sacred site, shows that Saturn did not altogether lose his honour.

By 776 B.C. regular history begins here with the Olympiads and names of the winners, and we do not lose that guidance till nearly 400 A.D. Historians count from this, Thucydides for instance saying that such an event took place in the year X won the Pancration, which is much as if a serious contemporary historian should fix the premiership of Lord Salisbury by the year that Ormonde won the Derby. Usually men dated by the winners of the foot-race, the recognized 'blue ribbon' of the whole, though other contests were at least as early. Thus, by 776 B.C. what had begun as a local matter was already pan-Hellenic and the lists of Olympian victors show how wide her circle of influence had already become.

Of course, there were no temples at first. There was an *altis* or sacred grove of olive and plane, and possibly a little *temenos* or sacred enclosure in it. A *prytaneion*, or lodging for resident priests and authorities, seems to have existed, and the ever-burning sacred fire was to be found on its hearth. That flame was only allowed to go out in spring, when it was relighted solemnly by 'a spark from heaven' (that is, kindled, probably, by a fire-stick) and it shows the continuity of things that this rite of 'the Holy Fire' should be one of the most venerated ceremonies in the Orthodox Church today.[1] There were altars of Kronos, Zeus and Pelops in the *temenos*, at the last of which offerings were made with a 'blood-trench' in true Homeric style, while the altar of Zeus was the home of the Olympian oracle. They were made (as those for 'burnt-offerings' usually were) in the roughest style, which is why hardly any remain.[2] A mere rough wall of stones, say four feet high, and enclosing a small circle of perhaps ten feet in diameter, was all that was wanted. It might be filled with rough stones, or the ashes of the flame might themselves

---

[1] It is quite general, and not by any means confined, as is sometimes thought, either to the most conspicuous instance of the rite at Jerusalem, or for that matter to the Greek church.

[2] An instance at Eleusis and one at Tiryns are all that we are aware of.

make the hearth. In this instance, the ashes of the 'ever-burning fire', when that was put out, were taken from the hearth and mixed with the (very hard) water of the Cladeus to form a sort of cement pavement round the altar. When anyone wished to consult the oracle, there was a sacrifice of a bull or bulls at this place, and the hides were thrown on the fire, where the omen was drawn, by the local priestly families of the Iamidae and Clytiadae, from the way the skins crackled and twisted.

There was also an Artemis Orthia ceremony here, when the candidates for manhood, the Ephebi, were put through the same contest of endurance as at Sparta; and at one time there seems to have been a human sacrifice, in the shape of a fight absolutely to the death between two selected young warriors.

With these ceremonies then the athletic festival that came once every four years at the full moon of August or September[1] had to be duly inaugurated. By about the year 700, when as we have seen the solemnity was already general, we get the first built temple on the site, one which still fortunately survives as what we call today the Heraeon. Originally it was that of Zeus and Hera, and the lady was only present by grace, and as the consort of her husband. Their statues stood side by side on the long-shaped base we see today. When however Zeus acquired a much finer house just over the way, he withdrew from this, and Hera remained in possession, though her husband's statue was by her side still. She was represented by a very archaic figure of 'acro-lithic' type, of which the face—probably the only part that was of marble—is preserved in the museum today. The fabric of the temple was of mud brick on the surviving stone *socle* and its peristyle was of wooden pillars, which were only gradually replaced by others of stone of very varying pattern. Pausanias saw a wooden one still *in situ* in his day. The roof of course was of wood also, and the ceiling was flat. The *naos* was divided into 'bays' internally, as Bassae was, but in ruder style, and no doubt this assisted in the construction of the roof.

Here, among a crowd of other votive offerings of far greater intrinsic value, was one treasure that has been preserved to us by the very fact that the fabric of the temple was mud, and so buried it when it collapsed. It is the priceless Hermes of Praxiteles, now in the

---

[1] All of the great Pan-Hellenic festivals (the Pythia, the Carneia, the Great Panathenaea, and the Olympian), came at about that season (when farming is at its slackest), and each four years. Probably it was arranged that one should come each year.

local museum. It may be taken as some evidence of the vanished wealth of Olympia that, whereas all know that this is a figure which men come from all over the world to see and marvel at, a good judge like Pausanias in his long account of the place passes it over with just half a line of notice: 'an image of Hermes with Dionysus; a work of Praxiteles, in stone.' What, one wonders, was the quality of the other contents of this temple, to which he devotes two chapters and a half? Olympia, we may mention, has the whole of one of his ten books.

Of course, the High Priestess of Hera was one of the great dignitaries of Olympia. She had a staff of sixteen matrons and as many maiden priestesses under her, besides minor officials. Their duty was, like that of their colleagues at Athens, to weave the robe or *peplos* for the adornment of the ancient figure of Hera, and they had various high rights and privileges that will be mentioned in due course.

The period 600–350 B.C. was the time of the most real greatness, though not of the highest splendour, of Olympia. Athletics were at their best, still in the 'amateur' stage, and the Persian War had shown their value. Greece had a sense of union in herself, while each State was independent and free to outdo any other in art if it could, and the inevitable decline had not yet begun. Hence the finest, if not the most showy of her monuments are of this period.

The Metroon, or Temple of the Great Mother, was the next to be erected after that of Hera, but this has little importance. It was in this case not a revival of anything that was ancient in the land, but an importation of orgiastic worship from Anatolia; it was felt to be so un-Greek, and struck so little root, that all the world consented to see the temple transformed later into a fane of Augustus and Rome.

The Great Temple of Zeus was built in the years 468–57 B.C., and was really the fruit of the ancient rivalry between Elis and Pisa, being built with the plunder of the latter when she went down before her enemy. It is a melancholy comment on a fine Olympian rule, that in the precinct there ought to be no trophy of victory for battles between Hellene and Hellene. As a building, it is about the size of the Parthenon, but without the miraculous delicacy that we know there. It is, for instance, of stone not of marble: a shell conglomerate from local quarries, which in old days was covered with a white stucco, while the *annuli* or rings just below the capitals of the Doric columns were painted red. Externally it was the usual *cella* and peristyle, and internally divided into 'nave and aisles' by internal colonnades that carried the roof. The whole of its sanctuary was occupied by the famous Zeus of Pheidias,[1] that 'wonder of the world' of which it could be said that it really fulfilled good men's ideal of the Divine, in that they could look at it, and feel that they were seeing 'The Father of Gods and of Men'. 'The majesty of the work', says Quintilian, who saw it in place, 'is equal to the God who is represented.' Again we have secured, in modern days, what may give us some idea of the original, even if it be no better an idea than the Varvakeion Athena gives us of Pheidias' other great work, or a modern cast does of a Michelangelo. The Head of Zeus recently discovered at Cyrene, is believed to be a copy of that of Olympia. The figure, made in the period 438–32, remained in its place at least till after 100 A.D., for we know that Caligula tried to remove it to Rome, but 'the cranes broke, and the statue smiled at his impotent efforts'. Later, however, it was taken to Constantinople by Theodosius, where it seems to have perished in one of the numerous conflagrations of that city.

The external sculptures, the metopes and pediments, have been largely recovered in fragments from the ruins and reconstructed in the local museum. They represented, in the eastern pediment, the start for the great chariot race of Pelops and Oenomaus, and in the western, the combat of the Centaurs and Lapithae. Zeus and Apollo —each, of course, supposedly unseen—preside over the two contests. Pausanias was told that the carvings of the eastern group were by Paeonius—of whose work we shall find a wonderful instance elsewhere—and the western by Alcamenes, a great Athenian sculptor who was a younger contemporary, and some said the equal, of Pheidias himself. That, however, is a mere 'guide's statement', and about as reliable as those made by modern guides at Athens often are! They are generally held now to be the product of a native school of Elean sculptors, and fine though they are, the stiff groups and archaic mannerisms show that here in the provinces men had not reached the standard set at Athens. Such carved metopes as there were on the building—and that was only at the ends, the rest being

---

[1] This colossal figure was erected in the 'workshop' that still stands in the *temenos*, and which is of the exact dimensions of the Sanctuary, so that the artist could judge of the effect of his scheme as he worked. It could seemingly be taken to pieces—like the Athena at Athens—and re-erected in its proper place. The building became an Orthodox Church in the sixth century and still retains the fittings and arrangement of that date—a very unusual survival. We may be pardoned for noting the fact that these early arrangements resemble those of a modern Anglican church much more closely than do those of a modern church of the Orthodox Communion.

left plain or merely coloured—have also been rescued and placed in the Museum. They represent the labours of Heracles.

Outside in the precinct there were statues in plenty. In a place of honour in front of the temple, and on a high triangular base, stood the marvellous Victory of Paeonius, the Messenians' trophy for their day of revenge at Sphacteria; she flaunted herself in the face of any Spartan who came to the shrine. The goddess, flying down from heaven, has just lighted on a mountain top, seeming rather borne up by her wings than resting on solid earth and rock—a *tour-de-force* of sculpture that astonished men then as even in her mutilated and shattered state she amazes us now in the Museum. When first she was put up, the inscription on her base ran: 'For the victory of the Messenians over the Spartans', but this was objected to, on the ground that this was not the place for any triumphing of Greek over Greek. 'Well, let it be "The victory of the Messenians over their enemies" ', said the donors. 'It is no great matter, for all the world knows that we Messenians have only one.'

Statues of victors no doubt there were, but not so many as one would expect, for it was not till you had won your third triumph that you were entitled so to commemorate yourself. On the other hand, any breach of the rules or any foul was punished by the order to put up a *zan*, a statue of Zeus that everyone knew the meaning of, and the name of the offender went on that. It is to the credit of all concerned that there are so very few of these, and they were put where they would do most good by their example, on the way from the precinct to the Stadium.

Other figures represented a thankoffering of some city for good service done. The town of Lampsacus, for instance, set up one to the orator Anaximenes, who saved them from the wrath of Alexander. The city had offended the king somehow, and he was threatening destruction on them; so when he heard that they had briefed this advocate, he took a solemn vow to do the precise opposite of what he asked. Anaximenes accordingly set out his case, and was heard in grim silence. 'What do you want me to do?' said Alexander gruffly at last. 'King, in your mercy, kill every man, enslave all the women, and raze the city to the ground,' said the pleader, who had heard of the king's vow. Alexander, though furious for the moment, burst out laughing at his own expense, and the town received the royal pardon.

Other buildings may be traced, such as the Great Colonnade on ground where previously the actual contests took place; the

Bouleuterion or council hall; and the *Leonidaeon*, the gift of a man of Elis in the fourth century, to serve as a lodging for distinguished guests at the festival.

The general decline of all higher matters in the days of the Peloponnesian War affected Olympia also. Professionalism crept in, and in 400 we get the first case of a bane of modern sport, the buying of a good professional by a rival town that could give him a higher salary. Be it owned that when Syracuse played this trick by tempting the boxer Astylus away from Croton, Croton promptly pulled down the man's house and built a gaol on the site. With professionalism came in also over-specialization at one branch of sport so that the original object of training fine all-round men was quite lost sight of.

With the Macedonian age, decline goes further yet. The authorities may invite Alexander to compete, thereby paying that plain barbarian (we quote Demosthenes as to the status of the Macedonian) the compliment of recognizing him as a Greek. Alexander said he would be delighted—if they gave him kings to race with! Soon the erection of the *Philippeion* (a temple to the house of Macedon, with Philip and Alexander there in the chryselephantine statues that had hitherto been reserved for gods) shows Olympia consenting to the apotheosis of her conqueror. And a little later the Roman Mummius is allowed to decorate the temple with the loot of Corinth, and a big statue is put up to him as 'the hero who restored order in Hellas'.

In Roman days, there is prosperity and magnificence, but the soul has gone out of the festival. Augustus (we do not think of him as a sportsman, but he really loved a good prize fight) made his own Games of Victory at Actium a copy of Olympia, and gave Olympia a duplicate of his own great trophy there.[1] It became the proper thing to patronize the place, and Tiberius and Germanicus both drove in the chariot race, as did Nero also. By way of beating all records, he appeared in a chariot with ten horses, but got tangled up with such a team and came a cropper. However, he was picked up and declared winner somehow, and so the emperor went off, presumably with the crown, certainly with five hundred statues that he collected in the precinct. That was Olympia's reward for the new house that she built for Nero when he declared his intent of visiting the place.

[1] It was an amazing trophy of victory—a peasant driving a donkey, in bronze. The fact is that as Augustus went down to his ship on the day of Actium, he met the or ginal of it. 'What is your name, old boy?' said he. 'Eutyches' said the peasant. 'And the donkey's name?' 'His name's Nikon.' 'Eutyches and Nikon. Fortunate and Victorious,' cried Augustus; 'I accept the omen.' And peasant and donkey became the trophy of that day.

By 265 A.D. the Pax Romana had broken down and the Barbarians got in to ravage, and in 393 Theodosius, who stopped the mysteries of Eleusis, stopped also the Olympic Games. By an odd coincidence, the last of the victors in the foot-race was a Persian, one Varazdates.

In the days of Justinian a series of great earthquakes brought ruin on the temples and the emperor put one of his many big fortified monasteries on the site, the north wall of the old temple of Zeus being part of its boundary, and the workshop of Pheidias its church. Some of the other buildings had to serve as quarries then, though the fallen columns of the temple were spared and lie in order crying for replacement. So we pass to mediaeval days, when the monastery perished, and a slight rise of the coast deprived the rivers Alpheus and Cladeus of their outfall, so that a combination of swamp and malaria made the place almost uninhabitable, and floods brought down débris that buried the site twenty feet deep. Even its name was lost, and Olympia became the wretched village of Andilalo and was practically forgotten.

It was a German, Winkelmann, who identified the site at last in 1768, but he was unable to realize his dream and dig there; and though the French found a few objects in 1829, including one of the metopes, now in the Louvre, it was not till 1874–80 that the Germans under Prof. Curtius (the Crown-Prince Frederick being the moving spirit in the work) were able to get leave to complete the task which they carried out with characteristic thoroughness and skill.

When we try to depict the great Olympian festival, we must remember that the athletics of Greece presuppose a leisured class who have no books to occupy them, are debarred from all trade and handicraft, and have the services of a huge proletariat of slaves. The result was what Galen could see even as late as the Antonine age, when he declared that he could find youths as beautiful as any of the statues any day in the gymnasium. The reflex effect on artists who could constantly watch picked young men at their sports, unburdened by any clothes and naked with the unconsciousness of habit, can be guessed.[1] It was the very best of such specimens that were trained for the Games, for nine months at home, for one month either at Elis or in the gymnasium at Olympia itself, under the eyes

[1] Probably Greeks liked bronzes so much just because the natural colour of the metal without any artificial patina, well polished, is nearly the colour which the human skin assumes—in white races—when it is well browned by constant exposure to all weathers, and at the same time well oiled.

of the *Hellanodikai* who would have to judge the contests, and who must have been able to pick the winners with some certainty before the event came off.

Just before the feast, for which sacred truce had been already proclaimed, candidates and officials marched from Elis to Olympia, there to find the great crowd already assembled; official delegations, sight-seers, foreigners, artists—it was like a gigantic fair, with booths everywhere, even in the western half of the *temenos* itself. Water-sellers did a roaring trade, for the little Cladeus which runs just by the site was pretty well dry at that time, and 'Olympian Thirst' was a proverb. Herodes Atticus for once won real popularity by bringing water in an aqueduct from a spring six miles off, and distributing it in conduits about the place. They made his wife Regilla honorary priestess of Hera as a compliment, as a marble bull in the Museum proclaims today. At the great feast, however, women were taboo in the *temenos*, as their presence was supposed to exercise a deteriorating influence on the competitors. Any woman found trespassing was liable to be thrown from the cliff over which Pelops kicked Myrtilus. Still, we find at least one taking a chance in the matter. It was the lady Pherenike of Rhodes, who came in disguised as her husband's trainer and passed scrutiny—and then gave her own show away because when her husband had won his race she jumped into the arena and kissed him! She was let off, but a new rule made, that trainers in future were to wear no more clothes than the competitors, who wore none at all, so that the trick could not be tried again. Still, women had their chance, for every five years came the girls' games, when they had their competition, with 'exactly the same sports as the men'. The reference is, we presume, to the *Pentathlon*, for the jumping, racing, diskos and javelin throwing, and even the wrestling of that 'five-fold contest' were all well within their compass, though such rough sports as boxing, and even more the *Pancration*, do seem a little out of the picture for them. Girls raced in a short tunic reaching to the knee, and we are told with their hair loose. The statue of the 'Spartan Girl' in the Vatican is now believed to be one of those figures that we know were put up in honour of the Olympian victress. The Priestess of Hera had the right of presiding at the Games.

On the first day the competitors formally entered their names before the *Hellenodikai* in the *Bouleuterion* and both they and the judges took the oath. The competitors' oath was that they were true Hellenes—a condition afterwards stretched to include Romans,

191

Macedonians, and even Persians—that they had been properly trained, that they would play fair, and that they would abide by the rulings of the umpires. The judges swore that they would judge fairly and—a rule that shows real knowledge of humanity—that they would never discuss their rulings with anybody.

That oath once taken, no excuse was accepted for non-appearance at the competition for which you had entered. You must show up, or pay a heavy fine and be publicly proclaimed coward. There was the case of the man Theagenes, who entered his name for the boxing and for the *Pancration*. Victor in the first, he was left in such a state that he could not stand up, far less face such a terrible contest as the other one. Yet he had to pay the penalty all the same.

After the ceremony of the oath there was nothing official that day, save perhaps the 'blood-offering of the Ephebi' in the Pelopeion, which was probably a popular exhibition. There were, however, plenty of other interests, for this was the time when authors read their works, preferably in the *opistho-domos* or west portico of the temple. So it is there that we may place a scene which we know took place here in the year 445, and picture the respectable Athenian Olorus asking a friend 'are you coming to hear that man from Halicarnassus, Herodotus, read his new history? I have my son here; Thucydides his name is, and he will not rest till he has heard him'. It was on this day, too, that the official deputations were received, so that we may picture Themistocles being cheered by all Greece assembled there, and Alcibiades coming in with the seven chariots and the pomp that he declared was an advertisement that was itself a great service to Athens. Once, too, Dionysius the Tyrant of Syracuse appeared here, prepared to read a poem and race with a chariot. However, the poem and the tyrant were both hissed by the crowd, and the chariot got upset in the race.

The second day was the great day of the games, beginning with the chariot race, in the Hippodrome that must have been somewhere out on the open plain between the precinct and the River Alpheios. There was a grand march round in procession to begin with; then the chariots—often forty in number, with four horses abreast in each—deployed into line, and 'the Eagle rose and the Dolphin dived', which was the signal for the start, given by some sort of counterpoise arrangement, and the great race began. It was a nine-mile course, and the *spina* had to be turned twelve times, so that there were twenty-three turns in all round the points where the 'Demon Scare-horse' or Taraxhippos had his special dwelling-place.

16. Bassae: Temple of Apollo

17. Source of the Styx

There seem to have been more spills than even in a Grand National Steeplechase, for of forty competitors it was not uncommon for only one to finish—though when Alcibiades was there we know that at least four got home. The owner led up his chariot with the charioteer in it, to the *Hellanodikai*, and the victor was proclaimed. Of course, this was only a rich man's race, and at Syracuse we often get gold coins struck in honour of a victor.

Horse races followed, in which the jockeys rode bare-back, and there was no weight rule. Further, as it was specifically a horse that was racing, when one of them—as happened once—got rid of his rider and finished the course, coming in first, he was acclaimed the winner! Races for two-horse chariots, for colts, and for mules followed. There was a case when the Tyrant of Rhegium, having won the last, required a poem from Simonides in honour of it. The poet was in a dilemma, for to write in honour of mules was shame unbearable, but yet the fee was too big to refuse. He wrote, and his first line was:

All hail, ye children of the wind-swift mares,

and there was no other allusion to mules in the whole poem.

Then there must have followed a grand scurry of all the world from the Hippodrome to the Stadium, for the *Pentathlon* followed next, and in that place. The Stadium—which has been buried so deep that it has not been worth while to excavate it, beyond the starting line that is exposed to view—was far less elaborate here than, for example, at Athens or Delphi. It was no more than a stretch of level ground with the slope of the Cronion Hill on the northern side, where was placed the only seat provided in the whole —a marble bench for the High Priestess of Hera, the only woman who was allowed to be present at the solemnity. As for the course, we are specially told it was covered deep with soft sand, so that when we hear that the speed was so great that you could hardly see the men, we must be rather sceptical. One does not like to suggest that it was the dust that made them invisible!

The Five-fold Contest—consisting of foot-race, disk-throwing, javelin-hurling, leaping, and wrestling—was specially designed to bring out the all-round athlete, and to make style and rhythm count for more than mere muscle. You counted by points, and of course if any one man won three events outright, he had won the rubber; boxing settled it, in the event of a tie. The foot-race needs no description, and familiar statues give the attitude of the Discobolus, but the weight of the eight-inch discus is a question. One account gives us four pounds and another twelve, a difference which makes it difficult to estimate the worth of the record of about 100 feet. You had to throw the javelin to music, and were allowed to use a thong (*amentum*) to sling it, but distance and not direction was what counted. There was no target. The jump was a standing jump, and the only extra impetus allowed was that given by the dumb-bell weights (*halteres*, of which one survives) which you swung with either hand. The trick was, to fling them backwards at the very instant that you sprang, gaining some extra push by the act. Even so the reputed record for this standing jump, held by Phayllus of Croton, fifty feet, or over double our university record with a run to help, is we fear quite beyond our powers of belief!

The third day was given up to the boys' races and other competitions, a 'boy' according to the Nicopolis or Actium rules being over seventeen and under twenty years of age. Still there is record of a 'boy' who, being disqualified because he was over eighteen, after winning his race, raced again next day against men and beat them. Hence we cannot be sure of the regulation.

The fourth day was given up to extra events, the real 'Olympian contest' being over on the second day. There were foot races, short and long; there was the race 'in heavy marching order', that is in full armour, with helmet, shield and greaves. The judges provided shields, all of one standard weight, but the rest of the kit was your own. There was wrestling, in which a 'bout' consisted of three fair falls, and—as we see in a familiar group—it was 'no fall' unless both shoulder blades were got to the ground. Sculptures show that what our age knows as the 'cross-buttock' and the 'flying mare' were familiar enough to the Greeks.

The boxing must have been rather a brutal business, for all were in one class with no weight rule; the *cestus* was a most appallingly punishing weapon, and there was little science beyond hard hitting. It was said that after a good boxing bout, your own dog would not know you! If this was brutal to our ideas, however, the *Pancration* was worse. This was a contest of the 'all-in' variety, with no rules and no fouls. The competitors were turned naked into the arena, and you could do what you liked to your opponent, subject only to his right to do what he could to you. Biting and gouging were sometimes barred, and such a rule shows what the contest could be like. It was in this contest that we read of Arrichion the Spartan knocking his opponent out and dropping dead across him.

194

On this day, too, any athlete who was about could exhibit any trick feats for the sake of the kudos won. Milo of Crotona, for instance, strode into the arena, to break cords round his chest and head by the expansion of the pectoral muscles and those of his temples. It was on one of these occasions that Bubon 'put up' the big stone that still bears his name, and is in the Museum. Judging by the grip provided on the block, he must have lifted it with one hand and raised it above his head. As its weight is 316 pounds, or over $22\frac{1}{2}$ stones, the feat was a fine one, but is surpassed by that recorded on a block that is still to be seen on the island of Santorin, which weighs 1,100 pounds, or roughly half a ton, and bears the inscription: 'Eumastes lifted me.'

The last day saw the distribution of the prizes, those olive wreaths which carried with them so much glory and very often substantial privileges at home. An Olympian victor at Athens could claim free board in the Prytaneum for life, that compliment which Socrates could count as the high honour of which he was really worthy from his fellow citizens. A Spartan had the right to stand next to his king in the battle-line.

Grand feasts were a matter of course, and sacrifices that ran to many hecatombs, suggesting that the Hellenes were a strong stomached race, for the *temenos* on those occasions must have had much resemblance to a shambles. However, the same might be said of the Temple at Jerusalem, and in both cases the sacrifices were the highest expression of religious devotion of the age, even if we keep an attitude of scepticism towards the tradition propagated by the authorities of both shrines, namely that never, no matter what the number of the offerings, was any fly ever seen within the borders of the holy precinct.

X

THE GULF OF CORINTH

Patras—The Gulf—Megaspelaeon

Train will probably take the traveller from Olympia to Patras, over country that has but little interest, save for one distant glimpse of the castle of Clarentza. This hold of the Latins, which stands up much like Bamborough on an isolated rock that commands a low-lying coast, has a certain amount of interest for English folk, as having been probably the original of one of the ducal titles of our royal house—Clarence; though the name was transferred to an English site from this Greek one.

At Patras we are once more on the Gulf of Corinth, and the mountains that we see on the northern side of it are those over which the hunt of the great boar of Calydon once wandered. The modern town, though it is a prosperous centre of the currant and wine trade, contains little to interest a tourist. But the city of Patras is old enough, for it has borne that name continuously since before the days of Homer, though it is not long since the civic fathers of the place had to be reminded of the fact, when they desired to change the name to Andreopolis. They had this much excuse for their idea, that Patras or Patrae is by very ancient tradition the site of the martyrdom of that Apostle. He is said to have been arrested at a certain spring, on which occasion he borrowed a sword from one of the soldiers who guarded him and smote, not at any man but at the rock. The great perpendicular gash that marks the face of the Mount of Calydon on the opposite side of the gulf is the token of the strength of the Apostle's arm. Then he yielded peaceably to martyrdom. As for the spring, it was a holy fountain long enough before the Apostle came here, for it was shown to Pausanias as a very ancient Oracle. If any fell sick, those interested in their fate might come here to enquire,

196

and the 'Querist' had to let down a mirror by a cord till the flat surface of the metal just touched the water. Then, when he drew it up and looked in, the 'Querist' saw not his own face but that of the 'Quesited'. If the face was living, the sick person would recover; if he appeared as dead, then there was no help for him. To this day something of the sort is done at times at this *agiasma* or holy well, and it has, men say, some mysterious spiritual power as well. Over it there is a modern version of an ancient inscription, which you can read forwards or backwards at pleasure, thus:

ΝΙΨΟΝ ΑΝΟΜΗΜΑΤΑ ΜΗ ΜΟΝΑΝ ΟΨΙΝ

'Cleanse thy sins not thy face only.'

There is plenty of record of ancient things in Patras, for they had primitive customs here that were so grim that even a king who turned up just after the Trojan War—and folk were not particular at that age —felt it needful to reform them. Nowhere else did the Great Mother receive such awful tribute. Nothing, however, is to be seen above ground from either primitive or classical days, and the only monument of the 'silver age' of the land that did come down to our own period met with a doleful fate. This was a small Odeon which Pausanias describes as second only to the great one at Athens, and far more elegant and beautiful than that ever was. It was uncovered, in all its completeness, quite lately, with its marble seating and pavement quite complete; that was in the year 1910. But nothing that the small foreign colony could do would induce the municipal authorities to take any steps whatever to preserve it. So, all the marble gradually vanished, being used locally for wash-basins, door-steps, and even meaner uses, till nothing but the brick core of the unique building was left. Now, by way of giving a literal illustration of an old proverb, they have put a gate on the place and locked it up.

Actually, then, the main interest of the town is mediaeval, for a port that was so easily reached from Venice was a stronghold of Latin influence during their rule in Greece. Hence it is that the treasured relics of St. Andrew are now at Rome, not Patras, and hence the fine castle of late date that stands over the town—which the 'hyper-Hellenic' town council were anxious to destroy not long ago 'as a monument of slavery'.

As a Latin stronghold, in 1364 or thereabouts it was the home of Carlo Zeno, the Venetian, one of those men in whose careers Clio, muse of history, sets out to show that when she really gives her mind to it she can easily outdo both romance and probability. We

197

find this hero of romance at Patras as a rather juvenile canon of the Cathedral, that being the provision that an annoyed family had made for him after he had gambled away allowance, books and clothing at Padua University, and had afterwards, feeling a delicacy about going home, put in two or three years with the *condottieri* of the day. Family councils had decided that Carlo's career was to be the Church; so he accepted Orders enough—it was probably a very low minimum —to enable him to hold his prebend at Patras, and had just entered into residence there when the Greeks attacked the place. At once, the canon took command of the garrison, and his 'aggressive defence' sent the enemy flying. However, some mere layman was insolent enough to say that the act might be good service but was scantly clerical. Shall a canon allow his cloth to be aspersed? Perish the thought! Dom Carlo Zeno challenged his traducer to a duel and slew him, but coming to the conclusion afterwards that the fellow had some right on his side, he resigned the clerical career for the military one for which he felt much better suited, and ordered special prayers for the soul of his late adversary. For his further adventures, manifold and incredible, but absolutely historical, we must refer readers to the history of Venice.

History does not end here with the Latin occupation, for the blue gulf off Patras was the real scene of the great battle of Lepanto, A.D. 1575, though it takes its name from that corrupt version of the classical Naupactus, which was where the relics of the Turkish fleet could find refuge that day. Though the victory was not improved, that day marked the fact that the high water mark of Ottoman power on the sea was past, so that it was a true instinct that made even Protestants regard it as a triumph for Christendom; a wave of feeling that reached even as far north as Scotland, and made King James VI of that land commemorate it in a poem of over one thousand thoroughly bad Latin hexameters. (It was a task in classic composition, laid upon him by his tutor Buchanan.) It was also the end of a military age, for it was the last great battle fought by two fleets of galleys, in the waters where that armament had been supreme since history and seamanship began. It is true that even that day showed that their career was done—for Don John of Austria had their beaks chopped off before going into action. Gun and arquebus, not the ram, decided that battle.

Thus, if you want old ways and monuments at Patras, you must look for them in the ways and habits of the people, where they certainly abound. Not, perhaps, to a greater extent here than elsewhere in Greece, but the writer happens to have had better opportunity of access to them here. Here then it was that an English lady, who had dismissed a very unsatisfactory and disagreeable servant for open theft, found all the rest of the household begging for forgiveness for her, in spite of the fact that they had hated her before. The thief was turned out, however, and then at last things came clear enough: 'Kyria! She is a witch, and a Thessalian witch! And she left the house in anger! Kyria, for heaven's sake wear garlic.' Garlic is a great preventive of all evil influences, spiritual and material. When there is a birth in a house and the 'Wise Woman' comes to do her duty, then if she knows anything of her business she will wear this herb and see to it that her patient does too, for the hour when life begins is naturally the time when all enemies and evil spirits will seek to do the new-born a mischief; the mother too needs special guarding at such a time. That garlic is a real preventive of and cure for at least one definite evil, *viz.* malaria, is a fact for which we can vouch personally.

Means of harmful magic, as well as preventive, are remembered and practised here. We remember how an English lady once resident in Patras found her housemaid brandishing a revolver, and proclaiming that she meant to be revenged on a faithless swain, who had got her into trouble and abandoned her; she would shoot him first and herself after. The Englishwoman rose finely to the occasion, addressing her maid most severely: 'Theodora, if I find you doing anything of the sort, I shall dismiss you at once! Give me that pistol.' That awful threat so impressed the servant that she gave up the revolver quite meekly and took to magic instead. Students of Theocritus will remember the Eclogue *Pharmaceutria*, in which poor Simaetha stands at the cross-roads, working her spells with whirling wheel and wry-neck, and chanting her haunting refrain: 'Wheel, magic wheel, draw this man back to me.' Theodora in like case worked precisely the same spell (which no doubt is far older than 200 B.C., which is the date of Theocritus), with the trifling exception that she used a hoopoe instead of a wry-neck. Alas, the magic did not work, and faithless Andreas married another. Still, Theodora was at least believed to have got even with him, for folk suspected her grievously of being the person that wove the spell that prevented the perjured lover from 'getting any good' of his marriage. Someone, this was certain, got into the bridal chamber that morning and left there a twist of cord with three knots tied in it, and the scrawl: 'I bind Andreas and Maria, and the Devil in between 'em.' It was found there when the couple were led in by the *paranymphos*, or best man, and there was no getting out of that! The only person who can unbind such a spell is the person who will confess to having bound it, and that is naturally a hard thing to find.

When it is time to go on from Patras up the gulf towards Athens, it is best to go by sea if that be possible. Boats go regularly, and the sea passage is much more interesting and beautiful than the railway, at any rate by day, and not so very much slower. Further, for classical students, one of the boats that wander from side to side of the gulf will have the advantage of taking the traveller over the 'field' of other great battles, those which Phormio won for his country in the Peloponnesian War. This officer was, as we have called him elsewhere, the 'Cochrane of Athens', and one who had better fortune than Cochrane himself had when he served Greece in the War of Independence. That is to say he, as a leader, took what looked like impossible odds and awful chances, but in a spirit that was the very reverse of recklessness. There was a cool calculation of risks and a deliberate planning of action that usually brought off a victory at an amazingly low cost. In 429 B.C., Phormio with a squadron of twenty ships was lying at Naupactus, the refuge of the exiled Messenians that was a safe base for any power that was fighting Sparta, while a big fleet of the enemy was trying to concentrate at Leucas and act against the Acarnanian coast. Phormio with his twenty caught forty-seven of the Spartans out in the comparatively open water where Lepanto was fought later, outside the narrows of the gulf. The Corinthians (for most of the Spartan fleet was drawn from them) paid the Athenians the compliment of standing on the defensive in a 'globe' formation while Phormio with his perfectly trained men rowed round and round them, repeatedly threatening an attack yet never pushing one home, till the 'globe' got confused and began to break formation, and the morning breeze, on which he had calculated, finished the work. Then the attack was pushed home and ended in a rout of the forty-seven by the twenty, several being sunk and twelve taken.

Sparta was furious as she had some excuse for being, and raised the numbers of the fleet to seventy-seven, sending orders to the Admiral, Cnemus, to 'fight again, and win this time'. Cnemus took post at Aegion (the port where a traveller going as we have advised is most likely to land on this voyage), inside the narrows of the straits, while Phormio with his twenty remained outside, but even with odds of four to one in his favour the Spartan did not care to face the terrible skill of the Athenian in manoeuvre out in the open, while Phormio was too prudent to be caught in narrow waters where that skill would hardly avail. For a week they faced one another, and then Cnemus decided to force on an action by an attack on Naupactus, and this move on his ally and his own base brought Phormio up to give help. Hence he had to accept the risk of action in the strait, where numbers were bound to tell. Nine of his twenty ships were driven ashore, where the Messenians saved their crews and prevented the Spartans from carrying off the prizes, while eleven had to run for it to Naupactus, with all the twenty fastest of the Peloponnesian fleet in full cry behind them. As they approached the safety of the harbour they saw a neutral merchant craft lying in the mouth of the bay, and the rearmost of the Athenians, which was very close pressed by her pursuer, suddenly circled that ship and was able to ram and sink her leading enemy before an attack was expected. The sudden shock staggered the whole pursuit and instantly the Athenians turned to the attack and the eleven routed the twenty, capturing six besides sinking the one mentioned. The bulk of the Spartan fleet was too flabbergasted at the sudden change of the battle to do anything at all, and Phormio now rescued his own nine disabled craft, and returned in triumph to Naupactus. It is no wonder that this was counted the most daring naval exploit of the whole war, and the only reason why we hear no more of so gallant an admiral must be that he died very soon after, very possibly in the great plague that we know attacked Athens in the course of the following year.

What impresses one most in the action, however, is the amazing endurance of the Athenian rowers. From Rhion—the narrows—to Naupactus is just five miles. There was obviously a bit of a fight at the first point, and then the distance to Naupactus had to be done at racing speed to avoid capture (the University boat race course, we will remind readers, is four miles), yet even the last and slowest of the Athenian squadron had still got a spurt left in her men which would enable her to ram her opponent, and all of them were still capable of a second and fairly brisk action. Yet Aristophanes suggests that the standard ration was only barley bread and onions! As for the planning of the actions, it will be seen that Phormio, without losing one of his twenty ships, defeated a very superior enemy twice, and took or destroyed triremes to an even greater number than that of his own whole force. Had he lived longer, the Peloponnesian War might have had a different ending.

201

THE GULF OF CORINTH

Some of the highest mountains in 'old Greece', the range of Erymanthus (along the ridge of which Heracles pursued the big boar), run along the southern shore of the Corinthian Gulf. Cyllene, the highest peak, runs up to 8,000 feet, and carries snow till almost the end of the summer. Two rivers, of which one, the Vistitsa that comes out at Aegion, is the ancient Styx, pierce the range in their descent from the Arcadian plateau, and their gorges afford the most splendid scenery of the country and some of the finest of the type that the writer has the pleasure of having seen. Though the Styx is well worth a visit, for such as can tramp the ravine on foot, it is the second, the Kalavryta or ancient Buraikos, to which we propose to introduce readers now, for whatever the position of the River Styx in Hellenic mythology, folk are hardly likely to find Charon's ferry-boat up its course now, while the Kalavryta stands for much in the mediaeval and modern history of the land.

A railway, branching off from the main line at Diakophto, goes up the gorge, and so narrow is it and so precipitous its sides, that this is actually the only way of ascending it. Investment of the price of a first-class ticket wins—or used to win—permission to walk up or down the track, and that talisman secures that the gates that guard the tunnels will be opened to the foot passenger. Otherwise, one of the most splendid pieces of scenery in the land cannot be seen, for the mule-track that does ascend the valley keeps high up on the hills at the side, and one can see little from the windows of the railway carriages. Once through the gorge, the valley widens a little, and you are in a sort of mountain citadel that once gave an almost inaccessible refuge to two of the greatest of the mediaeval monasteries of Hellas.

One of these is Kalavryta, the place that gives its name to the river and is a spot sacred to every Greek now, for it was there that the standard was first raised by the Bishop Germanus—a prelate whose statue deservedly stands at Patras and also at Athens—in the beginning of the War of Independence. It was literally a raising of the standard, for the flag that was used that day is preserved as one of the most treasured heirlooms in the monastery today.[1] Otherwise, the present building has little to attract a visitor, for its picturesqueness can easily be matched elsewhere.

[1] The first national flag was different from the present one, being red and gold in colour. The blue and white stripes of the national standard of today have a somewhat homely derivation, though none the worse for that. They are generally said to have been taken from the white kilts of the land soldiers and the blue breeches of the sailors.

Lower down the valley, though still above the highest point of the gorge, and indeed just where it begins to widen out into the possibility of cultivation, we find the premier monastery of the older Greece, the house known popularly as Megaspelaeon, the monastery of the Great Cave. Its position is a wonder in itself. Just at the widening point of the vale there is, as is usual enough in limestone scenery, a great beetling cliff, crowning the long steep slope of the débris that has fallen from it in past ages. At the top of that slope is a good-sized cavern, which actually contains the church of the monastery, and not improbably served as church before the present fabric was built, while the rest of the monastic buildings are plastered like a colony of swallows' nests against the precipice, often actually backing upon the rock. It can be reached by a winding mule-track without difficulty, though the slope is as steep as it well can be.

According to the legend—which is recorded only in two abstracts from the older Chronicles, that were saved in 1640 from a fire that then destroyed the bulk of the buildings, and left only the church—there were two holy monks of Jerusalem in the days of the apostate Julian, who were warned by a vision of the Panagia to leave their own homes and wander to Aegion in Greece, where it was promised that further guidance would be given them. There they met a shepherdess, a girl of the name of Euphrosyne, who told them how she had been led, while seeking a stray goat, to a cave in the mountains, where was a most holy Eikon of the Blessed Virgin, embedded in the ivy. Under the girl's guidance, the Eikon was duly found, and proved to be a 'far finer thing than Pheidias ever wrought', while there was definite proof available—the character of the proof is unfortunately not given—that it was the actual work of St. Luke, who had written his gospel in that cavern, and produced this Eikon to confound the Eikonoclasts in anticipation. A dragon which appeared on the scene as the guardian of the holy picture having been killed by the prayers of the fathers (at all events his bones were shown till the fire of 1640), the monastery was founded, and the girl Euphrosyne became an anchoress in the neighbourhood, while some additional sanctity was secured by the fact that the two monks were opportunely martyred by the wicked persecutor Julian, and indeed, everything needful for the future prosperity of the monastery was secured. As for the facts, the Eikon is certainly of an unusual type, for it is some sort of wax composition—or so it appears, for we naturally have never handled or tested it—and in fairly high relief and of a type rather unlike the usual conventional 'Panagia' of Byzantine art. The tradition that St. Luke was a painter goes back certainly as far as the fourth century, but the identification of this with any supposed work of his is shadowy in the extreme. A 'Chrysobull' of the emperor John Cantacuzene, dating from 1350 and quoted in the abstract referred to above, assumes that the Gospel was undoubtedly written here, and points out that, in that case, it is quite certain that the evangelist would have given a special copy to the 'Excellent Theophilus' to whom it is addressed, and who may have been governor of the province of Achaia at the time. If he did this, is it not natural to suppose that he would have given him a portrait of the Blessed Virgin as well, and what else can it be but this one?

Personally, we do not venture any opinion as to the age of the relic, and only suggest that, being in high relief which is exceptional in the Orthodox Church, it may possibly be of older date than the Eikonoclastic controversy, after which the convention of flat surfaces prevailed.

Of course, the genuineness of the Eikon soon became a matter of honour to the monks of the monastery, the full title of which is 'The monastery of the Repose (*Koemesis*) of the all-holy Theotokos, the Stauropegîon which possesses the holy Eikon wrought by St. Luke'. A Stauropegîon, it may be well to explain, is a monastery which is outside all diocesan authority, and depends directly and solely on the Oecumenical Patriarch at Constantinople. It is a privilege which many monasteries sought to obtain in every land, though in the West the object was to obtain a grant of similar dependence solely on the Pope; but, fortunately perhaps for the continuance of the monastic institution in Orthodox lands, a privilege that was very often demoralizing in effect was granted here much more rarely than with us.

The fact that the place was burned down as late as 1640, in which fire all the records perished, implies that the Megaspelaeon has no history previous to that date, the earliest documents surviving being a formal letter from the Patriarch of Constantinople confirming all the old privileges of which record had been lost, and a *firman* from the then Sultan 'directing' the rebuilding of it. It should be understood that in old Turkey a *firman* was not so much a command as a permission—the standing order being 'thou shalt do nothing at all' — and only implied that local officials were not to prevent Christians from rebuilding the ruined monastery at their own expense.

It must have been shortly after the fire that an episode occurred which is the pride of the house to this day, as the most recent and by no means the least of their miracles. Pirates of some undefined school were haunting the Gulf of Corinth, and they somehow penetrated the mountains and levied a heavy forced contribution on the monastery. This, however, had the after-effect of bringing the monks into serious trouble with the Turkish authorities, who naturally regarded the fact that they had not protected the *Rayahs* (subjects) from the pirates as somehow implying guilty connivance on those *Rayahs'* part. Abbot and prior were both ordered for immediate execution, but—the sword broke upon their holy necks. So impressed were the Turkish Pasha and his followers by this miracle, that they spared both the victims and their monastery, and only made them pay for the broken sword! That last touch is so characteristically and uninventably Turkish—as those will know who have had the pleasure of being conducted to prison by the police of that land, and then found that they had to pay all the expenses of their own journey to gaol, plus the cost of a return ticket for the policeman—that for its sake we accept also the story of the miracle in which it is imbedded! Do they not show the broken blade to this day? What better proof can anyone desire?

This mountain district of the Morea was the stronghold of the Greeks during their War of Independence, and that fact, in the light of the additional one that it was the bishops and clergy who were the soul of the rising throughout, brought Ibrahim Pasha against this monastery, in the course of the struggle. His letter of summons to surrender, written in most execrable Greek upon a scrap of paper that is none too clean, is now one of the trophies and treasures of the place. The reply of the monks was, that they were bound by the most terrible of oaths to accept nothing but freedom or death, and that therefore they were bound to resist. If Ibrahim should capture the place, to cut the throats of a handful of monks would add but little to the fame of so great a general, while if he should fail, as by the power of heaven they were convinced that he would, that would be shame unspeakable for him, and the fact would rouse the spirit of all the Greeks in the land. Wherefore they begged him to leave them in peace.

Naturally, Ibrahim attacked the monastery on receipt of this defiance, but found it by no means the easy job he had anticipated. His artillery could only be brought to bear directly upon the monastery from the opposite side of the valley, here of considerable width, and though of course the first shell from a modern gun would have blown the buildings clean out of their cave, it was quite beyond the range of the cannon of 1825. An attempt to breach the walls by fire from below and to storm the place was repulsed, while the fact that Kolokotronis, the general of the insurgents, was in the near neighbourhood and could cut up Ibrahim's provision and munition convoys at pleasure in the mountains, made it very difficult to maintain the siege. Presently, the Pasha adopted a scheme that shows how little hope he now had of succeeding, for he sent men up to the top of the great cliff that rises above the monastery, with instructions to roll rocks upon it and crush the defenders. Even this proved impossible, for the great precipice 'beetles' and projects so far that the rocks fell clear of the buildings, which no doubt in those days projected a shorter distance from the rock than they do at present. Disappointed and disgusted, Ibrahim gave up the siege and withdrew, leaving the monks to a very natural joy in their triumph.

Note.—Alas, the traveller will not find, now, the Megaspelaeon that we describe. In 1940 an accidental fire—started by a monk who was doing some cooking in his cell and went to sleep over it—destroyed the whole monastery save a modern guest-house. Only the famous Eikon of the Panagia seems to have been saved. One questions if much of historical interest can have perished, as nothing was saved from the holocaust of 1640, but a most picturesque monument has vanished. No doubt the monastery will continue, but most probably on a far smaller scale and—to judge from like cases elsewhere—in buildings more convenient but far less beautiful.

XI

CRETE

Travel in Crete—Modern customs—Turkish rule—Brigands—
Classic and Roman Crete—The Gortyna Code—Titus and Christi-
anity—Byzantine rule—Saracen, Venetian and Turkish conquests—
Union with Greece—Ancient Crete—Minos and Atlantis legends—
Minoan civilization, commerce and art—Palaces—Water supply—
Habits of life—Women's position—The Labyrinth—Taurokathapsia
—Religion—Cult of the Great Mother—Earthquake cult—Zagreus
legend—Fall of Minoan kingdom—Cretans in Egypt—The Dorians

Crete is always a special expedition, and one that—save in
summer, when an island in that latitude may be hot—is very
apt to imply a rough crossing. As voyagers like the apostle
Paul have found, weather there can be tricky, for to quote another
mariner of experience, 'the wind can come down from those
mountains as if it wanted to blow the ship out of the water.' Once
there, however, there are few pleasanter places in which to travel.
It is true that you will find—save of course at the ports—few hotels,
but there are village inns, and there are the houses of the leading
villagers and there are the monasteries, where the only ill that you
are likely to suffer from is over-kindness.

Cretans have been given an ill name in history, even by inspired
apostles, but the writer, who has always found Greeks most kindly
folk to travel among, owns to a special fondness for the Cretan among
the Greeks. As for their reputation—it must be owned that it is hard
to be called liars all the world over just for asserting what is a bare
fact, and to you a perfectly familiar and undeniable one. Greeks
gave them the name for asserting that they had among them the
tomb of Zeus, which was, of course a patent absurdity—but nevertheless a simple fact. Anyone who approaches Candia—or Heracleion

to give it its proper name—which is the port to which all visitors come who wish to see the ruins of Knossos, can hardly avoid seeing both the tomb and Father Zeus recumbent thereon, particularly if they make their approach from the north or north-west. The fact is that the sky-line of the hill of Juktas, the most conspicuous object in the landscape thereabout, gives the profile of a bearded and recumbent giant from that aspect; and it is a fine face too, though we own that the nose—the weak point of the whole—has not been improved by the devotion which has put a little whitewashed church on the tip of it. That, to every Cretan of old, was the Tomb of Zeus, who to them was the Son-Husband of the Great Mother, and only later won identification with the Sky-God of the Hellenes and rank as Father of Gods and Men. On entering the harbour, one passes the little Isle of Dia, or Zeus. Here, according to local tradition, the god kept a 'bachelor establishment', for use on those numerous occasions when Hera's temper had become—quite justifiably—intolerable.

As a people who, fortunately for themselves, are still what other nations call backward, they have kept their old costume, at least in the country districts, and many of their old customs and superstitions. The Cretan's costume—which is really more Turkish than original Cretan, and certainly is more ample than what the pictures tell us was in vogue in Minoan days—consists of a dark blue 'Zouave' coat, and breeches—if indeed we ought to use the dual number for a garment that is not divided—of a really magnificent bagginess. We have seen a worthy Mahommedan, who was doing his marketing, stow two kettles and a saucepan in the seat of that garment, and walk away, clanking a little, certainly, but quite at his ease. A voluminous waist-band, as tight as those that his Minoan ancestors used to wear, covers the gap between coat and trousers, and his legs are covered with stout top-boots, which are a most practical thing to wear in a land so thorny as is Crete. A small hiatus is *de rigueur* between the top of the boot and the garter-band of the breeches.

Personally, the Cretan has kept the build and often the feature of his Minoan forebears, being tall and rather slender of bone, with the curious slim waist and 'forward-growing' beard of the ancient frescoes. However many immigrants there may have been in the last three thousand years, the land has taken them in and made them its own.[1]

[1] English lady anthropologists bear this out. They made a habit of measuring skulls in all villages, which excited some suspicion till it became a game and any unmeasured head had to be brought in and put under the

18. Megaspelaeon

19a. Knossos. The grand Stairway

19b. Knossos. The 'Theatral Area' or 'dancing floor' known to
Homer in ancient Crete and now unearthed. A settlement of the
ground has disturbed the levels. The 'steps' in the background are the
seats for spectators.

Quaint superstitions present a field for the folk-lorist that has hardly been even touched as yet, and we give just one specimen of them. Folk in a certain village complained bitterly to an English excavator that 'those wicked Mahommedans' had scraped off the eyes of the holy eikons in the Church. Examination proved that this had been done in truth, and an artist was produced to make things right again; but alas, next year, 'those scoundrels had done it again.' This time, however, the Englishman instituted an enquiry, which proved that though it may well have been Moslems who were guilty of the act, they had done it not so much *qua* Mahommedan as *qua* natural and human man. The eyes of the saints, properly scraped off, and duly administered, make an infallible and irresistible love-philtre! Though sympathetic, the Englishman refused to provide a constant supply of this article.

Ottoman rule was never very complete in Greece as we have seen, and was still less so in Crete, where only the lowlands were Turkish at all, and the hills, often very rugged, were left to the Christians, who, in spite of their repeated revolts, remained under the Turkish flag till 1912. There were constantly awful happenings, from the time of the War of Greek Independence in 1820 onwards—sanguinary risings and reprisals as sanguinary. Cretans will still show you the Cave of Suffocation, where five hundred men, women and children were penned in 1829, and a fire lighted at the mouth, so that the smoke poured in and every soul was smothered.

Arcadîa Monastery has a tale, the consummation of which is pictured in many a restaurant all up and down continental Greece, for the episode has been unforgettable. The place was held against the Ottomans in one of the many revolts, abbot and monks taking their full share in the fighting. Presently, it became clear that the abbey was no longer tenable, and that the storming by the besieging soldiers and *bashi-bozouks* must come in a very short time. The abbot gathered his whole garrison—men, women and children—in the solidly built refectory of the monastery that had served as powder magazine. There the heads of the big powder-barrels were knocked out, the abbot rose in the midst, ceremonial taper in hand, gave solemn absolution to all present, and with his own hand fired

tape. While there has been so much Venetian immigration that about one name in six in the isle is of that derivation, the proportion of broad Italian skulls is negligible. The Italian immigrants—and other types too—have become Cretan.

o   209   H.T.

the powder and sent all there to eternity together, just as the enemy burst in. It is one of the episodes that make one understand the grip the Orthodox Church still has on the hearts of her people.

The Christians of Crete then were rather apt to be 'brigands' and to raid Turks, particularly during their long struggles for unity with Greece. It was a habit that they found it hard to give up even after the union, though the Athens authorities expostulated with them seriously. 'But we have always raided those Turks,' said the Cretans. 'We did it even while we were under the Sultan, whom we had to respect even if we hated him. Do you think that we shall stop now, when we are under a set of—minutely but unquotably described— lawyers whom we do not respect?'

That ingenuous explanation was offered about 1920, and since then much has happened. Owing to the 'Exchange of Populations', there were practically no Turks left in the island, and further, a man whom they did respect became the Prime Minister at Athens. This respect was not given because he happened to be a statesman of European reputation, which goes for nothing in Crete. He was a Cretan born (even though his name of Venizelos would seem to argue Venetian ancestry) and, what is more, one who in younger days when the Turks ruled here was an honoured 'brigand'—outlaw is what we should say—himself. That is to say, he took to the hills after a disagreement with the Ottoman authorities, and made his reputation there by holding aloft the unlawful Greek flag after it had been struck down by a shell from a British cruiser. Naturally, Cretans felt that they could obey such a man without loss of self-respect.

Thus, the island became as orderly as Greece, and even while there were still some outlaws in the hills, the ordinary tourist ran little risk from them.

To give any clear idea of the ancient history of Crete is not quite easy. Definite civilization has existed there for six thousand years, and development has been continuous since Neolithic days, whether the ruling power has been Minoan, Hellenic, Roman, Byzantine, Saracen, Venetian, Turk or modern Greek. It will be easiest to begin near the end of this magnificently lengthy story, in those relatively modern days which saw the foundation of Rome and the date of the first Olympiad, about 750 B.C. We may say something of the later history of Crete, before turning back to that earlier period, of which we know so much of the culture and so little of the history, the period of the Minoan Empire.

CRETE IN THE CLASSIC PERIOD

In all the classical period, Crete was powerless and unimportant, because of her utterly divided state. Though there were memories of great chiefs who brought their contingents to Troy thence, men like Idomeneus and Meriones, the 'hundred cities' had come to mean nothing but division. Yet even so the first great authentic document of Hellenic culture is Cretan, the wonderful Code of Gortyna; this code of laws presupposes some history behind it, for much of it deals with the important matter of the necessity of giving heiresses in marriage within the tribe, so as to prevent the break-up of families. It still stands in its original form of ten great 'tables' close to the church of the village from which it is named, and is written in the ancient *boustrophêdon* script, going 'back and forth' across the marble, like the ox-plough across the field.

Crete hardly appears at all in Greek history as taught in schools, but it fell under Rome soon after the rest of the country had done so, though in a very different manner. Metellus Creticus, who conquered it in 66 B.C. had quite as much hard fighting as even a Roman general could desire, when the mountaineers stood against him in their country covered with its forests of cedar and cypress, and seamed with deep gorges with perpendicular sides, the bottoms of which were choked with thickets of oleander and giant heliotrope.[1] Yet, Rome meant the coming of an order strange to Crete since the empire of Minos had passed away, and Christianity came in her train and perhaps with her soldiers. Titus, the apostle of the land, sleeps in the church at Gortyna, under the shadow of the great code, and close to a temple of Isis that still keeps the little crypt that seems to have played a part in the initiation of postulants into her mysteries.[2]

History there is none, till in 823 A.D., when Crete was officially part of the Empire of Constantinople, the Saracen raiders landed and at least went so far towards conquering the island that they turned out the Byzantine administration. Further than that they hardly seem to have gone, though they established a great pirate stronghold

---

[1] The two last-named remain in all their luxuriance, in the gorges described, and the lowland districts abound with vine and olive: the mountains, even if some of them still bear the name of 'Cedar Hills' are bare of trees, and every plant upon them, even the little blue chicory familiar to us in England, has taken to growing formidable thorns as the only possible defence against the Cretan goat! The general look of the hills is summed up in the verdict of a friend with whom the writer once wandered over them; 'it's like a photograph of lunar scenery.'

[2] There is an arrangement by which water could be admitted to rise to the very lips of a man standing in the little 'cell', and then flow away through a syphon.

at a port that took its name, Kandia, from the great ditch (*khandaq*) and palisade with which they defended it. It must be allowed that the 'ditch' in question, the huge moat that still surrounds the town, is a fine piece of engineering work.

About a century and a half later, in 975, Kandia was won back for the empire, after a siege rather longer than that of Troy, by Nicephorus Phocas, the great re-organizer of Constantinople. However, even this service to Roman civilization, and the additional fact that he was the real founder of the first and greatest of the monasteries of Mount Athos, could hardly win him pardon in ecclesiastical circles then for the fact that he had renounced an early aspiration of becoming a monk in company with a friend of his boyhood (whom he had established on the 'Holy Mountain') and had so declined to worldly ways as to 'put an earthly crown on his head, instead of a heavenly one' in the shape of the tonsure.

Constantinople was set fairly on its feet again by the work of Nicephorus, and Crete remained in the hands of imperial authority, and served as a base for the checking of Saracen sea-raids, till the dolorous year 1204. Then the Fourth Crusade, which started to redeem the Sepulchre of the Lord from the infidel, turned aside to shatter the great bulwark of Christianity; it sacked Constantinople, and by its destruction of the Greek Empire was responsible for the ultimate conquest of half Europe by the Turk. Venice (a power which really took the rôle of Mephistopheles in the whole disgraceful business) was wise enough to take only such portions of the loot as she knew she could manage and keep—islands and trading harbours. Crete therefore fell to her, and she ruled in Candia and other coastal towns till 1669, leaving abundant witness of her rule in fortifications and winged lions of St. Mark. In the year named, however (when the wars of Louis XIV against the empire gave the Turk the sort of chance of which he was never slow to take advantage), Crete passed under the Crescent again, though it must be owned that the Venetians put up a heroic defence, seeing that Candia, under Morosini, held out for what we believe to be actually the longest regular siege in history, twenty-one years, from 1648 to 1669.

So Crete was ruled by the Turk, to remain forever restless and half-conquered, rising when Greece rose, and taking every opportunity of a Turko-Greek war thereafter to claim that union which her unquenchable sense of Greek nationality told her was hers by right. It was a sense of nationality that seems to date, not from classic days (when, as we have seen, the connexion between Crete and

212

Hellas was of the slightest), but from that thousand years of the Christian Empire of Constantinople which counted for so much more than (until lately) historians were wont to allow. At last, in 1912, what she had claimed so often became hers at last.

Turning now to the prehistoric civilization of Crete, the re-discovery of which has been one of the great archaeological feats of our time, it is best to recall first the legends on the subject that were current in the classical age of Hellas, remembering that excavation of traditional sites has almost always been found to confirm those legends in general outline, if not always in detail. Greeks then had a folk-memory of a great king in Crete, whom they called Minos, who was in some sense a son of Zeus, and who ruled by the power of the first fleet in story, over the isles of the sea. He kept a mysterious 'labyrinth' in which lived the fearful 'man-bull' or 'tauro-centaur', the Minotaur, and he drew at intervals the tribute of youths and maidens from Athens who were cast to that monster, till Theseus the hero slew it. There were further stories of Theseus' dive into the sea to fetch up the gold ring, of Ariadne the princess, and of Talus, the bronze giant—the first mechanical 'robot'—who guarded the coasts.

A second group of tales spoke of Daedalus the cunning artificer, who fled from Athens and 'in Knossos wrought the wondrous dancing-floor for fair-haired Ariadne', and who ultimately escaped by means of the first 'glider'.

Third we must remember another account, given to Solon when he was in Egypt by the priests of that land, and preserved for us by Plato. Here Minos appears again as son of Zeus, his mother being Europa, so bringing in the bull-motif in connexion with him once more. He is at once the great king, priest and law-giver, who rules in Atlantis over the great sea to the west, beyond the Pillars of Hercules, and who is taken back to Zeus his father after nine years of rule. In the courtyard of his palace, which was also the temple court, men hunted wild bulls with nooses, and he was the greatest of all kings. Yet suddenly all the glory came to an end, when Atlantis sank in the sea and was lost to man.

Apropos of this, it may be interesting to recall that Schliemann, whose marvellous flair in archaeology every student knows of, was convinced that Crete was the real Atlantis, long before any dis-coveries were made there, and pointed out that to an Egyptian the 'Great Sea' was not the Atlantic but the Mediterranean, while the expression 'beyond the Pillars of Hercules' need not be construed as a literal reference to Gibraltar, but only as meaning 'far away'. It was Schliemann's hope to excavate in Crete, where he was always sure that great discoveries would be made. At least his mantle fell on the shoulders of a worthy successor.

Fourth, we may remember the description that Homer gives in the *Odyssey*, of the Palace of Alcinoos, with its gold-plated doors and jambs of silver, and decorations of blue *kyanos* enamel. It is true that Phaeacia may or may not be Corfu—always supposing that it is not somewhere in fairyland—but there is probably no question that the picture of the luxury of the greatest and wisest of kings is drawn from the general tradition of the Cretan Palace, where we find so many of these details in actual fact.

These, then, are the legends as preserved in the folk-memory of classic and pre-classic Greece, and now we may ask, how far archaeology confirms them, and generally, what does it tell us of what we may call the Minoan civilization. Broadly we may say this: of the life, the habits, and in a measure the ideas, of these people we know much; of their history, nothing at all. It is much as if all that a future explorer had to go upon for his knowledge of England were a mutilated catalogue of the Army and Navy stores, and the cellars of Buckingham Palace, with a little of the ground floor, after the building had been most thoroughly looted.

It is certain that we have in Knossos the capital of a great sea-power, for what appears is a great unfortified palace-city, in the midst of a large town that was similarly open. While far richer than 'Mycenae, rich in gold', it lay exposed to any foe who dared to come, trusting to its ships to guard it. Minos may be a terror to foreigners, but he lives unguarded among his own people. The kingdom of which this is the capital extends, at least in its developed form, all over the land. Roman-like roads connect it with all other cities, being detected by the trained eye of an archaeologist who happened to be also a road-surveyor.[1] Viaducts that are carried on corbelled arches take these roads over the rivers, and the monuments give us proof enough of wheeled traffic, while one of the earliest imports of which we have evidence is a horse. Much of the merchandise that went on these ways came from Egypt, for there was direct connexion with that land by a port on the southern side of the island. Statues of Egyptian work and Syenite vases, whose material at least came from up the Nile, are found in the ruins, while in Egypt pictures of the

[1] The late Sir Arthur Evans.

Keftiu who come as ambassadors have now a meaning that they failed to yield at first, and it even seems that the great palace of Hawara which Herodotus saw was the work of an architect who had at least seen and studied that of Knossos. Not that their commerce was confined to Egypt, or for that matter to the Mediterranean, where we know that it extended. Axes of jade and nephrite that were found in the excavations can have come from no nearer place than China, and bear witness to some sort of touch with that land.

These Minoans could certainly write, for we have evidence of no fewer than three distinct scripts existing among them, none of which are hieroglyphic, though that type is also found. The only writings preserved are on clay tablets which were the labels on big chests of stores, tablets which have been preserved by the agency of the very fire that destroyed what they indicated with the rest of the palace, but has burned them hard. Clay tablets, however, were not the usual medium of writing here, though they were in Mesopotamia. The writing on them is done with a reed, and a scribe whose usual instrument is a reed writes on paper or parchment in some form. The Babylonian scribe with his mud tablet used a *style*.

Here in Crete we have an alphabet that is certainly far older than that introduced into Greece by Cadmus—and which somehow we do not think that wandering Phoenician really invented himself, though he may conceivably have simplified it, as his kin simplified cuneiform in their own land. Unhappily, it cannot be read as yet, though every archaeologist who works at the problem hopes that it may be his lot to find that bi-lingual inscription that will give the key to it, and which the fitness of things surely requires to exist somewhere.[1]

Crete had its system of weights, and the fact that its surviving standard, which bears an octopus as token, is the same as the Babylonian and Jewish talent, suggests early trading intercourse between them. They had even their coinage, in an age when gold ingots or material oxen were the units elsewhere, and their method of producing it (that of making flat slicings or 'skillings', which is the

---

[1] The clay tablets give the numerals with some certainty, with symbols for units, tens and hundreds. This is evidence that the Cretan had—what the Roman never acquired—a decimal system of notation.

As for the bi-lingual inscription, the Swedes who excavated Asine near Nauplia (a Minoan colony) found a *graffito* of eight Cretan words in the Greek script which is said to show a kinship between Cretan and Albanian, and the Cretan mercenaries in Egyptian service left *graffiti* on the temple at Beth-shan.

original of our English shilling, from a golden bar) is the one that was in use in England up to the late Middle Ages.

If the Minoans were thus a commercial and seafaring folk, it is most interesting to find in their houses surviving evidence of a high level of domestic comfort. In any royal palace you may find evidence of a luxury that nobody else in the land could have, but a comfort that could be general is a much rarer thing, and one that was not found again—with the possible exception of some of the greater cities of Magna Graecia in their great days—until the England of the late nineteenth century. Thus we find in the palace a drainage system and general sanitary appliances which a French savant to whom they were exhibited could only describe as being '*vraiment anglais*', and which, in at least one of the palaces, still works after an interval of perhaps four thousand years. It was far superior to anything available at Edinburgh (or for that matter, at Versailles) until the date given. This must be coupled with a water supply drawn from the hills by pipes and brought to the palace across a valley by a 'siphon system' which, if Rome ever knew, she certainly did not use in her great aqueducts. This extends to other houses than the palace, and both houses and palace are planned on a system better suited to the climate than anything ever evolved in the great Roman palace on the Palatine, for their 'light-well' system gives illumination enough for that latitude, while securing that at least the living rooms shall be cool in the trying summer. It must be owned that the Cretan never seems to have troubled about external effect or a grand façade, arguing perhaps that people lived inside their houses and not outside them. The plan of his palace does resemble the maze later folk thought it to be. That he could produce real dignity in what he judged the proper place is plain enough from the many-flighted stairway that Sir Arthur Evans' wonderful restoration has preserved for us to see, a staircase with steps so designed that a king can move up or down them in his robes, without danger to his royal dignity. How did William the Conqueror manage a stately procession down from his living apartments in his Tower of London?

As for the ordinary houses, we know that they went up to three storeys in height, though their structure—roughish masonry and wooden tie-beams—was hardly such as to resist the earthquakes to which they were often exposed. Their windows, as the surviving picture-plaques on porcelain show, were filled with oiled parchment to admit light, and the way in which the doors swung back into a proper recess so as not to be an obstacle when opened, shows care for comfort in all ranks of life.

When we come to the habits of life which all this argues, we may fairly draw a contrast between what we see here, and what we next meet in the houses of Homer's heroes. In the *Odyssey*, it would seem to be natural to have the slaughter-house and kitchen in the dining room; that Ctesippos of Samê should throw the hoof of the ox at Ulysses during dinner (*Odyss*. xx, 299) is a breach of good manners, but that the hoof should be lying there is only what was to be expected. Contrast that with the refinement of which we get evidence at Knossos. In Homer, the menu would appear to be 'straight meat', either boiled or roast; but in Knossos you have a *batterie de cuisine* that seems to indicate an elaborate bill of fare. When Ulysses takes him a wife, he goes about furnishing the house with a bed, beginning with an axe and the standing olive tree, and he has no other tool and seemingly no other furniture. Here we get not only the oldest throne in Europe but regular low seats for women, hollowed out for comfort, and couches and chests with porcelain plaques for adornment. The king's gaming board is a marvel of inlay in gold, silver and blue enamel, while what looks at first glance like a kitchen tumbler that has met with misfortune is seen on examination to be a royal goblet of rock crystal. The elaborate tools which fashioned these articles of luxury still remain in part. The walls, carefully plastered, are adorned with the frescoes that are our wonder in the museum, and not all of them by any means come from the palace. Some of the best are from a private dwelling, and from the inn or rest-house over the way. Crete was the original home of the Tyrian dye that the murex yielded, which Clytemnestra in later days spread before her lord; while in such work as that of the goldsmith or the ivory carver, it is admitted that Benvenuto Cellini in the sixteenth century of our era would have been proud to produce the Vaphio Cups of a Cretan artist of sixteen centuries before it, and it is doubtful if even he could have carved the ivory Bull-leaper. The Minoan—and we must think of Crete as the centre of an empire spread over most of the Aegean, and of 'Minos' as like 'Pharaoh', the title of the ruler rather than his personal name—seems to have been as it were the Japanese of that ancient day, a people of marvellous artistic instinct, which they tended to express rather on the miniature scale.

In social matters, at least so far as the position of women was concerned, the Minoan was far more advanced than the Greek a thousand years later. We have seen how dull a life a woman of good reputation was apt to lead even in Athens. In Crete, the only evidence that we have is from frescoes and seals, but there women appear at all public shows, unveiled, and it is a very significant thing that a betrothal was not the handing over of the female chattel to a new owner, but the hand-clasp of two equals. Their costumes, at least on ceremonial occasions, were of a modernity that makes the spectator gasp. The priestesses who remain in little faience figurines appear with elaborate flounced skirts to the ankle, a big picture hat, a very tightly laced waist, and a rather daring decolletage. No wonder a French visitor exclaimed on beholding them, 'Mon Dieu, mon ami, ce sont des Parisiennes!' We have evidence that in the matter of hairdressing Cretan ladies managed to achieve almost as many changes as we ourselves have known.

Women seem to have lived an indoor life, if that be a lawful inference from the fact that they are always represented with very white complexions, in contrast to the sunburnt red-brown which the male costume—nothing but a short kilt and a tight belt—showed to some advantage; this, however, did not prevent their driving chariots at times, and hunting, while there is even evidence that some of the noble maidens were trained for the perilous *taurokathapsia*, the bull-baiting sport which was obviously as popular in Crete as ever was its parallel in Spain, or England.

This is one of the points which shows that there was a sub-stratum of barbarism under the surface of the polished civilization that reached such a high level at so early a date. Athenians remembered how the Cretans used to collect captives from other nations, and cast them to some great man-bull monster, in a place that they called the Labyrinth, and we know now that the legend came very near indeed to being literal truth. The Labyrinth of tradition was the palace itself, the Place of the Labrys or 'double axe' which was a sacred symbol undoubtedly among the Cretans, for it survives in several instances. That the termination 'inth' is a locative, we know already, and it appears in such pre-Hellenic sites as Corinth and Tiryns. The Labyrinth then being the actual palace, we can easily see how, when it became a haunted ruin in after ages, men who knew that this maze-like place was so named, should make the word mean 'a maze'. Here these captives, who according to the tradition and the pictures were both youths and maidens, were trained for the bull-baiting sport, of which the final act was, that they were placed in the arena—the great court before the palace— with the huge sacred bull, which was the *bos primigenius*, half as

218

large again as the bull of our day, and they had to provoke and dodge his charges. The *chef d'oeuvre* of the performance, which we have pictured on more than one fresco and vase, was to catch the bull with one hand on either horn, just as he lowered his head to toss in his charge, and to spring up at the same instant. The acrobat then performed a somersault over the head of the beast, assisted of course by the lift of his head as he tossed, and came down with his or her feet on his back. As a sport, it was far more dangerous than any modern trick played by a toreador who has only to dodge the charging bull or play him with a cloth, and called for far more agility and accurate timing. If pictures go for anything, the performer failed often enough. How long the life of even a trained captive was likely to be at such a game we had better not ask too closely. According to the tradition, it was the skill and activity of that handsome barbarian captive, Theseus, at this sport, that won the heart of the Princess Ariadne, and when you have the actual arena, and the frescoes both of games and audience, to study, it does not take much imagination to reconstruct the scene.

The religion of these Minoans seems to have rested on grim and barbarous principles enough, yet the strange modernity that coloured all of that civilization showed up here too, for they had developed that quaint modern mixture of commerce and religion—the church furniture shop! Some seven miles to the east of Knossos at a place now known as Niru Khan, excavators have discovered the depot, where were stored some fifty tripod altars and a like number of ritual double axes, all ready for dedication when they should be wanted by the pious, who were to pay in some currency of Minoan gold 'shillings'.

The principal object of worship, for of course this nation was polytheistic, was that Great Mother who appears so often in the older strata of the religion of the mainland of Greece. She is the Lady of the Wild Wood and of the Wild Beasts, and so is the original of the later and more literary Artemis, and she is the giver and taker of life. By her side there is a male figure, Zagreus in the form that the Greeks made of his name. He is sometimes the husband, and sometimes the child of this grim Madonna, and as he grew more important, later comers could identify him with Zeus or less properly with Dionysus. The symbols of the Mother are first, the double axe or gavel, the *labrys*, that universal sign of power all the world over, and next the Horns of Consecration which we meet still as a means of averting evil, and which may be connected here with the sacred bull that was

219

so important in the lives of the worshippers. Two pillars—or sometimes three—are almost as universal a sign of 'the numinous' as the gavel, but here in Crete we find the Mother also using as one of her symbols the cross. What is symbolized in the mind of her worshippers one cannot even guess, but here it most certainly was, appearing—with the two figures of the Snake-goddess or her priestesses—in the little makeshift shrine that was all that could be put up, when worship had to be kept up somehow after some great disaster; for that reason it appears still, in the reconstructed shrine that now stands in the hall of the Museum. It may be another instance of the way in which prehistoric symbols revive in the folk-memory of a people who do not forget, that the cross of prehistoric Crete should be in the peculiar form, with all the four arms equal, which the Orthodox Church always prefers today.

As the Mother is a triple goddess, *Diva triformis*, ruling in heaven, earth and in the underworld, the animals that are sacred to her are those that represent those three kingdoms, doves for the air, lions or bulls for the earth, and snakes for the world below, and she appears herself on the impression of a seal—the seal has not survived itself—in a form that gives to us, as already suggested, the interpretation of the Lion Gate of a later age at Mycenae. She stands upon the mountain that is represented by a pillar there, and wild, primitive being though she is, has to be clad in the flounced skirt of a later civilization, while her lions ramp against the slope of the hill.

Old though the Mother is in Crete, yet there was a memory of the fact that she came to her island from over-sea, perhaps from Anatolia, though one would not like to hazard a guess how long ago that coming may have been. On an ancient seal she appears, arriving in a ship, though there she is not yet worried with the skirts that a later age made her wear. Imported somehow she must have been, we suppose, if what geologists say be true, that Crete has been an island since long before the appearance of *homo sapiens* on earth. No doubt 'the Minos' was her king-priest, perhaps in a sense the incarnation of either her or her son. We know from a surviving seal that he appeared at some functions wearing a bull-head mask, so that he exactly resembled the Minotaur that Greeks drew on vases later. Of course, the Mother had priestesses also, and it would seem from the seals that these ladies sometimes personated her. According to one old legend, 'the Minos' ruled for nine years and no more, after which he had to enter into the cave of Dicte on

Mount Ida,[1] where Father Zeus himself was born, where he brought
Europa to be wedded, and where Minos himself was born too, and
there the king had to receive 'renewal' after his time of rule. Was
it that the king, here as elsewhere, was regarded as a personification of the fertility of the land, and as such was liable to be sacrificed,
with his attendants, when his powers began to fail? In a later age,
a sacrifice of attendants or captives might have taken his place.
That is of course the merest conjecture, but it covers the facts
known.

Certainly there was a strong belief in a real future life, a much
more real and desirable one than the shadowy Hades of Homer.
Whether it was one definite form of belief is a thing that our present
knowledge does not enable us to say. Some of our scanty evidence—
that of the Hagia Triada Sarcophagus for instance—shows us
practices very much like those of Egypt, though they appear in a
Cretan dress; the Ring of Nestor on the other hand—a Cretan
object undoubtedly, though its discovery at Nestor's home gave it its
name—shows plainly that the artist who engraved it believed in the
future reunion of those who have loved and lost one another here,
and in their admission, perhaps after a trial and acquittal, to the bliss
of a heaven and the abodes of the gods.

That an earthquake region like Crete should have had a strong
'chthonic' side to its religion is only natural. The phenomenon itself
was known as the Roar of the Great Bull who was tossing the earth
on his horns, and the god's sacred animal was sacrificed to him when
the thing happened, for 'in bulls doth the Earth-shaker rejoice'. A
house that he had chosen to destroy was filled up and often abandoned after such sacrifices, and worship that might avert his anger
was carried on in underground crypts and caverns, and in those
'lustral basins' that we find in the ruins, which were turned into
shrines later. But usually it seems that the great temples or precincts
were on hill-tops, with only small shrines in palaces or houses. The
sacred tree, however, certainly had its own *temenos*, with altar and
labrys before it.

Of course Crete had, like any other primitive tribe and people, its
own Mystery Cult and rite of Initiation of Youth, and this, for the
men at any rate, was the initiation to Zagreus. We can only give this
in its later form, as it was known in Greece and told to the candidates

---

[1] Various caves on various mountains claimed to be this holy spot, and
each received its meed of votive offerings from its own people. There are
even two on Mount Ida.

there in Orphic lodges or *thiasi*. Zagreus, the heavenly youth, or *Kouros*, was the son of Zeus and Persephone, the gods of heaven and of the underworld. So soon as he was born, the earth-bred brood of Titans were after him to destroy him, and it was his youthful initiates and worshippers, the *Kouretes* or armed priests, who strove to protect him from them. They clashed their weapons to drown the infant's cries, and they tried to amuse him with toys and the like; this is the episode that we have shown us once for all in the famous Hermes of Praxiteles, in which the god, the ideal *Kouros*, is trying to amuse the infant who has, in that late age, been identified with Dionysus, but is really the primitive Zagreus. However, his adherents failed, for the child was lured away by the Titans and torn in pieces by them, and devoured, all save his heart. That was saved by Athena and swallowed by Zeus, to be born again of Theban Semele, as the god Dionysus. As for the Titans, they were struck by the thunderbolt and reduced to ashes, the white ash, *titanos*, with which the initiate was daubed in his preparation. It was from those ashes that mankind was born, and hence its double inheritance, sparks of the divine from Zagreus, and original sin from the evil Titan brood. When the *kouros* is initiated to Zagreus, a very grim ceremony or sacrament takes place. The initiates tear a bull-calf to pieces in their frenzy, and devour the still warm flesh, thereby taking part, as the Titans did, in the banquet on the god himself. As the calf thus sacrificed was tricked out in a boy's tunic and boots, it may well be that even this horrible rite was the softening down of something worse, and probably cannibalistic.

The version that we give, the only one we can give, is late, and we can trace in it plain attempts to identify the Cretan Zagreus with the Theban Dionysus, and even to mollify Athenian sentiment by giving their goddess an honourable rôle to fill. But whereas in Greece the Orphic mystery of Zagreus was only the private worship of a selected few, in Crete all youths were expected to participate in what was originally the Young Men's Dance and the initiation rite of the tribe. It was, too, closely connected with the Great Mother. In the one fragment that we possess of the *Cretans* of Euripides— and if we had the whole of that play we should probably know much more about the religion of the Minoans than we do—the Chorus there proclaim that, being initiates of Idean Zeus they are also initiates of Zagreus, whose 'red and bleeding feasts' they, who normally hold all meat as taboo, have fulfilled; in so doing they have also, as in duty bound, roved on the mountains and 'held up the torches to the Great Mountain Mother'. The connexion between the cults was obviously very close.[1]

This great Minoan Empire lasted from let us say 4500 B.C. till about 1500 B.C., three thousand years in all. The palaces in every place were destroyed and rebuilt more than once in that long period, and what had once been the hall of audience where stood the 'throne of Minos' was abandoned after one of the earthquakes we have told of. Then, with utter suddenness, came a cataclysm of destruction, about 1500 B.C. All the palaces are destroyed, and the Minoan civilization comes to an end in an orgy of plunder and fire. Little indications show how sudden that catastrophe was. The workman had finished one lamp of stone, and had just blocked out another, when the invader came and the artist was either slain or set to serve another lord. His lamps lay side by side in his workshop for 3,400 years. The plunderer who was carrying away priceless ivories dropped one in the corner of the great stairway, and the Bull-leaper remained for our age to find and marvel at. Who did the destruction nobody knows for certain, but we have found that Greek legends usually tell the truth or something like it in these matters, so let us hear what they have to say.

The Athenian version was that it was the doing of Theseus. An expedition and a fleet followed up that fugitive, when he went off with Ariadne, and their absence gave the opportunity for a dash of plunderers. Diodorus gives a fuller account, saying that when Daedalus got off on his extemporized 'glider', Minos followed him with a fleet, and found that his runaway artist had taken refuge with Kokalus, King of Kamikos in Sicily, whom he required to surrender him. The treacherous Kokalus invited Minos to a conference, and induced him to avail himself of the bath of ceremonial hospitality, where the daughters of his host were, as was usual, to attend and bathe him. Those faithless maidens, by command of their sire, drowned their guest in the bath, and the unprepared fleet was attacked and destroyed. Another great armada was sent in revenge, carrying all the force of Crete on board, the Lelegian mercenaries on whom they relied. Then when this was away, 'the enemy' fell on Crete and destroyed it.

Both accounts agree in a surprise attack that had a marvellous success, but neither says who did it, though Diodorus does add the

[1] The man who fortunately preserves us this fragment is Porphyry—in a tract advocating Vegetarianism!

223

detail that the only serious fighting was at the guard-house of the palace, where the prince Deucalion fought to the end with his guards, who were black men. Now excavation shows that the only fortification of the whole palace was a small guard-house at the northern side, and a fragment of pottery indicates that the Cretans did employ black troops, who by the look of them were Soudanese. One respects an authority who gets such unforeseen confirmation. Was it the Achaean civilization, rising under the shadow of Crete, that thus turned on the mother power and destroyed her? 'There were brave men before Agamemnon,' says Horace, and if this conjecture be correct, then one of these predecessors of the 'King of Men' led out an expedition that was much more profitable and successful than the ten years' ill-managed fighting at Troy. Whoever did it, done it was, and fragments of the plunder of the palace, like the Vaphio Cups and Nestor's Ring, turn up at intervals in Greece to this day, while the Greeks who certainly learnt the profitable business of piracy somewhere, and pretty early, went on plundering to Egypt as well as to Troy. Anyhow the great empire was struck down and its artists were scattered to carry their wonderful naturalistic art where they could.

Surely it cannot be coincidence that just about that date, the Pharaoh who was a heretic and a preacher of new ideas both in religion and in art, the strange figure Akhn-aten, found a supply of artists that could carry out his revolutionary dreams in the way that so startled the conventional painters of Egypt. We believe that it is agreed by students that it was Cretan artists and probably Cretan refugees, who executed or inspired the novel and very un-Egyptian paintings of Tel-Amarna.

Some sort of culture went on for a while on the spot, though in a painful state of decay, but it was not long before an even rougher invader than the Achaeans—if Achaeans they were, who plundered the place originally—came upon it from the same direction. This time it was the Dorians coming down from Balkan lands, men who like the Turks boasted that it was with the sword that they reaped corn, and whose swords were of the hard iron that the bronze user can never stand up against. Taking to the water after passing through Greece, they went on to Crete, there to destroy whatever culture was left or was reviving at ancient Knossos and Phaestos, but to shun the haunted site, so that the ruins of the palace that men had called for aeons the Place of the Labrys became the Labyrinth in its legendary interpretation. So the long story ends with this startling

20. Gortyna. The Code of Laws, approximate date 450 B.C., written in the 'ox-plough' script

21. Bronze base of golden 'Plataea tripod' erected by 'all Greece' at Delphi after the victory over Persia 479 B.C. Transferred to present site by Constantine. 'Obelisk of Theodosius' in background

GORTYNA INSCRIPTION

suddenness, at least until the discovery of that bi-lingual tablet that all seek shall make the Cretan records yield up the secrets that they hold.[1]

[1] A discovery made in 1939 by Professor W. Blegen, head of an expedition sent to Pylos by the University of Cincinnati, seems to have brought this very much nearer. A palace of Mycenean date, much resembling Tiryns, was brought to light there, and with it, its archive room. Here were found as many as 200 complete tablets, with fragments of 400 more, all with writing of 'Cretan' type. At Knossos, this would be described as of 'linear class B slightly modified', and would be dated XVth-XIVth cent. B.C. Here, it may be rather later, and of 1300–1200 B.C.

It is only too probable that the tablets may be merely inventory work, as those of Knossos certainly were, but at least they prove that the art of writing was not unknown in Greece at that date, and finally demolish the argument that Homer's poems 'cannot' have been put into writing before 600 B.C. because writing was not known in Greece till that date.

It is at least possible that, now that texts of some length have come to light, decipherment may be achieved. The fact that other events began to unroll themselves in the year 1939 has hitherto made work on this find, impossible, and the publication of the results of it, impossible, but archaeologists are distinctly hopeful (*Illustrated London News*, June 3rd, 1939).

Crete has not only the first of all known alphabets—as distinct from syllabaries—to its credit. It has also the best-known specimen of the earliest form of Greek writing, the 'Boustrophêdon' or 'ox-plough' Script. See page 211. This is so called because the text goes 'to and fro', first from left to right across the field of writing, and then back from right to left, like a plough across a field.

This inscription is at Gortyna in central Crete and is a code of laws, dating from 450 B.C. or possibly earlier.

The place is the traditional scene of the labours of Titus, companion of St. Paul, and the Church claims to have his tomb.

A temple of Isis also, with a crypt that was used in the Initiation rites of that goddess, has been found on the spot; one of the few local monuments of the Graeco-Roman stage of civilization, in this island.

XII

CONSTANTINOPLE

Approach to the City—St. Sophia, its plan and decoration; history and traditions; Crusading sack; Ottoman capture—The Burnt Column— The Hippodrome; its statuary; the 'Nika' riots and the Empress Theodora—The Janissaries—Little St. Sophia—Pope Vigilius— Theodora's Monastery—Fatih and Sulimanie Mosques—Roxelana and Jehangir—The Serai—Its Plan—Hall of Council—Armoury— Hall of Audience—Treasury—Harem and Kafess—Kaharieh Mosque—Roman Walls—The Sieges of Constantinople—Its Capture by the Ottomans—The Bosphorus—Yildiz Kiosk—Roumeli Hissar

A library has been written on the city of Constantinople[1] and to do justice to it in one chapter is impossible; yet as we have had in view in this book educated visitors to Greece and the Levant, who always go on to Istanbul, we wish to give some idea of at least some episodes in the marvellous story of a city which has been a great capital for over 1,600 years, and has played a part in history that is not over yet. Guides there are now far better than of old, better than in most places indeed, but Ottomans are apt to deal most with points of interest to their own national history, as is only natural. Yet Ottoman history is, after all, no more than the latest episode in a romantic tragedy that is being played still, on this stage; whereas many of the monuments belong to the earlier acts of the play, acts which are at least of equal interest to most of the procession of visitors; and it is to these that we direct attention, for the most part, in this chapter.

There is only one wrong way of approaching a city that has the finest site of any capital in the world, and which a man who had

[1] Now officially, Istanbul. When we refer to the historic city, we use the historic name; when to the modern political town, its modern title.

226

genius in that direction chose as the seat of his empire; and that is, to come by rail from Vienna. Come down the Bosphorus or up the Marmora, and the marvel of the position is unveiled in a way that you will never forget; even if you come from Anatolia, there is the Bosphorus to cross. The rail approach, generally bad in any city, is by comparison worst of all here, and no man should miss one of the few moments that will abide with him for all his life. Coming by sea you see the site that Constantine chose, a city that even then had a full thousand years of history behind it, and which, when he had made it a capital, stood for a full thousand years more as the shield of a re-crystallizing Europe, and as the embodiment of that Roman Empire that was the dominant fact of all political theory. Then, when it passed by fortune of war to men of another type, it moulded them too, remaining for near five centuries more the capital of an empire of another faith and culture, that stretched—as the founder of it saw in his vision—'like a jewelled girdle from Baghdad to Vienna, with the clasp where the sea-river divides Europe from Asia.' It is out of the picture for the moment, but is bound to be in focus again, for its position demands it.

Yet, the grim man who founded the Turkish Republic may well have been wise to leave it and its unsurpassed beauty for the bleak uplands of Anatolia. It was an old Turk before him who said of Constantinople: 'That city is a most lovely, but evil, woman. Many men have sought to win her, and she has refused herself to none; but she has drawn his manhood from each one of her lovers in turn.'

> *Let us return. Across the fatal strait*
> *Our fathers' glories beckon us once more.*
> *Back to the glories of the Khalifate,*
> *Back to the faith we loved, the dress we wore*
> *When in one age the world could well contain*
> *Harun-el-rashid and your Charlemagne.*[1]

Santa Sophia is sure to be the first object of the visitor's pilgrimage, one of the three great churches which Constantine—theist rather than Christian—built to 'the Wisdom of God', the 'Peace of God' and the 'Apostles of God'. The fabric that we see is the third that has stood on the site, for the Basilica of Constantine stood for less than a century, 320–412 A.D. Then John Chrysostom, a prelate whose zeal

[1] Houghton: *The Old Turk*. Ghazi Mustafa Kemal would not have subscribed to it quite as it stands!

was greater than his tact, felt all propriety outraged by the fact that an Empress with whom he had a quarrel had shared in a court ball, and proclaimed in a sermon, 'Again Herodias rages; again she dances; again she demands the head of John!' He was arrested and exiled, and in the riot that followed the church was burned. Its successor stood hardly longer, from 412 till 532, when it also was burned, in the 'Nika' riot to which we must return. Then the present fabric was erected by Justinian, one of those emperors who have proved able to choose the men to do the work wanted, whether it was war, law, or building; there can be no doubt that Anthemius his architect was one of the masters of his craft.

The problem set before him was this; men knew the Basilica plan well enough, and the dome also: how could they be united? It was not a case of squaring the circle, but of circling the square. Men had tried their hands at that problem before, as at Salonika for instance, where a forgotten genius erected the Church of the Holy Wisdom at that city; and it had been attempted by Anthemius himself on a smaller scale, in an essay that happily remains to us in the 'little Santa Sophia' of Constantinople, properly the Church of Ss. Sergius and Bacchus. There we see him trying the experiment on which his greater church depends: could the great central dome which was the main feature of his plan be carried safely on a series of semi-domes? Reassured on that point, he used his new knowledge on a scale of magnificent daring, with results that have had their effects all over the world both of Islam and of Greek Orthodoxy. Both have modelled their finest temples ever since on St. Sophia. Yet, when we realize that it was the first time the experiment was ever tried in anything like such dimensions, we stand amazed at the man's courage, for it was, like the Menai Bridge, the application of a new principle on a huge scale. A dome, approximately the same size as that of St. Paul's, is borne east and west on two semi-domes, of the same diameter as itself. Each of them is carried in its turn on three smaller semi-domes, the various parts of the whole being connected with one another by pendentives which are common enough now, but were a new expedient, if not absolutely an original one, then. Hence the great feature of the whole—the magnificent open space of the 'Nave'. No doubt, external effect is sacrificed, as unimportant; a dome that is 'right' from within a building necessarily looks low from without, and the effect is worsened, both by the big buttresses that have been added, though they were a structural necessity, and also, by the loss of the great *atrium* that should stand before the building. Further, external decoration, meant to be like that of St. Mark's, Venice, was never added at all. Smaller men, trying to correct the great pioneer's errors, might partly avoid that blunder, but it was not, we think, till the days of our English Wren that the right solution of a double dome (an inner one for inside effect, and an outer one of the right proportion to be seen from outside) was evolved and erected on any scale to compare with that of Anthemius. For the interior, we can only say that none has yet been designed to compare with the magnificent space of Santa Sophia. By the side of it, St. Peter's looks vulgar and Cologne cramped, and this is in a class by itself among the religious edifices of the world.

Its decoration was originally worthy of it, for the Emperor not only poured out the treasures of the empire on it, but used his power to plunder other fanes of their choicest beauties for the sake of this. Diana of the Ephesians and Zeus of Olympia had to give columns, and even the Parthenon of Athens was not spared. The huge monoliths of Syene granite, that once came down the Nile and over the Lebanon to Baal-bek, had to make that laborious journey to the sea once more, and be shipped to Constantinople. The marvellous mosaics that were the peculiar contribution of Byzantium to art, the finest of which adorned the walls of this church, are to come to light once more we rejoice to say, so that soon—as far as the fabric is concerned—we shall be able to see again what Justinian saw, when he burst out with: 'Glory be to God who hath counted me worthy to perform so great a work. Solomon, I have surpassed thee!' Yet even then there was an old hermit who came to tell the king that he had been bidden to convey the thanks of Heaven to the greatest of the contributors, and when the Emperor said that he was very highly honoured, replied: 'It was not you, sire, but the poor widow Euphrasia whom I was bidden to congratulate. She did what she could; she gave water to the oxen who drew the stones up the hill.'

We may try to picture, for a moment, some of the scenes this wonderful fane has seen. Here emperors worshipped for centuries, while—since the eleventh century at any rate—the Varangian Guards waited for him without, and when he came out 'greeted him, crying "Long live the Emperor" in their own barbarous language, which is English', for it was from our island that this Caesar drew his Praetorians. Here came the Bulgarian Embassy when in the ninth century that wild people was debating if it should accept the religion of civilization, and after seeing the Liturgy here, went back to report that in Constantinople Heaven was open on earth, and that angels came down to worship among men.[1] It was here, in 1054, that the Legates of the Pope of Rome solemnly laid the writ of excommunication on the high altar, and consummated that separation of East and West that has been the bane of Christendom ever since, declaring as they went out, 'Videat Dominus, et judicet'; and here that there came to pass one of the consequences of that great wrong, namely the Crusaders' sack of Constantinople in the year 1204.

Those 'Pilgrims' had started with the best of intentions, in that they were to win back Jerusalem for the Cross, and to travel thither on transports provided by the one power that could furnish them, the 'serene republic' of Venice. Unfortunately Venice cared nothing for the objects of the Crusade and much for her own trade and her own quarrels; hence when they found that the French knights could not pay more than half the sum agreed on for the chartering of the ships, they suggested first that they should do the republic a service by capturing for her the rebellious city of Zara, and then they would call it square. Before that was done came another suggestion from Venice and an exiled Greek prince combined; let them put back 'the rightful heir' on the imperial throne of Constantinople, and he would pay all expenses and bring the schismatic Greek Church into rightful obedience to our Lord the Pope; and the capture of Jerusalem would be easy after that. This was done, Constantinople being captured by the 'Frank' army, and when he was unable to pay, the Crusaders turned on this unhappy ally of theirs, put an end to him, and celebrated the Holy Week and Good Friday of 1204 by the most awful sack of a Christian town that had been seen till then. In Santa Sophia, the great cathedral that they had proposed to win back from heresy and schism to the only true obedience, the treasure that nine centuries of piety had accumulated was carried out of the church by the horse-load, and one of the camp-women enthroned upon the high altar. The Pope, Innocent III—who to do him justice had excommunicated the whole Crusade when it first commenced the siege of Zara and fought against Christians—could only accept the *fait accompli*, let his most just sentence lapse as ineffective, and congratulate the Crusaders on the fact that 'God had transferred the empire from the Greeks to the Latins'. A Venetian was installed as

[1] It is true that they made a condition for their acceptance of Christianity, and a council had to be held to debate it. 'Was it possible to be a Christian and to wear breeches?' The absence of that garment was then as much a test of civilization as its presence is now, though we must sympathize with those who, living in Balkan winds, desired to retain some defence against them!

Patriarch of Constantinople and nominal ruler of the Orthodox Church, and the Papacy accepted the union thus brought about, a union that has left behind it the legacy of hate that still subsists between the two churches of Greeks and Latins.

There is one last scene that we may try to picture—the midnight of May 28–29, 1453, the last Christian service in the great church. The Turk had been hammering for weeks at the half-ruined and half-defended walls that a wiser and greater age had built, and though the ignorant might try to persuade themselves into the delusion that a miracle must happen and the city could not be allowed to fall, the Emperor Constantine was not among them. He knew that the next day must see the end, the end that he had done all that in him lay to avert, even to a stretching of his conscience. He had brought himself—most unwillingly—to make some sort of submission to the Pope on the guarantee of assistance, and the reward that he had received had been a contingent of about two hundred men! Now, he had just come from the walls, where he had looked out over the Turkish lines and seen that all was ready for the great assault on the morrow, and it would begin at daybreak. For the last time he came to the great Liturgy, and standing before the Royal Doors before the altar received the Eucharist. With the elements in his hands he turned to the crowded congregation, solemnly asked their pardon for anything that he had done amiss in his rule, received the Sacrament and passed out of the church to the walls once more, where in the morning of that day he was to meet a death not unworthy of the long line of emperors that he represented. For that night and morning the church was crowded with agonized worshippers, praying for what they hardly dared to hope for now, and before noon word must have come that the Turks were in the city, and soon they were clamouring at the silver doors of the Cathedral. As the first of them broke in, a priest was just beginning the Mass, apparently at some little 'par-ecclesia' or side altar, in the gallery of the building. Men said that he took up the sacred vessels, and vanished through the wall, and for centuries they hoped that the day would come, when he would return and finish the holy rite that he had just begun.[1]

There were a few minutes of wild disorder, and securing of captives, and then Mahommed the Conqueror himself strode into the building with his escort, and by his order a Mollah stood upon the

---

[1] During some later repairs, a staircase the existence of which had been forgotten was discovered in the wall at the point in question.

altar and pronounced the prayers that made the cathedral into the mosque that it still is. Later legend said that the Sultan rode his charger into the church, and that the corpses were piled so high that he struck his bloody hand upon the wall at a point twenty feet up, and that the mark remains to this day. The mark is certainly there, a hand-like print upon the plaster, at a point where one of the marble veneering-slabs has fallen; but the rest is fiction. The only blood shed in the church itself that day was that of a Turkish soldier, who was breaking up the pavement with an axe when Mahommed cut his head off, for his disobedience to the order issued the previous night: 'The treasure and the captives, those are yours; but all the buildings in the place are for the Sultan.' There may have been something of the barbarian in 'the Conqueror', but at least he could appreciate the value of such a monument as St. Sophia.

It is true that he altered it a little, for some internal changes were necessary when the Christian church became a mosque. Internally, the Eikonostasis and the altar had to go, and the mosaics were hidden from sight as we have seen.[1] Externally, the little campanili at the four corners of the fabric were pulled down, and a minaret—not too well proportioned—went up on one of them. It was a century before the other three were added, in 1571, by Selim 'the Sot', as the sin-offering that he felt must be required after the disaster of Lepanto.

Before long, Mahommedan legends gathered round the trophy of which they were so proud, though it could never become one of their great religious shrines. Here, it was said, the prophet Elijah, 'Khudr Elias', always stays to worship when his never-ending wanderings round the earth bring him to Istanbul. He will always be able to worship here, for the great dome can never fall; a hair from the beard of the Prophet (upon him be peace!) was embedded in the mortar when the place was built. Naturally, such trifles as dates are irrelevant to a legend of this sort; but as we have been solemnly assured (by English folk) that Santa Sophia was modelled on the mosques of Islam, it may be well to remind readers that the great monument was built rather before Mahommed the Prophet was born.

From Santa Sophia the visitor turns naturally to the Hippodrome, but before entering it, it is well to spare a glance for a monument of

---

[1] Justinian's mosaics were mostly crosses on a gold background, not figures. These were often disguised rather than hidden and can still be traced in many places.

old Constantinople that is often neglected. This is the 'Hooped' or 'Burnt' column, which now stands in one of the main streets of the modern town, but was in the centre of the forum of Constantine, much as the similar column of Trajan stood in the older Rome. Here, that enigmatic man the founder of the city put his own statue, and with it objects that illustrate the confused working of a mind which expressed its religion thus—that a power that had shown itself more powerful than the empire, as Christianity certainly had, must be itself somehow divine. The statue had, as a halo round its head, metal spikes that were supposed to be the nails of the true cross of Christ,[1] while under the base of the column there were buried —the Magdalen's alabaster box of ointment, the adze which Noah used in the construction of the Ark, and the ancient Palladium of Troy!

The place certainly seems to have been regarded as in a sense the heart of the city. During the last siege, when all were demanding the miracle that was to save it, there was a general belief that the Infidel was to penetrate into the inviolate town up to this point, but that then an angel would descend from heaven with a sword, which he would put into the hand of a poor man who was seated at the foot of the pillar, who would take it and drive the unbeliever not only out of Constantinople, but also even beyond the mountains of Taurus.

Yet it was the Hippodrome that was the real centre of the civic and political life—as distinct from the religious—of ancient Constantinople. Politics and sport were mixed up there, and up to the time of the Latin conquest at least the *spina* of the racecourse was the spinal column of the city. After the Ottoman conquest, it preserved its name indeed (for 'At-meidan' is just a translation of Hippodrome) but it lost its importance. It was not originally the work of Constantine, for Septimius Severus gave to the town of Byzantium its first racecourse, as a sort of solatium for the very stern discipline to which he had subjected the inhabitants. It was much enlarged by Constantine, however, who inserted into it the great imperial box or *Kathisma*, which was quite inaccessible from the rest of the area but was provided with a covered way running from it to the precincts of the imperial palace just behind. This was about opposite to the present Fountain of the German Emperor. The *spina* (which recent excavation shows was a railed area rather than a raised

[1] Another account says that Constantine used these relics, one for the ornament of his helmet, one for the bit of his favourite charger.

233

platform) was also the museum where were deposited all the most wonderful sculptures of the ancient world, which had been collected from their homes and gathered at the capital. Here once stood the Horses that now stand over the doors of St. Mark, much travelled steeds that Mummius brought from their original home at Corinth to Rome, and that wandered from thence to Constantinople before finding a place at Venice. Venetians said that it was an intolerable outrage that another conqueror should remove them to Paris, though the difference in title is not so very clear! Here also were once the Roman Wolf with Romulus and Remus, the trophy of the Ass and his Driver that Augustus put up at Actium, and the colossal Athena Promachos from the Acropolis. These all remained safe till the time of the Latin conquest, when the apostles of Latin culture and orthodoxy melted them down to make copper coins for their own payment. Somehow they spared one monument that is still left us, though in a mutilated state; this is the bronze base of the golden tripod of Delphi, formed of three twined serpents, the Greek memorial of Salamis and Plataea, which still bears the names of the cities that took their part in that great struggle.[1] Tradition still says that this monument stood uninjured till the Turkish entrance, when Mahommed the Conqueror smote off the heads of one of the three serpents as he rode past on his way to Santa Sophia; as, however, Lady Mary Wortley Montague saw the three heads still in position in 1718, the conqueror must be acquitted of this act of vandalism.

The only other two objects that remain there are two obelisks, one of which was brought from Egypt by Theodosius the Great in 380 A.D., though it is itself some nineteen centuries older; while the other is the work of Constantine Porphyrogenitus, of the ninth century, and principally interesting as having been the place of the execution of Alexius Mourtzouphlos, the miserable instrument of the Crusading conquest. He had failed to produce all the cash that his employers expected of him, so they—having put up ladders and scaffolding against this monument for the easier removal of its bronze plating—made their own work serve as a gallows for the hanging of the man whom they had intended to make an emperor.

Of the many episodes in the story of Constantinople that this place

---

[1] The names cannot be seen now, but a 'rubbing' produces them, and incidentally gives testimony to the accuracy of Herodotus, who tells us that two of the list were added later, when the cities in question (Tenos and Siphnos) gave proof that they had the right to be there. Those names have been added later, and in smaller lettering than the others. One of the missing serpent-heads is in the National Museum.

234

has seen, we can choose only two, and one of them shall be the great 'Nika' riot that we have referred to above. Imperial Constantinople was 'sport-mad' to an even greater extent than later capitals, and as it was never allowed an amphitheatre or gladiatorial contests, it took to chariot racing instead. The four colours that were customary in the four chariots that contended in each 'heat' (red, white, blue and green) became convenient pegs on which any political faction at any moment might hang itself, and of the four the two dominant ones (who knows the 'why' of any vagary of fashion?) were the Blue and Green. Authority could usually trust their division, and maintain a certain amount of public order accordingly, but in the year 532, for some reason that was never clear even to themselves, they suddenly elected to combine against the Emperor Justinian. Thus the whole Hippodrome was filled with a crowd who were yelling at the emperor instead of one another, and what might very well be a revolution blazed up without either cause or warning. The Emperor appeared in the great *Kathisma* to speak to the mob, but when he began by saying 'I have always tried to govern well', somebody in the arena shouted 'You lie, you jackass', and the whole populace took up the cry.

The Emperor got back to his palace with more haste than dignity, grateful enough for Constantine's covered way, and the whole capital was aflame. Justinian's nerve failed him utterly, and he had prepared for a flight to Asia, for which the ships were actually ready just below his palace, when he was stopped and brought to better ways by his wife and Empress, Theodora.

The marvellous personality of this woman seems to stand outside all recognized rules, for in the days of her youth—not long past then—she had been the most notorious *danseuse* in the Capital in a period when actress and courtesan were interchangeable terms, and had been accustomed to appear on the stage in costumes—or in an absence of all costume—that would be counted as extreme in a Parisian music-hall today. Yet Justinian, a man who otherwise gives the impression of never having been young in his life, fell once for all in love with her when he was already 'Caesar' or Heir-designate to the empire, and made use of his position to pass a law to enable a man of senatorial rank, as he was, to marry a woman of the 'infamous' position of actress—a thing illegal before. When Emperor he at once made his wife 'Augusta', co-Emperor with himself, and her first act in her new dignity was to found the first home in history for those 'fallen women' from whose ranks she had raised herself so

CONSTANTINOPLE

wonderfully. Now, when emperor and ministers alike failed in this crisis, it was she who sprang up in council and declared that she at any rate was not going to run away. 'You made me Augusta, sire, and I will never live to see the day when men do not salute me as such. As for death—we all die once, and I hold by the old proverb: "Imperial purple makes the finest shroud!"' There could be no more talk of flight in her presence, and it seems to have been the Empress who called up a young guardsman with a good record, Belisarius by name, and bade him take charge of the situation. He did so at once. The mob had crowded in the Hippodrome to crown a noble of the name of Hypatius as emperor, and Belisarius was able to shut the gates, let the imperial guard (who only wanted a leader) in at one end, and bid them cut their way out at the other. Forty thousand corpses were taken from the Hippodrome in the next two days, and the 'factions' gave no more trouble to Justinian.

The same place, some fourteen centuries later, saw another great destruction, the massacre of the Janissaries in 1826. This wonderful corps, originally the invention of Orkhan, the second Amir—not yet Sultan—of the Osmanlis, was a scheme of diabolical cleverness by which the 'rayahs' or Christian subjects of the Ottoman, were made to hold themselves in subjection by the training of the pick of them as Moslems in the service of their ruler. A levy of 'tribute children' was laid upon them and in the year 1333 the first detachment of one thousand lads was brought to a famous Dervish, Haji Bekhtash of Khorassan, for his blessing. Drawing the long sleeve of his white robe over the head of the leader, he said, 'I name this corps the "new soldiery" (*Yeni Askeri*), and may they ever be the terror of the Infidel.' The system was kept up, new recruits being collected periodically by the 'Crane-keeper' of the royal household, and all so selected at the age of from four to eight years were brought up in strict discipline and the faith of Islam. All were affiliated members of the Bekhtashi order of Dervishes, and formed originally a military brotherhood, drawing rations and clothes from the Sultan, but no pay. They were the boys of his house, and the titles of their officers, the Chorbaji and the Kahwaji (Soup-maker and Coffee-maker) bore witness to the fact. They were to live an ascetic life in which marriage was not allowed till they retired on a pension, and all plunder, even arms, were divided among all. There does not seem to have been any uniformity of equipment at first, save only the shaven face and the long flap of white felt that depended from their caps, that represented the white sleeve of Haji Bekhtash. Volunteers

236

THE JANISSARIES

might join them, and many a Serb and Albanian,[1] on whom his ancestral religion sat lightly, did so; but no born Moslem or Turk was at first admitted to their ranks. It marked a distinct decline when under Sulieman, 1574, the sons of Janissaries and Moslem volunteers were admitted to what thus became a privileged military caste, and soon men got enrolled for a fee, and practised their trades while in the corps, so that its quality declined. In its great days, however, it was the *corps d'élite* of the finest army in the then world, and like Napoleon's guard was reserved for the final blow in battles. The first act of each Sultan on his inauguration (i.e. the girding with the Sword of Osman) was to go to the Janissary barracks and drink to their health, 'and to our merry meeting at the Red Apple,' which meant, at Rome!

Gradually, they became a disorderly body of Praetorians, who often mutinied; the sign of mutiny was, overturning the big copper camp-kettles and banging the bottoms of them with the huge ladles. This 'beating of the kettle-drums', and the implied refusal of the Sultan's rations, could only be appeased with a big *bakhshish*, and not uncommonly by the head of the Grand Vizir and a few other ministers. The person of the Sultan was always sacrosanct. If there was any delay in the matter, they enforced the protest by firing a quarter of Constantinople!

Naturally they became a nuisance in time, for in 1800 there were over 135,000 men on their roll, drawing rations, privileges, and by that time pay also. They always refused all reforms, till at last in 1826, Mahommed 'the Terrible', who had been bullied more than usual by them at his accession, and was also employed in reorganizing his mediaeval army on Napoleonic lines, simply gave them the choice, reform or massacre! The decree was published at the big Ahmedieh Mosque in the Hippodrome, and when the Janissaries came swarming out of their barracks at the end of that space in open mutiny, 'Kara Jehannum', the Grand Vizir, ordered the

[1] So strong was the *esprit de corps* of this wonderful body, that there is only record of one individual reverting to the religion and nationality of his fathers, when once admitted to their ranks. It is true that this one was Scanderbeg. Those who volunteered in later life and abandoned their own religion naturally kept at times remembrance of it. In 1557 for instance, one Mehmed Sokolovic (in Scots, McEarne), thus 'verted, and rose to the rank of Grand Vizir, there being no distinction between military and civil in Turkey. As such he secured 'auto-cephalous' privileges for the church of his own Serbian land and secured that his own brother, the monk Macarius, should be Patriarch, of the See of Ipek. After many historical adventures, this dignity still survives in the Serbian Church today!

237

artillery to open fire on them with grape, from the Santa Sophia end of the Meidan. As they rushed at the guns, the artillerymen hesitated to obey the order to fire, and when 'Black Hell' (for that is the meaning of the name given him) himself put the match to the nearest gun, it refused to explode. For an instant it looked as if the mutineers had got into the battery, but 'Kara Jehannum' shot the artillery commander with one pistol and discharged a gun by the firing of the second. The Janissaries checked for an instant, and then the whole battery was discharged, and for the rest, it was merely a massacre. Every active member of the corps was put to death, and they became simply a memory in the new Turkish Army.

From 1826 we drop back abruptly to 530, for from the Hippodrome we go down a steep hill under the terminal wall of the race-course itself, to the beautiful church of 'Little Santa Sophia', properly that of Ss. Sergius and Bacchus. It was originally one sanctuary with another church of similarly double dedication, Ss. Peter and Paul, and they had a common *narthex* and *atrium*, now represented by a square of doleful slum, but once adjoining the grand palace of the Boucoleon, or Hormisdas.[1]

We have already described the architectural history of this little church as the experiment that made possible the building of Santa Sophia; historically it was a thank-offering, offered by both Justinian and his uncle and predecessor Justin for their delivery from a political danger, and it bears both their names and that of Theodora on the inscription that runs round the spring of the dome. They had been plotting against the Emperor Anastasius, and had been put under arrest for it, but were delivered by a dream that that Emperor had, in which St. Sergius appeared to him and ordered the release of the captives. Later, in the last days of Justinian, it served as a sanctuary for an unfortunate Pope of Rome, Vigilius.

That unlucky prelate had got mixed up in a politico-religious dispute of his day, in the following fashion. The Council of Chalcedon, in the year 451, had given a decision on the 'Christological' question submitted to it, which was satisfactory enough to the Greek and Latin portions of the empire, but was quite the reverse to 'the Orient' and to Egypt, where Syriac and Coptic were the vernaculars, and where men thought that they had had a little more than enough

---

[1] The Church of the Anastasis, where St. Gregory Nazianzen revived Nicene Orthodoxy in the fourth century, was also in this quarter, but has perished.

of Greek dictation in Church matters. The open discontent of those big provinces—which in after days enabled Islam to overrun them with ease—was a real political difficulty; but while every man there was waving the flag of 'down with Chalcedon and its accursed Council', it was hard to find a formula that would reconcile them without at the same time enraging all Greek and Latin-speaking districts, who revered the Council in question. (These theological problems were also national: that was why men fought so over them.) A previous Pope, Agapetus, had come to the Capital to discuss that question, bringing Vigilius as his secretary, and as it happened had died there; Theodora, who loved Church politics and was personally an opponent of Chalcedon, had her own game to play, and believed that if she could only get all the Church to anathematize the memory of certain men, long dead, but objectionable to her friends, these last would swallow their objections to the Council that the Emperor could not abandon. Let Vigilius get the Church of Rome to oblige them in this and he should be Pope as reward. Unfortunately, Vigilius found it far easier to promise this in Constantinople than to execute it in Rome, so when he came back as Pope, to attend the Council that was to pass the condemnation, he had to say that he was unable to meet the bill that he had signed. Followed a 'row royal', for Justinian (Theodora was by then dead) meant to carry her policy through, and had a short way with any bishop who opposed him. After some tergeversation that did him little honour, Vigilius took sanctuary in this church, which was quite close to the residence where his permanent representative in the Capital had his abode, and sought a refuge absolutely under the altar. Justinian's soldiers hauled him out of that, upsetting the Holy Table itself in the scuffle, but did not force him to leave the building. Ultimately, Vigilius consented to sign what the Emperor asked, attributing all his previous doubts to the Devil, and he was able, after a good deal of disputing, to get the Western Church to accept the condemnation of men whom they had hardly known of and cared nothing about. In other parts of the world it was a different story! To find the scene of that sixth century scuffle between the soldiers and the Pope so nearly unaltered has its interest for students. The scene of the martyrdom of Thomas Becket has been changed much more drastically, in less than half the interval.

Close to this, in the Palace of the Boucoleon which stood between this church and the sea, was once one of the most remarkable monasteries of all history, for here the ever-interesting Empress

Theodora kept her collection of heretical hermits and bishops! We have seen that the prejudices of that active lady were against the Council of Chalcedon which her husband the Emperor supported; so when he exiled all the bishops and monastic agitators of the obnoxious party, the Augusta co-Empress received them here, and gave a palace to be their monastery. There was no secrecy about it, for the place was one of the sights of Constantinople, and a historian who went to visit it declares that 'when these holy hermits are at their devotions, the whole palace resounds night and day with groaning and weeping and lamentation. A man would think that he was in heaven already to hear them'. Each man is, we suppose, entitled to form his own notion of celestial bliss, but this does seem to be an original one.

Justinian's object in the theological game was to 'squeeze out' the malcontents by preventing them from getting bishops, the necessity of whom was axiomatic; so Theodora, playing her hand against her husband, smuggled bishops out when they were wanted. She selected one John, and ordered him to go to Syria as Metropolitan, and conduct ordinations. Now one would expect things to go easily when one has an empress as accomplice, and that empress so unusually efficient a lady as Theodora; but it would seem that John, however excellent he may have been as hermit and prelate, was yet a very poor conspirator, for he so bungled his escape that the imperial police had to take measures for his arrest, and he could find no better refuge than the imperial hall of audience, where he begged protection. 'The divine Empress', says the chronicler with delightful naïveté, 'was very cross', and it seems probable that she was. Her opposition to imperial policy might be diplomatically ignored, but it needed concealment; this bungler had advertised it. Certainly Theodora, whatever her failings in some respects, would never have mismanaged a practical matter so egregiously! However, her second choice of a prelate to organize dissent in the provinces was much more successful. She sent out Jacobus Baradaeus, the founder of the present 'Jacobite' communion in those parts.

Leaving the joys of ancient theology, we wander up the hill once more, to the finest site in the whole Capital, where Constantine put one of his great churches, that of the Apostles. This church, the Westminster Abbey of Constantinople, in which were all the imperial tombs, was given by Mahommed the Conqueror to Gennadius, the Greek Patriarch, after the capture of the city, as his cathedral, and his verbal gift was an indefeasible title for all time. Yet within a

22. The Kaharieh Mosque, Constantinople. A typical XIIth Century Byzantine Church

23. The Roumeli Hissar on the Bosphorus

year, the Patriarch was asking the Conqueror to resume a gift of priceless historic value, because it was inconveniently far from the quarter down by the Golden Horn where most of the Greeks had then congregated. Naturally, Mahommed took back what the Greeks did not seem to want, and as the tombs of the Emperors had little interest for him, he pulled the whole place down and ordered the erection of a great mosque (called 'El Fatih', 'the Conqueror's') on the site. He employed a Greek, Christodoulos, as his architect, and the result was a copy in all essentials of St. Sophia, though later fire and restoration in the eighteenth century have altered the Conqueror's fine work rather dolefully. As a fee, he gave Christodoulos a street of houses, and as that street contained a church, the little fane of St. Mary of the Mongols was given by its new owner to the Orthodox Patriarch. That fact, that it was thus indirectly given by the Conqueror, was sufficient to save it in later days, when fanaticism wished to deprive the Christians of its use. No one could take away what the Sultan had given.

The mosque has been so much altered as to have little interest now, but in its precincts are two tombs of two women that merit a passing note. In one of them lies Irene, the Christian slave whom Mahommed so loved that he was ready to make her his empress, if only she would abandon Christianity. When she would not, the grim Conqueror ordered her immediate execution, because he could not trust himself. 'Irene is dearer to me than life, but I give my life for Islam', he said, and ordered the woman whom he must honour to be buried with the burial of a queen.

By the other, that of the French wife of a later Sultan, Ibrahim II, there hangs this strange tale. Late in the eighteenth century two Creole girls (offspring of French parents in the West Indies) who were both famous for their beauty, and were to sail in the same ship from Martinique for France in a few days, went to an old Negro mammy to have their fortunes told. The Obeah woman worked her spells, and stared at the two girls in real terror. 'I can only say what the spirits say', she said; 'Aimée de Rivery, you will be a queen, and the mother of a great king. Marie-Joseph de la Paganie, you will be greater than any queen, but you will outlive that greatness.' Marie de la Paganie fell ill, and could not sail with her friend, which was as well for her, for the ship was taken by a Barbary corsair, and poor Aimée de Rivery was sold in the market of Tangier. The prophecy was fulfilled nevertheless, for an agent bought her for her beauty and sent her to Istanbul, to the harem of the Sultan, Ibrahim. Becoming the mother of his son, she was recognized as Empress, and her son was Mahommed the Terrible, of whose exploits we have told. As for Marie-Joseph, she went to France, where she married an undistinguished man, who left her a widow with one son, but well off. Then, to the anger of her family, she took a second husband, a man who was hardly French; a gunner who had several black marks against him just then, and no prospects. As he did not like her name, he always called her Josephine, by which appellation we know her, for the man's own name was Napoleon Buonaparte. The words of the Obeah woman came true.

A far finer mosque to see and study is the Sulimanieh, finest of all the buildings built as mosques in the city. Work of the tenth Sultan of the Ottomans and fourth of Istanbul, it carried four minarets and ten galleries to mark the fact, and its architect was one Sinan (a Janissary and therefore not a Turk), who is said to have declared that when he designed the mosque of Sultan Selim—elsewhere in the city—he was a good entered apprentice. The Sulimanieh is the work of one who has really won rank as a Fellow of his craft. (His masterpiece, however, is the great mosque of Adrianople.)

Its creator is the greatest and most terrible of the long line of Sultans, the man who captured Rhodes, Buda, Belgrade and Baghdad, and who only just failed before Vienna. On the sea he was equally formidable, for the greatest of the pirate kings of Africa, Khair-ed-din Barbarossa, was his admiral.[1] Like his contemporary, Philip of Spain, he executed his own heir-apparent, yet he could govern the whole of his vast empire so well, that Elizabeth of England sent a special representative to study the administration of justice in his realms, so that she might be able to imitate him.[2] Yet it is with this great ruler that the seeds of decline first begin to show themselves in the empire; the harem influence, from which the Ottoman rulers, soldiers all, had hitherto been singularly free, begins to work; and it is seen in one of the few romances in the life of the Turkish rulers, the tale of Roxelana. This woman, a Russian or as some say an Italian slave girl, could capture the heart of Sulieman, and—the story is told again and again where polygamy prevails—she was bitterly jealous of the son of the other wife and ambitious for her own child, the Prince Jehangir. Constantly she instilled suspicion of his

---

[1] The tomb of this great fighter at Beshik Tash on the Bosphorus is worthy of remembrance.
[2] We call this Sultan Sulieman 'the Magnificent'. Turks name him 'the Law-giver'.

heir Mustapha into the heart of Sulieman, till at last her work was done: Mustapha was summoned from his province to an interview with his father, but when he entered the tent where he was expecting to meet him he found awaiting him—the mutes with the fatal bow-string. Mustapha died, but to the absolute amazement of Roxelana, the son for whose sake she had plotted died too, literally of grief for the death of his senior. It is true that her second son acceded, but he is that Selim whom historians call 'the Sot', the first of the feeble Sultans of the empire.

In Sulieman's day, too, we get the first instance of what is soon to be, for some generations a characteristic of the Ottoman rule—the great Grand Vizir. Hitherto the prime minister has been nothing but a servant of the real ruler, but Ibrahim Pasha was for fourteen years *alter ego* of Sulieman, who slept in his room and ate from his table, by whose advice all things were done. A real 'dynasty' of great Vizirs follows him in later days. Yet Roxelana could be as jealous of him as of another heir, so that she could sow suspicion there too, and get the Sultan to believe in her. Hence there came the day in March, 1553, when Ibrahim went to the palace as usual for his evening audience with the Sultan, with whom, as always, he dined. When men entered the private dining room next day, Ibrahim lay there among the cushions, dead and strangled, with signs of a struggle all around him. They took him away and buried him, none asking questions of the Sultan, who gave no explanation.

It is appropriate that Roxelana should be the person to bring about another very significant change in the palace. Before her time, the harem had not been within its borders, but away at the Old Serai, close to the Sulimanieh mosque. Roxelana was able to get it established within the inner court of the Serai, where we shall soon have to see it. Yet she kept her rule over Sulieman to the very end, and when he died at last—his death was concealed for several weeks by his Vizir, till the Heir-Apparent could arrive and take command, the Vizir 'taking his instructions' daily from the litter where the corpse lay—he was laid by Roxelana, first recognized Queen and wife of the Sultan, in the court of the great mosque that he built.

Other mosques are less interesting, even if they be of the first order, like those of Ahmed on the At-Meidan, or of Sultan Bayazid by the modern War Office. They are fine enough, and are called 'gems of Turkish architecture', but none of them would have existed in that shape had it not been for Santa Sophia. For human interest we turn from them to the Palace, the Serai, which lies on the point of the old city, where the Bosphorus and the Golden Horn merge in the Marmora. Here was the palace of the old Emperors, but in early mediaeval days it seems to have been abandoned and the residence of the court set at Blachernae, at the other end of the city, on the landward walls. There were only ruins here when Constantinople fell to the Turk, but it was here, with a true instinct, that the Sultans put their seat, only residing at Adrianople or in the Old Serai till their new palace was ready to receive them. The days of the Sultanate were numbered when they left this for Dolma Baghche, or Yildiz Kiosk.

It is only in very recent years that one of the most interesting places in Europe, the embodiment and memorial of a very great institution that has now passed away for ever, the Sultanate of the Ottomans, has been thrown open to public inspection, and a visitor can now enter freely to a palace to which entry was once only given as the rarest and most costly of favours, by a special firman of the Sultan. Practically all the palace can now be visited and each year more and more of its endless treasures come to light.[1]

We enter by the great portal on the south side of St. Sophia, the 'Sublime Porte' which has been so famous in diplomatic language, as meaning the Sultan of Turkey. Actually the phrase is a term of immemorial antiquity in the East for the place where the King sits to do justice and exercise government; we first find it in use in Egypt, for the word Pharaoh has that meaning, and it was already customary long before the Sassanid dynasty came to rule in Persia, and 'Jamshid gloried and drank deep', though it was through them that the Ottomans received it. In the large court to which it gives entrance there are two main objects. One of them is the former Church of St. Eirene, of 'Holy Peace', which Constantine founded, though the present fabric, which has gone through

[1] We give one instance of a recent discovery, viz., the map drawn in 1493 by Columbus' first officer, to show the new discoveries in the west. That gentleman had the not uncommon misfortune of being captured by Barbary pirates and sent as a slave to Istanbul. There he was made to draw a map of all the new islands and he put them in quite accurately, but as attached—as Columbus and every one else then thought them to be—to the coast of China, not of a new continent. Haiti appears as the land of Cipangu, which is Japan. He also puts in a final episode of the voyage; sailing south, the sailors saw high mountains ahead, and at the same time found that the water round the ships was fresh, not salt. Clearly they had reached the Islands of the Blessed, which are distinguished by those signs, and as such they went on the map. Actually, the fresh water came from the river Orinoco, and the mountains were those of Venezuela and Trinidad.

various vicissitudes, dates from Leo I and the year 740 A.D. It is a very fine basilica of its date, and practically unaltered structurally, retaining its *atrium*, the women's galleries, and the apse for the altar and the seats of the clergy. It is true that the banners, etc., that decorate it rather disguise the lines of the architecture, for it serves as a military museum now, after having been an arsenal for many years. As such it is crowded with objects that deserve detailed study, but the visitor ought to spare an instant to comprehend so interesting a fabric.

The second object is, the remains of a very ancient plane tree, now supported by props. In this court in old days was one of the main barracks of the Janissary corps, and it was generally arranged that when any foreign ambassador was to have an audience of the Sultan, he was admitted just when rations were being issued. More than one 'High Excellency' was badly scared—as he was meant to be—by the sight of 'those wild men rushing out like so many wolves' to the kettles where their meal was waiting, the kettles that were sometimes overturned and beaten as sign of mutiny; after which the plane tree came in useful for the necessary hangings that ensued!

The Gate of the Divan leads from the first to the second court, from the military to the business part of the palace, and it is here that visitors leave their carriages now. At this spot—they have now been unfortunately abolished—were the 'stones of example', dwarf classical columns on the capitals of which were exposed the heads of Grand Vizirs and other ministers who had met what was almost the natural end for those who attained that high office. All people liked to see them, and the palace executioner, who united with that high function the office of head gardener, made quite a large part of his income by the perquisites chargeable for the purpose.[1]

The Palace that we now enter is in all its essentials the work of Mohammed the Conqueror, though the harem part is later than his date, and naturally each ruler in his turn has added a pavilion or kiosk. Hence it embodies the great Sultanate that held sway here over one of the great empires of the world for a period of four

---

[1] Ex-ministers were not always executed, and the alternative shows that liking for a grim practical joke that is a characteristic of the Turk. If the Sultan allowed it, the ex-cabinet minister was allowed to race the executioner from this spot down to the Fish Gate which was somewhere on the edge of the sea below. If he got there first, his punishment was reduced to exile. If otherwise—the bow-string and the subsequent exposure of his head at the gate, even as if it had been Temple Bar!

hundred years, and what we see reflected here is—the nomad instinct of the Ottoman, who has the Tartar in his blood and make. He is a tent-dweller by age-long heredity, and when he builds a palace on the ground that his sword has won, he covers a whole stretch of ground with one-storey buildings, the black tents of his fathers translated into masonry and containing as those tents used to do, the spoil that he had won and the weapons that had won it. If fortune shall change, he can leave it all, and go back to the plains whence he came. The stone-built tents (for they are hardly more) are roofed with lead, the metal of royalty. Even if you depose a Sultan, you must keep him in the lead-roofed building, for the short time that is left him.

On the right hand as you advance is a long row of kitchens, which are worth a glance, but one is apt to go straight to the Pavilion of Council where the ministers of the Sultan met to discuss policy, with a place for His Majesty in the midst. Not that he always occupied it, for above it is a window, obscured with wooden lattice work, where the Sultan could, if he willed, be present unseen, and hear exactly what his ministers really said and perhaps, thought! The councillors never knew that their master was not there.

Yet, underneath the autocracy of the Sultan, there was a democratic equality for all Turks that we do not achieve in the West. The ceremony of the Selamlik, the weekly procession to prayer, was intended to allow any man a chance of submitting a petition to his lord, unhindered by officials; this, it must be owned, was a survival from Byzantine days. There is, further, a tale of how a burly Turk strode one day into the council of ministers, looked round on them and asked gruffly, 'Hangissy Hunkiar?' 'Which o' ye's the Man-Killer?' (The Sultan.)[1] That the Sultan had the right to kill him if he would was understood, and if that were his 'Kismet', he was ready; but the peasant had also the right to speak with the Sultan, man to man.

---

[1] Literally, 'the Blood-drinker', i.e., the man whose right it is to kill; a title of high honour. By old custom the Sultan had the right—execution of justice apart—to kill not more than nineteen men per day, because that was his pleasure. On the other hand 'Kismet' does not mean quite that man must submit to fate, because 'it is helped and you must eat'. It is rather this, that in perfect and cheerful submission to Creative Will, man finds his real happiness.

The Selamlik in Istanbul was really a modification of a Byzantine habit, but in Abdul Hamid's day it had degenerated sadly. It was no more the ride of a Sultan on his charger, at a walk, to give all men the chance of approach. A ruler who feared his best servants was driven in a carriage at full speed. A melancholy parody of a very fine custom.

Next door to the Pavilion of Council is the Armoury, a marvellous collection of trophies and curio weapons rather than an arsenal. It contains—and this is we think its unique feature—a collection of Tartar bows, many of them probably made by Sultans. Custom decreed that the Prince must learn a trade, and most of them chose that of 'Bowyer and Fletcher' (i.e. arrow-maker) as our fathers put it.[1]

It is the third court, that reached by the Gate of Felicity, that contains the really private portions of the palace. Within its narrow limits lived a population of nearly 2,000 souls—at its greatest period of development—all of whom were kept in a state of compulsory celibacy, save only the solitary lord of the whole. Once in, no inmate, save only the Grand Vizir, was ever allowed to go out again. The Corps of Imperial Pages, for instance, were admitted at the age of perhaps twelve years, and spent fourteen years in the precinct. Their time of service done, they might get promotion elsewhere, but for that time they never crossed the threshold to go out, and after it, never crossed it again to come in.

Immediately within the gate is the Hall of Audience, whither ambassadors who had private audience with the Sultan might penetrate. The ambassador was led up to this gate, and given a sumptuous banquet in one of the halls adjoining, on the priceless green china still shown in the great collection,[2] and which had this property, that it always neutralized any poison in the viands! The most nervous of ambassadors might therefore eat without fear. He was then clad with a robe of honour, and report made to the Sultan in his hall. According to the story, the Sultan then asked solemnly, 'Has the Dog been fed?' Assured on that point, he asked further, 'Is it decently clad?' 'Then, admit it.' Two attendants then took the

[1] The Turkish bow is worth study; it is a horseman's bow, to be drawn from the saddle, and so is very short. As they hang in the armoury, they are of a 'C' shape, and were strung by bending them, under the thigh, to the reverse curve, so that when ready for use they looked like 'brackets'. Of course no wood can stand this, and wood is not available in Tartary, so they are made of horn and sinew. The arrow is short compared with the English 'cloth-yard shaft' and very light. It was drawn, not just to the head but well beyond it, lying in a 'rest' of which several are shown, within the arc of the bow. The 'rest' was secured to the left wrist. As the bow was very stiff, it was not drawn by the fingers as with us, but by a 'hook-ring' on the right thumb. The range was very long, for records of over 600 yards remain, but we doubt if the arrow had the penetration of our 'cloth-yard shaft'. Richard I found that the cross-bow had a greater *effective* range than the Tartar 'horse-bow'.

[2] By custom, the Emperor of China gave periodical gifts of china to his Turkish brother, huge quantities of which have been preserved and are shown.

ambassador by either arm, and 'frog-marched' him into the presence
—a precaution said to have been observed since the day of Kossovo,
when the Serbian desperado, Milosh, sought an audience with the
Sultan Murad, and stabbed him in his tent.

There is a little fountain in the Hall of Audience, and while
Sultan and ambassador were conversing privately, this was set
playing, to make it impossible for eavesdroppers to overhear. The
precaution, however, was of little use, for secrets always did leak out.
Selim the Grim always took counsel with his Vizir when they were
alone on hillsides out hunting, but even then the Grand Master of
the Knights of Rhodes had a secret service that got at the information that he needed! Perhaps Mahommed the Conqueror was more
successful. It is said that once, when he was preparing for war
against somebody, his Grand Vizir suggested that he would be better
able to give effect to the plans of his august sovereign, if he knew
against whom they were directed. Mahommed gave him one look:
'If I thought a hair of my beard knew that, I would pluck it out and
cast it into the fire.' The Vizir asked no more questions![1]

The Treasure of the Sultans, now shown, is a collection of priceless
marvels, of value intrinsic and historic; and of gimcrack trinkets.
You may range from the Sword of Osman, with which every Sultan
was girded, to the last set of field-glasses and chiming clocks; from
the captured throne of the ancient Shahs of Persia, to a silver beer-
mug set with specimens of German coins. You may see the inaugural
robes of all the Sultans, from those of Mahommed the Conqueror to
the Frenchified uniform of Mahommed the Terrible. There is the
marvellous suit of armour the last warrior Sultan wore in the field.
Almost the only thing not shown—save perhaps as a special favour
to guests of the faith of Islam—are the Sacred Relics, which are
kept in a treasury of their own. These, the Palladia of the Khalifate
—the Banner of the Prophet, his cloak and seal, and a hair of his
beard—came down the centuries as the heirlooms of his 'Successors'
(Khalifs) through the ages. When Selim the Grim conquered Egypt
in the early sixteenth century, the last of the 'Fatimid' rulers surrendered these to his conqueror, and here they are still. Place and
things are still holy, though Turkey may be a religionless republic
now. The Forty Pages of the Royal Bedchamber, who read the
Koran perpetually, in relays, before these relics, have been abolished
now, of course; but Forty Curators of the Sacred Relics, who are the
same people as of old, still keep up the same observance. In the other

[1] This tale is told also of Murad IV: it fits the characters of both men.

buildings of the palace, and in the mazes of the harem, one can see the gradual process of Europeanization doing its work, and the old interest departing, till at last a painfully 'Victorian' kiosk closes the series, and the Sultan leaves the palace for ever.

In one wing, however, the Kafess, the 'Cage' where the Princes of the House of Osman resided in old days, one is back in the old grim age once more. Here once lived, up to the beginning of the nineteenth century, in a stately confinement, all of the sons of the reigning Sultan. Elders there were none, for till then it was the custom of the House that the Sultan killed off all his brothers on his accession, because there must be no rival near the throne. 'Better a prince dead than a province wasted', ran the saying. It was an existence under the shadow of death, for all knew that the day must come when one of the number would be ruler, and all the rest would die; and few Sultans were long-lived! If drones in the bee-hive had foresight, their lot would be like that of an Ottoman prince in the older days. Here, for instance, in 1650, lived Ibrahim, heir of the terrible Murad IV, who is said really to have used the right of the Hunkiar, and to have enjoyed acting as executioner himself,[1] either with sword or with bow-string. Ibrahim lived expecting execution daily for years in these narrow rooms, occupying himself in perpetual copying of Korans; and was only saved from death when his terrible old father lay dying by the fact that he was reported dead already. When once the breath was out of the Sultan's body, the ministers rushed to the Kafess to salute his successor—and he in panic piled the furniture against the door, for he was sure it was the executioners come to fetch him!

And if that was the life of the Princes, was that of the Sultan much better? He could have female toys by the hundred, but never a wife; slaves by the thousand, but never a friend. His first act had to be to kill all his own brothers. It was a life of splendid solitude. Yet most of the long series of holders of that office, of which the average tenure was just about three years, must have been the kindly person that the ordinary Turk is, save when he is frightened. What sort of life was it for them? Let one of the greatest of them, Selim the Grim, speak for himself and for others:

I have read life's riddle, emptied its nine pitchers to the end.
Never shall I, Sultan Selim, find on earth one faithful friend.

[1] His kiosk, where he sat and enjoyed archery practice on the persons of passers-by, is still on the outer wall of the palace garden.

From the palace, which has brought us right up to the beginning of the nineteenth century, we go to the furthest end of the city and to the greatest and oldest of its monuments, the grand Roman walls, which fortunately still stand and bound the city in that direction, though after the revolution of 1907 the Young Turks wished to show how civilized and European they were, by destroying that wonderful monument and substituting a boulevard! They had to be begged not to do away with one of the great memorials of their own nation's history and valour.

When approaching them, however, the visitor is sure to be taken to see what is described as the most ancient church of Constantinople and is one of the most interesting. Known now as the Kaharieh Mosque, and previously as the Church of the Redeemer *en chorais,* 'in the fields', it is the parallel to our own St. Martin in the Fields of Trafalgar Square. In both cases the city has crept round the church that was out in the country once. The walls enclose it now, but it was originally some distance outside them. It is believed to stand on the site of an ancient *martyrium* of a certain St. Babylas, who was put to death in the year 298, and in that sense is by far the oldest church of the place. There is, however, not a trace of the ancient building left in the modern fabric, which has undergone various vicissitudes. Justinian rebuilt it once, in basilica form, and endowed it by the ingenious and economical expedient of making a rich general—who had got into some political trouble—turn monk in it and present it with all his property. Then the present fabric was built at the approximate date of 1100 A.D. and after being left a ruin at the close of the Latin occupation in 1265, was repaired about the year 1300 by 'the chief accountant of the Treasury, Theodore Metochites'. The mosaics which form its principal attraction date from this period, and therefore come rather late in the history of the art, though they are a very fine specimen of their period and an interesting link in the story of its development.

The church was a special shrine in the time of the great Turkish siege of 1453, for it contained a specially holy Eikon, Panagia Odegêtria, or Our Lady of Guidance, which was considered to have saved the city from Russians and Bulgarians, and it was believed would do the same against the Turk. Alas on this occasion it failed to do so, and the Eikon only received this much of honour from its enemies, that when they looted the church after the capture they cut the picture up to make charms.

It was the Vizir of the Sultan Bayazid, about 1500 A.D., who got leave from the Sultan to make a mosque of the building, though it does not appear to have been in use as a church at that time, but to have been derelict. He, like a good Moslem, covered the wonderful mosaics with plaster, which at least had the effect of preserving those that the weather had spared. It was in 1860 that Italian archaeologists discovered their beauty and got leave to uncover them, on condition that those in the mosque itself (as distinct from those in the old *narthex*) should be covered during the hours of prayer. This has been a useful precedent to justify the work now being done on the far more important mosaics of St. Sophia.

Constantinople has had a series of walls to defend it. Putting aside those of Byzantium, and those built by Septimius Severus, the merest traces of which can be found in our day, Constantine naturally fortified his new capital. Legend has it that as he traced the circuit of the new wall in ancient style, spear in hand, he enclosed so large an area that his followers asked in amazement: 'When do you mean to stop?' 'Only when he shall stop who goeth before me', said the Emperor; but whoever this mysterious guide may have been, he seems to have lacked sufficient boldness, for the line that he traced was nothing like large enough, and the area had to be doubled only eighty years later. The walls run from the Marmora to the Golden Horn, as well as round the harbour fronts, and form one of the most wonderful monuments of the later Roman Empire in the world. The bulk of them date from the period 400–450 A.D. and are the work of the Emperor Theodosius II. At the Marmora end, however, they have been remodelled by the great Turkish castle of the Seven Towers, and here they also embody the Golden Gate of Constantine, a great marble arch that originally stood, like the Arc de Triomphe, in solitary grandeur. There is a brief length, too, at the other end, towards the Golden Horn, which dates from Manuel Comnenus and the year 1150, when the line was remodelled so as to include the Blachernae Palace, which had then become the imperial residence. The great body of the system however is of the fifth century, and a marvellous piece of military engineering it is. The backbone of it is the Great Wall, a rampart some forty feet high, with towers at hundred-foot intervals rising twenty feet above it. In front of it is what was known as a *peribolus*, an open space sixty feet wide, in which troops could march, and beyond it the Lesser Wall of a height of twenty-five feet—so as to be thoroughly commanded by the larger one—and with its own complement of towers. After a second *peribolus* came the third line of defence, a breastwork (of four feet only) rising above the moat, sixty feet wide and twenty feet deep, which was separated into sections by dividing walls (*diataphrismata*) so that the water was retained in spite of the undulations over which the line had to run. An enemy had thus to penetrate a fortified area of 220 feet in depth on this front, though on the Marmora and harbour walls a single line was sufficient. In a thousand years of service (450–1453) this defence resisted seventeen great sieges, of which the first, that of Ayub the Saracen, lasted fully seven years, 672–680. Greatest perhaps was that of 717, when Constantinople took the brunt of the great assault made by the Crescent on Europe. We westerns think a good deal of the victory won at Poitiers over the Saracen by Charles Martel just about that time, but that was only just a 'back-lash' of the great wave of invasion, and the real attack came here. In the eighteen months that the siege lasted, the Khalif brought 180,000 stout soldiers into the field, and when it was over he withdrew baffled with some 30,000 disease-ridden survivors. Thereafter, it was the Eastern empire that held back the advance of Islam, till Europe was strong enough to resist alone, and it was only European treachery that weakened the barrier at the last.

Of the seventeen sieges, only two were successful, and one of those was the Crusading attack in 1203. On that occasion, the line of wall was defended by the Varangers, the English guards that we have spoken of above, and the Crusading assault came to nothing before their axes. It was over the harbour wall that the Venetians got in, laying their ships alongside the rampart and using their yard-arms as boarding bridges, with blind old Dandolo—who was at least a real fighter—to lead them. Then the Emperor surrendered and the sack that we have spoken of elsewhere could begin. As for the Varangers, they held out as long as there was an Emperor to fight for, and only then did they make terms with their 'Frank' kin. It is some satisfaction that the only people who have a decent record in all that disgraceful business were the only English that were there.

The Turkish siege of 1453 (April 6th–May 29th) found the wall in a thorough state of disrepair, and hardly defensible. Money had been given for the purpose of putting it into a proper state, but some misbegotten monks embezzled that and hid it in their monastery, where it is a satisfaction to record that it was found by the Janissaries during the sack! The moat had been allowed to run dry by the neglect of the *diataphrismata* and the Great Wall was a mere ruin. All the fighting was at the Second Wall. The defending force was ridiculously small, barely 8,000 for a circuit of over nine miles, while Mahommed the

Conqueror, though his real attack was made at the Valley of the Lycus on the land front—always the 'Achilles heel' of the defence, and the only breach in the line to this day—had so many that he could threaten everywhere, and every point had to be guarded. Yet, for all his great force and his magnificent artillery—his bronze guns of 24-inch calibre still lie at St. Eirene, though the 36-inch gun[1] that was certainly used proved too cumbrous for effect—he could not overcome the defence. Hence his resort to the expedient of hauling his ships (or at least his lighter craft) overland and launching them on the upper waters of the harbour to threaten that wall. The ships in question were hauled ashore at the present Top-hana in Galata, and up the steep hill of Kumbaraji Lane over the crest where Pera now is. The admiral, a Bulgarian named Baltoglu, declared it was impossible to proceed when a swamp intervened in the track selected, on which Mahommed sent him a bow-string, with the simple message, 'Twenty-four hours!', and the impassable obstacle was overcome. The ships came down the hill easily enough, and were launched about where the Upper Bridge now lies. Actually, they made no attack on the Harbour wall, but their presence was decisive, both by moral effect and by the fact that so many of the scanty garrison had to be withdrawn to guard a line that could be neglected before, that the remainder were insufficient to resist the last great assault. Yet even so, it was said that 'a trifle would have turned the scale'. Many of Mahommed's advisers were in despair of success, and it was only the young Sultan himself (he was no more than twenty-two) who determined on the last assault. It was prepared, on the usual Turkish terms, 'Free plunder of the city for all and a province for the first man on the wall', and with that spur, after the inferior troops had worn down the strength of the defenders, the rush of the Janissaries got in at last, at the breach, at a forgotten postern, and at the Adrianople Gate.

A visitor to Constantinople always goes up the Bosphorus, even if he does not penetrate between the Symplegades rocks at the head of it, where Argo went through in the days of the world's youth. He goes up past a series of palaces, between Europe and Asia, among which one may note Yildiz Kiosk on the European shore, with its high double walls between which paced perpetually the Albanian sentries who protected Abdul Hamid from his constant fear of assassination. (Hard is the lot of an autocrat, whom fate has also

---

[1] One of the stone balls fired from this portentous weapon is still kept in St. Eirene. It could only fire thrice in 24 hours, and burst when in use.

made a constitutional coward!) Here that last one of the real Sultans lived like a spider in his web, of which the threads were telegraph wires, and ruled his empire by messages sent by that means, often to subordinate officials, because he would not trust his own governors-general. It is said that, till he gave the order where the guardian mastiffs that he kept were to be chained that night, no man ever knew in which of the many bedrooms that were ready for him he would sleep. On the Asiatic shore is the palace of Begler Bey, where Abdul Hamid spent the last years of his life after his fall, being at least the first of his house to survive deposition. In that palace the fallen Emperor, who had always been proud of his skill as a cabinet-maker and artisan, occupied himself with amateur dentistry, the four wives and other slaves which the Committee had allowed him being the *corpora vilia* on which he practised that science.

On the way up, there are two great castles opposite to one another which no man can avoid seeing, those 'of Europe' and 'of Asia', the Roumeli Hissar and the Anatoli Hissar, the two keys of the strait, without leave from which no ship went up or down the passage. When they were first finished, they sunk a merchant ship or two, just to make sure!

The Anatoli Hissar is the older, having been built fifty-seven years before Constantinople passed to the Turk—a proof how near they were to the city on both shores of the strait, before it actually fell. The Roumeli Hissar, far the finer of the two, is the work of Mahommed the Conqueror, built only just before the great siege, and actually planned to serve as his advanced base during the operation. El Fatih was too good a soldier to take chances, when they were not needed.

The unhappy Emperor Constantine, seeing this fortress going up within five miles of his own palace, could not mistake its intent; and he sent a mild protest, to say that to put such a castle there was not a really friendly act. Mahommed, who of course did not intend to have peace, sent back word that it was a very novel doctrine that a prince could not build a castle on his own domains without asking leave of a neighbour, but if his Brother did not like it, he could always declare war. He added a postscript to the effect that if any more messages as impertinent as that were sent him, he would flay the ambassador alive! So the castle went up, being planned, it is said—though we own that we never could read it—to reproduce in its plan the Arabic letters of the builder's name.[1]

[1] Old and new always touch. Robert College, the great American educational institution, is just by Roumeli Hissar.

ROUMELI HISSAR

As a base, the castle was never wanted, and after the capture of Constantinople it became just a garrison of Janissaries, whose descendants are said to live still in that most picturesque of the survivals of old Istanbul that can still be seen within its walls. As such, it became a prison, like the Seven Towers on the main wall, and like it was used at times for hapless foreign ambassadors and their suites. In old days, if an ambassador was not able to keep the 'princely' power that he represented from the folly of making war on 'imperial' Sultans—these are the technical words used—he was not politely handed his passports, but he and his went to one of the Turkish prisons, if not to the galleys. What that was like one can read in the memoirs of one who endured it, Wenceslas von Wratislaw, who underwent that fate in the year 1593 under the Sultan Murad III, and whose name we may still read on the walls of this dungeon, which was grimly called the Grave of the Living. 'Oh you poor prisoners, what can you have done to deserve so severe a prison as this? Nevertheless come in!', were the cheering words of the commandant when he received the ambassadorial suite, and still one can see the 'cage of beams' where that group of educated men lay in chains like beasts for four long years, undergoing torments that make grim reading in the memoirs that his lineal descendant has translated for us. 'Unless you accept Islam, you will never come out of this alive,' they were always told, 'while if you do, a fine career is open to you.' For years that was dinned into their ears day and night —and not one would buy his life on those terms. Of course their friends tried to help them, both by influence and by sending money which might alleviate their lot, but little could be done. 'Of four thousand two hundred ducats my friends sent me, I only got one hundred and fifty, and those I was obliged to give away', says poor Wenceslas. One is glad to say that at last it was 'John Burton, Ambassador of the Queen of England', who put their case to the Sultan, and actually got him to say that as they were plainly innocent they might be released. The good Englishman received them, and the first thing he did, being English, was to offer them a bath, which they needed! Yet even so, they were still a long way from freedom and home. In all that one sees at Constantinople or Istanbul, there is a note of deep tragedy running through.

We must leave the subject there, but let no one suppose that we claim to have touched on one tenth of what Constantinople and Istanbul have to show. We have not touched on the wonders of the museums, classic, national and religious; on the bazaars or the great cisterns, on mosques like Ayub, on churches like the Phanar, the Studium, the Pantokrator. The street fountains are a study in themselves, the aqueducts a separate subject. We have only tried to make what a visitor can see in two or three days (that is all he is apt to allow himself) a little more living to him than it is apt to be; so that he may perhaps be tempted to give some real study to a place where the classic age runs on into the modern, and where the East meets the West, and where human passions and human greatness have combined to write such a story as no other city in the world can show.

ALBANIA

YUGOSLAVIA

L. Ohrida
L. Presba • Monastir
• Florina
R. Vardar

Salonica L. Lankada L. Besik

R. Vistritza
• Kozani

ATHOS

Gulf of Salonica

KASSANDRA

• Metsovo

• Jannina

THESSALY

Meteora Monasteries

R. Arta

G. of Arta

• Dodona

Larissa

Volo
G. of Volo

Lamia

EUBOEA ISLAND

Thermopylae

LEUCAS

Amblema Pass
Chaeronaea
Libadoes

ITHACA

Rhion
G. of Patras

Naupactus
Itea
Delphi

Copais

Aegosthena
Thebes

Chaleis

Deceleia

Marathon

CEPHALONIA

Patras

Gulf of Corinth

Megara

Eleusis

Raphti

ZANTE

Elis

Megaspeleion

Corinth
CANAL

SALAMIS

AEGINA

Athens

Mantinea
Tegea

Namaea
Derbenaki Pass

Ratina

Pyrgos Olympia
Mt. Lycaeon
Tripolis

Epidaurus
Mycenae

C. Sunium
(Colonni)

Katakolon

Bassae

Argos
Lerna
Megalopolis

Tiryns
Nauplia

Asine

MEDITERRANEAN

Gulf of Arcadia

Messene
• Ithome

Sparta

SEA

Pylos

Kalamata

Gythion

Monemvasia

C. Taenaron

C. Malea

Southern
GREECE
Scale 1 in. = 54 miles
5 10 15 20 25   50

KYTHERA Is

C. Spada) —to C. Malea
Akratiri   60 miles approx.
• Canea Suda Bay

STANDIA

CRETE
to same scale

△ White Mts

Rethymno

Heraclion

• Sfakia   △ Mt. Ida   • Knossos

Is. of CLAUDA
(Gauda)

R   H.T.

INDEX

Acciajuoli, Florentine rulers of Athens, 1400, 75
Acharnae, village in Attica, 105
Acrocorinthus, Citadel of Corinth, 133, 135, 138, 139
Aegina, island state, 98-101
Aegion, port on Gulf of Corinth, 200, 202
Aegospotami, Battle of, 29, 37
Aegosthena, port on Gulf of Corinth, 92-93
Aethra, 121
Agiasma, holy well, Patras, 197
Agora, Athens, market-place, 42, 62
Agraulos, sacred Precinct, Athens, 26, 40
Agrilaesa, quarry, Sunium, 95
Agrippa Monument, 19–20
Agrippa, Vipsanius, General of Augustus, 20
Alcamenes, sculptor, 53, 87
Alcibiades, 22, 34, 37
  House of, 64–5
  at Nemea, 140
  at Olympia, 193
Alcippe, ancient goddess, 'daughter of Ares', 47
Alexander, Emperor, 53
  Corinth Canal, 131
  Olympia, 188
Alonia, cave at Delphi, 119
Alpheus, River of, 178, 182, 190
Amphictyomic Council, meeting place at Delphi, 116
Amynos, ancient shrine, Athens, 36
Anastasius, Emperor of Constantinople, 238
Anaximenes, orator, 188
Andanian Mysteries, Messene, 174
Andilalo, Olympia, Slav name for, 190
Andrew, Saint, at Patras, 196
Andritsaena, town of, 178, 182
Andronicus, builder of 'Tower of Winds', Athens, 62

Anthemius, architect of St. Sophia, 228
Anthesteria, Feast of All Souls, Athens, 35–6
Antiochus Epiphanes, 58
Antipater, poet, poem on fall of Corinth, 136 n.
Aphaea, Temple of, Aegina, 102–3
Aphrodite, Pandemos, 33
  of the Gardens, 26
  of Daphne, 76
  in Corinthian legend, 138
  of Kanathos, 147
  shrines of, 101
Apollo, Altar of, at Athens, 40
  Temple of, Daphne, 74
  capture of Delphi, 117
Arachova, 115
Arcadia, Monastery in Crete, 209
Areopagus, Hill and Court, Athens, 43, 44
Ares, Temple of, 62
Argive Heraeum, Shrine of Hera, 147–8
Argos, City of, 142, 152
Aristides, of Athens, 62 n.
  his 'Ostrakon', 68
  'the Orator', Epidauros, 151
Aristion, defender of Athens against Sulla, 26 n.
Aristodemos ⎫ Messenian heroes,
Aristomenes ⎭ 172–3
Aristogeiton, Athenian hero, 19
Aristophanes, comic poet, 30, 35, 38, 39, 90
Artemis, Brauronia, 20–1
  Orthia, Sparta, 161–3
  Laphria, Great Mother, 197
  at Olympia, 185
Asclepius, Precinct of, Athens, 47–8
  Legend of, at Epidauros, 149–50
  Shrine of, Epidauros, 149–51
  cures recorded, 151
Asinë, City of, 148
Asopus, River, 133

INDEX

Aster, archer at Athens, 65
Atalanta, Scopas' figure on Temple, Tegea, 155
Athena, 'Nike', 21–2
  'Healthgiver', 23
  'Promachos', 23
  'Lemnian', 23
  of Pheidias, 28
  'Pronaea', at Delphi, 122–6
Attalus, Stoa of, 62
Augustus, 29
  Actium trophy at Olympia, 175, 189
  the Strong, of Saxony, 31 n.
'Aunts', the, statues of priestesses of Athena, 24
Auxesia (see 'Damia and Auxesia'), 100

Baal-bek, source of Syenite Columns, St. Sophia, 239
Babylas, St. ancient martyrium, Constantinople, 250
Barathron, pit for bodies of criminals, Athens, 37–8
Bases of the Athletes, Archae. Museum, Athens, 67
Basil the Bulgar slayer, 1000 A.D. app., Emperor, Constantinople, 31
Bassae, Temple of Apollo at, 179–80
Bayazid, Sultan of Constantinople, 250
Bekhtash, Haji, dervish, 236
Bekhtashis, Order of, 62
Belisarius, General of Justinian, 236
Beulé Gate, Athens, Acropolis, 19
Bomo-nikes, in Orthia Rite, Sparta, 162
Boucoleon, palace, Constantinople, 239–40
Bouphonîa, bull-killing ceremony, Athens, 29–30
Boustropêdon, ancient script, 225 n.
Bromios, Thracian Dionysus, 49
Brutus, 19
Burton, John, Ambassador at Constantinople, 255
Byron, Lord, 16, 54, 95, 139
Byzantine Churches, Athens, 70–2

Caesar, Julius, at Corinth, 136–7
Cadmus of Thebes, 'inventor' of alphabet, 215

Calydon, Boar of, 196
Cario, slave in 'Plutus', Aristophanes, 47–8
Cassius, 19
Castalia, spring at Delphi, 129
Catalans, mediaeval invaders of Greece, 108, 110–11
Cathedral of Athens, 136–7
Centaurs, 49–50
  modern belief in, 114–58
Cephisodotus, sculptor, 45
Ceramicus, Cemetery of, 64–9
Chaeronea, Battle of, and monument, 111
  Maenads at, 50
  Scape-goat Ceremony at, 38
Charon, present belief in, 157
Choes & Chutroi, Feast of 'Pitchers and Pots', Athens, 35
Choragic Monuments, Athens, 55–6
Chryseis, Priestess of Hera, 148
Chrysostom, John, Bishop of Constantinople, 49, 227–8
Cicero at Athens, 65–6, 80, 91
Cithaeron, mountain range, 105
Cleobis and Biton, Argive twins, 148
Cleoetas, 23
Cleombrotus, Spartan king, 94
Cleon, Athenian demagogue, 169
Clepsydra, spring on Acropolis, 19, 40
Clodius, 80
Cock-fighting in theatre of Dionysus, 55
Codrington, British admiral, Navarino, 171
Columbus, his chart at Constantinople, 244 n.
Commodus, initiate at Eleusis, 80
Conon, Athenian admiral, 23, 37
Constantine, Emperor, 176, 241
  Palaeologus, last emperor, 231
  King of Greece, 1910–28, 72
Constantinople, 226–56
  St. Sophia, 227–32
  Varangian guard, 229
  Hippodrome, 233
  Janissary Corps, 236–7
  Little St. Sophia, 238–9
  Boucoleon Palace, 239
  Mosque of the Conqueror, 240
  Sulimanieh Mosque, 243
  Serai (Palace of Sultans), 244 f.

260

INDEX